Developing Teachers and Teaching

Series Editor: **Christopher Day**, Reader in Education Management and Director of Advanced Post-Graduate Courses in the School of Education, University of Nottingham.

Teachers and schools will wish not only to survive but also to flourish in a period which holds increased opportunities for self-management – albeit within centrally designed guidelines – combined with increased public and professional accountability. Each of the authors in this series provides perspectives which will both challenge and support practitioners at all levels who wish to extend their critical skills, qualities and knowledge of schools, pupils and teachers.

Current titles:

Angela Anning: *The First Years at School*
Les Bell and Chris Day (eds): *Managing the Professional Development of Teachers*
Joan Dean: *Professional Development in School*
C. T. Patrick Diamond: *Teacher Education as Transformation*
John Elliott: *Action Research for Educational Change*

Managing the professional development of teachers

Edited by
Les Bell and Chris Day

Open University Press
Milton Keynes · Philadelphia

Open University Press
Celtic Court
22 Ballmoor
Buckingham
MK18 1XW

and
1900 Frost Road, Suite 101
Bristol, PA 19007, USA

First Published 1991

British Library Cataloguing in Publication Data

Managing the professional development of teachers.—
    (Developing teachers and teaching)
    1. Teachers. In service training
    I. Bell, Les   II. Day, Christopher, *1943–*   III. Series
    371.146

    ISBN 0-335-09598-4 (hb)
    ISBN 0-335-09597-6 (pb)

Library of Congress Cataloging-in-Publication Data

Managing the professional development of teachers/edited by Les Bell
    and Chris Day.
      p.   cm.—(Developing teachers and teaching series)
    Includes index.
    ISBN 0-335-09598-4.—ISBN 0-335-09597-6 (pbk.)
    1. Teachers—In-service training—Great Britain.   2. Teachers—
    —Great Britain—Rating of.   I. Bell, Les, 1942–   .   II. Day,
    Christopher, ACP.   III. Series.
    LB1731.M33   1991
    371.1'46'0941—dc20   90-22955
                                                                         CIP

Typeset by Rowland Phototypesetting Ltd
Bury St Edmunds, Suffolk
Printed in Great Britain by Biddles Ltd
Guildford and King's Lynn

Contents

List of figures and tables   vii
Notes on contributors   viii
Introduction   xi

Part I   Supporting professional development for teachers   1

1   Approaches to the professional development of teachers   3
    Les Bell
2   The management of professional development in a Local
    Education Authority   23
    Eric Needham
3   The role of an advisory service   38
    David Wilkins
4   The role of the advisory teacher in staff development   49
    Shirley Andrews

Part II   Professional development in schools   65

5   The management of the GRIST initiative   67
    Beryl Lockwood
6   INSET in primary schools   80
    Julie Moore
7   'Teachers as experts': a case study of school-based staff
    development   88
    Bruce Douglas
8   Staff development in further education   110
    Maureen Woodward

Part III   Professional development in the 1990s   123

9   Monitoring and evaluating school-centred staff development   125
     Norman Thomas

10   Promoting teachers' professional development: a pilot project
     for primary schools   137
     Chris Day

11   The role of appraisal in staff development   164
     Helen McMullen

12   Staff development, local management of schools and governors   176
     Derek Esp

Index   187

List of figures and tables

Figure 1.1   The school development plan   18
Figure 5.1   A cycle for managing INSET at LEA level   69
Figure 6 1   INSET as a cyclical process   86
Figure 10.1 Variables in the success of externally initiated,
             self-managed staff development and school
             improvement   160

Table 1.1   Individualistic approaches to the professional
             development of teachers   9
Table 1.2   Group approaches to the professional development of
             teachers   13
Table 1.3   The professional development model   17
Table 6.1   LEAs visited   81
Table 6.2   Overall framework for planning   83

Notes on contributors

Shirley Andrews is Head of Music at Caludon Castle Comprehensive School, Coventry. She was previously in the Music Department at Foxford School, Coventry and an advisory teacher for Coventry Local Education Authority with special responsibility for developing the use of technology in music. She has extensive experience in running in-service courses on electronic music and is the author of *Practical Experiments in Recording* which is part of the Longman Music Topics Series.

Les Bell is Senior Lecturer in Education at the University of Warwick. He began his career teaching in primary and secondary schools before moving into teacher education. His research interests include school organization and management, teacher professional development and the application of management skills in schools. He provides management training courses for a wide range of schools, colleges and LEAs and has extensive experience of working abroad. His recent publications include *Appraising Teachers in Schools*, Routledge 1988 and *Management Skills in Primary Schools*, Routledge 1990.

Christopher Day is Reader in Education Management and Director of Advanced Post-Graduate Courses in the School of Education, University of Nottingham. He has worked as a teacher, initial teacher trainer and local education authority adviser. His research interests centre on school-based curriculum and professional development and in-service education. Recent publications include *Reconceptualizing School-Based Curriculum Development* (with C. Marsh, L. Hannay, and G. McCutcheon) Falmer Press 1990 and *Managing Primary Schools in the 1990s* (with P. Whitaker and D. Johnston) Paul Chapman 1990.

Bruce Douglas is Principal of Branston School and Community College in Lincolnshire which was a pilot school for financial delegation. He is on the

National Council of the Secondary Headteachers' Association and a Fellow of the British Institute of Management. He is author of *Quality Control and the Management of Schools* (1984) and *The Local Management of Schools* (1989) which are both published by the Centre for Educational Management and Administration at Sheffield City Polytechnic.

Derek Esp, formerly Director of Education in Lincolnshire, began work as an Education Consultant in April 1988. His main areas of interest include the training of head-teachers, local financial management in schools and colleges, education finance and management at LEA level, quality monitoring and control in schools and colleges, and strategies for school improvement. He is also involved in education policy review projects at home and abroad. He is associated with Nottingham University, Sheffield Polytechnic and the National Development Centre for School Management Training at Bristol University. He is Series Editor for the BEMAS/Longman books on the Education Reform Act. He lectures extensively and has been a contributor to several education publications.

Beryl Lockwood is the Headteacher of Bilton High School in Warwickshire. After completing her teacher training at Gloucester College she spent four years teaching in Malawi. On returning to England she taught home economics and became head of department during which time she took an Open University degree. In 1984 she became deputy headteacher in a North Warwickshire school and in 1989 she successfully completed a Master's degree at the University of Warwick. Her chapter is based on her dissertation for that degree.

Helen McMullen is General Primary Adviser for East Sussex, having previously taught in infant and junior schools and been headteacher of a large mainstream primary school with an attached special unit for pupils with emotional and behavioural difficulties in Hampshire. She is especially interested in staff development and has contributed to in-service activities and policy both in her present and previous posts.

Julie Moore is General Inspector of Primary Education for the London Borough of Barking and Dagenham. She has extensive experience of primary school teaching in Warwickshire and Solihull and was formerly the headteacher of Nethersoles Church of England First School, Warwickshire and a member of the Warwickshire Primary Whole School INSET team. She has contributed to a variety of journals including *Education 3–13*, *Mental Handicap* and *New South Wales Journal of Special Education*.

Eric Needham has had experience as a head of department in a Gloucester comprehensive school, a deputy head in a Leeds high school and was headteacher of a 12–18 high school in Rugby, Warwickshire for ten years. Since 1985 he has been county INSET co-ordinator for Warwickshire LEA with responsibility for professional development in schools, colleges and the youth service. He has contributed to staff training in his own and other LEAs and has been BPhil (Ed) course tutor at the University of Warwick.

Norman Thomas taught in primary schools for fifteen years, the last five as a headteacher. He joined Her Majesty's Inspectorate of Schools in 1962, retiring as Chief Inspector for Primary Education in 1981. He has since conducted a number of reviews of primary education and in-service training for a number of LEAs and advised a Parliamentary Select Committee for its 1986 report on primary education. He is an Honorary Professor of Education at the University of Warwick and Specialist Professor for Primary Education at the University of Nottingham.

David Wilkins is now a consultant with Nottingham University's Educational Management Development Unit. He spent three years in commerce and eleven years teaching before becoming a teacher educator at Loughborough College of Education. He became chief inspector of schools in Nottingham City with responsibility for curriculum and staff development programmes. This was followed by fifteen years as senior staff inspector in Nottinghamshire.

Maureen Woodward is Professional Tutor in the Centre for Continuing Education and Development at Tile Hill College, Coventry. She has extensive experience in education having previously worked in primary and secondary schools and community colleges. Her interest in professional development began when she carried out research in staff development in her own college for an MEd. dissertation. Her interests now include staff review and appraisal, training for staff development personnel and the effects that the European single market will have on further education.

Introduction

This book has been written for staff and students on educational management courses and for all of us within the education service with a responsibility for the professional development of teachers. This includes, of course, local education authority (LEA) inspectors and advisers, colleagues in higher education and others who provide and support professional development opportunities for teachers both inside and outside schools. It also includes the growing number of senior staff in schools who have, as part of their duties, a direct responsibility for the professional development of their colleagues. Further, it includes all of those teachers such as heads of department, heads of year and the many teachers in schools with curriculum or cross-curriculum responsibilities whose conditions of service include as one of their duties the facilitating of professional development of colleagues in a particular area of school activity. In short, this book will be of value to all in the education service.

The aims of the book are:

1 to deepen understanding of the concept of professional development of teachers
2 to identify the ways in which teacher professional development might be supported and enhanced
3 to explore the impact of the 1988 Educational Reform Act (ERA) on teacher professional development
4 to examine practical approaches to professional development in schools in the light of ERA and other recent initiatives.

The book is divided into three parts. In the first, 'Supporting Professional Development for Teachers', Bell deals, in Chapter 1, with the ways in which the concept of professional development has been interpreted and looks at the range of strategies which have been used to meet teachers' professional development needs. He concludes that LEAs will continue to have a crucial part to play in the management of in-service provision. This theme is explored further in Chapter 2 where Needham analyses one LEA's response to changes in funding for in-service education and in Chapter 3, by Wilkins, who looks in detail at the role of his LEA in supporting the professional development of its teachers. Finally in Part I, Andrews examines the ways in which advisory teachers, a relatively new group whose prime function is to initiate and support school-based curriculum development, can be used to support the work of teachers.

Part II, 'Professional Development in Schools', begins with an analysis by Lockwood of responses to new in-service funding initiatives by a group of secondary schools. This is followed, in Chapter 6, by a report from Moore on a range of professional development initiatives which are being adopted in primary schools. Douglas, in Chapter 7, examines in detail how one school set about establishing its own comprehensive programme of professional de-velopment over a three-year period. Woodward brings Part II to a close with her discussion of the need to identify staff development priorities effectively and of the impact of grant related in-service training (GRIST) funding on professional development provision in a college of further education.

In its concluding part, 'Professional Development in the 1990s', the book points the way forward by looking at the impact of ERA on professional development in schools. Thomas, who was the evaluator of the programme discussed in Chapter 2, opens this section, in Chapter 9, by examining the need to monitor and evaluate professional development provision. Day looks in detail, in Chapter 10, at how such an evaluation of a programme of professional development for primary school teachers' was monitored and evaluated. He raises some of the crucial methodological and conceptual issues that have to be considered. No volume on teacher professional development in the 1990s would be complete without paying some attention to staff appraisal. In Chapter 11 McMullen explores the relationship between staff appraisal and teacher professional development and argues that if it is conducted in a professional manner staff appraisal has a vital role to play in enhancing the professional development of teachers. This part, and the whole book, is concluded by Esp in a most appropriate way. In Chapter 11 he examines the impact of delegated budgets on the organization and management of teacher professional develop-ment and explores how, in the future, headteachers and their staff will have to work closely with governors in order to ensure that effective and relevant professional development is facilitated in all schools.

This final chapter makes explicit a series of main themes that run throughout the book. All schools now exist in a new climate that has been created by economic, demographic and ideological pressure expressed through legisla-tion and a radical shift in expectations about the nature and purpose of schools and schooling. The Education Reform Act was both the culmination of such pressures and a new departure. To the extent that it sought to redefine the structure and content of education in schools it was the product of a debate about education that was started by the Black Papers and had continued for two decades. To the extent that it produced a fundamental shift in the power relationships between various groups within the educational world it was a new departure.

The effect on the professional development of teachers has been twofold. In one way the professional autonomy of teachers, and therefore their professional development, has been curbed by a new contract, a national curriculum, new and extended forms of assessment and new forms of accountability. Much of the provision that has been made for teacher professional development has had to focus on preparing teachers for these changes. Resources have been devoted to implementing the national curriculum, to training for local management of schools and to preparing governors for their increased responsibility. Inevitably such an emphasis on helping teachers and others in schools to respond to national initiatives has limited the extent to which local, institutional and individual professional development needs have been identified and met.

At the same time one of the effects of these initiatives has been to increase the availability of professional development opportunities for many teachers and to link such opportunities directly to their work in school and classroom. The delegation of many new responsibilities to schools, the diminution of the role of the LEAs by central government and the increase in institutional accountability all require significant programmes of professional development for staff in schools that are planned and implemented with the specific needs of the particular school in mind. As a result many teachers find themselves both receivers and designers of professional development programmes. This can only highlight their awareness of their own professional development needs and those of their colleagues. This book traces the effect of such changes in teacher professional development over the last decade and points the way to meeting teachers' professional development needs even more effectively in the future.

Les Bell
Chris Day

Part I

Supporting professional development for teachers

Approaches to the professional development of teachers

Les Bell

This book is about the professional development of teachers. In this first chapter some of the basic approaches used to facilitate that development will be examined. The chapter will focus, in particular, on the interrelationship between the choices that teachers make about their own professional development or that of colleagues, and three different types of professional development provision. Each one of these three approaches consists of a set of responses to the professional development needs of teachers, but each is based on a different assumption about the appropriate relationship between need, choice and provision. The part played by the teacher in identifying professional development needs, making choices about priorities for meeting those needs and about the appropriate methods to be adopted to meet those needs is important in all of the approaches but is significantly different in each of them. In the first approach the teacher acts as a more or less isolated individual in identifying, prioritizing and finding ways of meeting his or her development needs. Hence this model has been termed the individualistic approach to the professional development of teachers. In the second model teachers act in groups as well as responding as individuals. This is, of course, the group approach to professional development. The third approach, the school development approach to professional development, is characterized by the extent to which teachers make choices about needs, priorities and provision at the whole-school level as well as at group and individual levels. In this model these choices form part of a coherent and planned process of school development. All of these approaches can be identified in teachers' professional development over the last three decades, but each has been predominant at particular times. In order to explore this further, however, it is first necessary to discuss what is meant by the professional development of teachers.

Professional development of teachers

Taylor (1975) identified two aspects of the professional development of teachers. These were staff development and further professional study. He defined further professional study as being orientated to the needs of individual teachers, while staff development was rooted in the needs of the institution. A year later, however, we find Watson arguing that 'The term staff development refers to the activity of ensuring the personal and professional development of the staff of the school' (Watson, 1976, p. 18). This definition identifies the fundamental role of the individual within the institution and implies the need to devise processes for professional development which will attempt to secure the professional growth of the teacher while improving the performance of both teachers and schools.

The reasoning behind the general support given to this approach to professional development in educational organizations appears to rest on the assumption that the interdependent relationship of the school and the teacher is crucial: a teacher cannot improve his or her performance consistently if the organization is in poor health, and the total functioning of the school rests on the sum of the individual teachers' contributions. Therefore, if the organization can harmonize the individuals' interests and wishes for personal and career development, with the requirements of the organization as derived from its educational aims, it will improve both individual and organizational performance. The teacher, the school and the pupils should benefit from such a process. Professional development in these terms implies the involvement of the whole staff in the operation and management of the school. It also implies that much of the work of staff development must be directed towards the improvement of the school as well as the professional advancement of individuals. Thus, it can be argued that professional development should embrace personal development (individualized learning) and staff development (the collegiality of group learning/co-learning).

The professional development of teachers should then, in any ideal world, be regarded as:

> a deliberate and continuous process involving the identification and discussion of present and anticipated needs of individual staff for furthering their job satisfaction and career prospects and of the institution for supporting its academic work and plans, and the implementation of programmes of staff activities designed for the harmonious satisfaction of needs.
>
> (Billings, 1977, p. 22)

Thus the process of development caters both for the individual needs of teachers and for the policy needs of the whole school and its constituent parts. I shall use the term professional development to encompass all such developmental activities within schools since my main intention is to explore the choices that are made about professional development by all those involved with schools and to examine some of the implications of those choices.

Such a view cannot conceal the conflicts that are inherent in any programme of professional development. Individual teachers will want a process that caters for their personal self-improvement and which acknowledges the difficulties and complexities of the job. On the other hand heads and senior staff will want a form of development that reflects their assessment of the needs of the school and the demands on it which emanate from parents, governors and other stakeholders in its activities. At the same time the local education authority (LEA) will want to ensure that its priorities are given prominence while the Department of Education and Science (DES) sets and resources its own national priorities for the development of teachers. These different perceptions influence the nature of the support that is and has been provided for teachers and helps to create a framework within which choices about professional development are made. Such choices depend upon and, at the same time reflect, sets of assumptions about the appropriate nature of and provision for teacher professional development.

Individual approaches to the professional development of teachers

Apprenticeship or process

My first experience of any form of professional development as a teacher took place in the early 1960s when, in my probationary year, I was given a classroom across the corridor from a dynamic and creative deputy headteacher in a primary school in Penge. I was so impressed by the impact of his visual display and his ability to stimulate a group of tough, cynical youngsters that I welcomed the opportunity to team-teach with him. We conducted a survey of a local beauty spot which involved taking 80 children to a wooded area in a large red bus. The work was planned in fine detail and the children, in mixed age and ability groups, were given specific tasks to complete on identified parts of the area in a limited time. The work was duly carried out as planned. We did not lose or gain a single child and caused no disturbance to any flora or fauna except for an unfortunate and embarrassing encounter with an early morning courting couple. Those city children came to realize how fascinating such a study could be and their subsequent work formed the basis for a mobile display at the local county show. I acquired skills of planning, organization and creating displays by working with my more experienced colleague and I felt that my development as a professional teacher had really started. This all happened entirely by accident as, I suspect, did much of the professional development of teachers at that time. I did, however, choose to become involved in the team-teaching process.

Much of the rest of my development as a teacher took place in the same random, almost haphazard, way through chance encounters with colleagues. My experience was typical of that of my peers. We tended to learn about our professional roles and to acquire the related skills by working alongside other teachers. This apprenticeship model of career development is characteristic of most occupations. However, for teachers it also builds on·their experience as students. Indeed, the sociological concept of anticipatory socialization sums up the way in which prospective entrants into an occupation consciously and unconsciously study the characteristics of the people whom they know already in a job and take on the attitudes, values, behaviour patterns and even appearance of members of that occupation. Many professional habits – good and bad – emerge during this process. Much of what we learned as teachers comes from our day-to-day contact with colleagues, but this is a limited and insufficient form of development. It is much less structured than, for example, the training of medical doctors, partly perhaps because the disaster criteria for school staff are not so instantly recognizable as they are in the hospital or surgery. It should be noted, however, that there are serious flaws in this approach to career development. For example:

- The role models which are available may not be appropriate for an inexperienced teacher to follow.
- The team of teachers may not be particularly united or effective.
- The experience that a particular member of staff may need in order to update his or her skills and knowledge may not be present in the school or local authority.
- A passive approach to staff development by which staff learn solely by association with colleagues is not consistent with the need to manage schools in a coherent, planned and structured way.

It is also arguable how far such experiences are truly developmental. They may help an individual teacher to acquire skills but such activity would be developmental only if it then enabled a teacher to make a planned contribution to the work for the school based on:

1 a self-analysis of professional needs and effectiveness;
2 an analysis of the needs and effectiveness of the school;
3 identifying and achieving a set of goals related to both levels of analysis.

My random apprenticeship met none of these criteria, yet it was professional enhancement of a sort and it was certainly individalistic in the sense that it reflected my needs and depended on the opportunities available to me. It was far less structured and coherent, however, than the other major approach to professional development at the individualistic level, which is dependent on courses provided outside the school.

Professional development through courses

The course-based model of professional development was, and still is, the most common and widely accepted approach to the development of teachers. For many, professional development *is* 'going on a course'. As Henderson (1979) has shown the notion of taking teachers out of school and instructing them in groups had its origins in the nineteenth century. Its rationale lay in the need to improve the education of relatively poorly educated teachers and, as such, it was probably highly effective. In more recent times, however, the treatment of newly qualified teachers, if not the rhetoric of the DES, LEAs and the training institutions, has been based on the assumption that their initial training has provided teachers with all the expertise they will require for the rest of their professional lives.

In-service courses tended, therefore, to fall into three groups. The first was for the enhancement of existing qualifications so that non-graduates could become graduates and those with degrees could obtain higher degrees or diplomas. These courses tended to be theoretical, located in institutions of higher education and based on what the staff of those institutions could and would provide rather than on any considered analysis of the needs of teachers and their schools. Here it was assumed that improved qualifications would in some way enhance professional performance. Until recently the provision of such long, full-time award-bearing courses for teachers on secondment provided a major source of employment for staff in education departments in institutions of higher education. The second and third types of courses are closely related and often indistinguishable. They are the top up and remedial courses. Top-up courses are intended to further develop existing professional skills while remedial courses help teachers in areas in which they are perceived to be experiencing difficulty. The current rash of primary school science courses generated by the demands of the national curriculum provides an example. Often these courses are run by LEA advisers, sometimes working with teachers, but universities and colleges are also significant providers along with a range of other agencies.

The provision of courses grew rapidly in the 1970s and course attendance by teachers increased dramatically (Henderson 1979). Professional development through attending courses became a panacea for improving the quality of schools and the education of children. In spite of this there was little evaluation of the impact of courses on the work of teachers in schools. The intention was that the teacher returning from the course would be able to identify those elements of the course work that were relevant to his or her classroom practice and that he or she would then be able to apply such expertise in the context of his or her day-to-day work. This, in turn, would then have an effect on colleagues within the school who would recognize the virtues of the good practice being demonstrated by the new, improved, course-stimulated teacher and would seek to emulate what they observed.

This approach to professional development assumes that change in schools can be brought about by changing selected or even randomly self-selected individuals within those schools who will then successfully generate change in others to such an extent that the school itself will be transformed. This is what Georgiades and Phillimore have termed:

> the myth of the hero-innovator: the idea that you can produce, by training, a knight in shining armour who, loins girded with new techno- logy and beliefs, will assault his organisational fortress and institute changes both in himself and others at stroke. Such a view is ingenuous. The fact of the matter is that organisations such as schools will, like dragons, eat hero-innovators for breakfast.
>
> (Georgiades and Phillimore, 1975, p. 134)

This was not the only limitation of professional development through INSET courses. Courses of this type tend to emphasize the expertise of those outside schools and to deny the legitimacy of the teacher-as-expert. This is almost inevitable and has the spin off of perpetuating the demand for courses in spite of there often being a mismatch between the needs of teachers and/or their schools and the content of the courses.

This was partly due to the almost total separation between course organizers and the teachers in their schools, partly because of inadequate course descrip- tions and partly through the attempt of course providers to maximize course membership. At the same time the provision of courses was unsystematic and unplanned, reflecting the existence of a plethora of providing agencies; the need of these agencies to offer what they had the expertise to provide rather than what teachers and schools needed and wanted; and the failure to establish appropriate feedback and follow-up mechanisms for such courses even when provided within and by LEAs.

Nevertheless, courses remain a popular mode of development for teachers. They do enable teachers to make choices. The most obvious choice that teachers can make is whether or not to become involved in any form of professional development activity. Those who do so choose can decide to enhance their qualifications, to develop existing skills or to acquire new skills. They can also choose when and where to undertake such courses. They are offered the possibility of secondment, although this is now unlikely to be available to the majority of teachers. Teachers can also, for most courses, make the choice for themselves as to what, if anything, they choose to apply and how they choose to apply it in their own schools. They may wish to practise new skills within the security of their own classroom. They may wish to work with other members of their team or department. They may wish to share with the whole school some of their expertise or they may choose to do nothing at all.

Teachers are thus now seeking to make more informed choices about courses and to relate these choices to planned professional development. At the same time more effort is being made in many schools to ensure that colleagues within the school benefit from the experience gained by the teacher attending the course. The impetus for this comes from the fact that attendance at courses may now be funded from the school's own budget and, even where this is not the case, attendance may have to be justified in terms of the overall development plan for the school. As a result teachers may be:

- briefed before attending courses about what they may be expected to do as a result of attending the course
- asked to produce an action plan as a result of attending the course
- required to make arrangements for applying new skills in their classroom or within the schools
- expected to provide in-service training within the school, based on their own expertise
- asked to provide an evaluation of the course in terms of its value to them and to their school.

Increasingly, therefore, attempts will be made to ensure that courses are relevant to the needs of teachers and their schools. The focus will be on how far

Table 1.1   Individualistic approaches of the professional development of teachers

Apprenticeship model

Advantages	Disadvantages	Assumptions
Immediacy	No coherent needs	That individuals can plan
Relevance	analysis	own development alone
Low cost	May be *ad hoc*	That what is good for the
Available in school	Needs may not be met	individual teacher is good
Focus on individual needs	May not be developmental	for the school
Teachers can make	Focus *only* on individual	Individuals can change
choices	needs	schools

Course-based model

Can increase knowledge	May be too theoretical	One teacher can influence
Can increase improve	Choices determined by	whole school or group of
skills	providers	colleagues
Teachers can make	May not reflect school	Theory can be translated
choices from what is	needs	into practice by teacher
offered	May not have practical	A wide variety of different
Provides opportunity to	application in the	needs can be met by the
reflect on professional	classroom	same course
practice	Ignores teacher expertise	
May be full-time	May be high cost	
Can lead to further	May require long time	
qualifications	commitment	
Can enhance promotion		
prospects		

those teachers who attend courses can make a more professional contribution to the effectiveness of their institution and to improving the quality of education that is provided for their pupils. As a result, the ownership of courses, their content, methodology and evaluation, is shifting away from the providers and towards the consumers. This is equally true whether the providers are universities, colleges, LEAs or other agencies. No longer are courses planned by providers alone. Teachers are being involved in planning and identifying appropriate topics for courses. The choices that practitioners make are determining the nature of the course provision in a very real way. Nevertheless, many of the weaknesses in this model of professional development provision still remain. A summary of the advantages, disadvantages and assumptions of the individual approach to professional development is provided in Table 1.1.

Group approaches to the professional development of teachers

As we have seen, there are major concerns surrounding the traditional course-based approach to professional development. These centre on the extent to which external courses are too theoretical and are not related to classroom practice; the degree to which such courses have little reference to school needs; the simplistic assumptions that are made about the ways in which schools change and can be changed; and the major role played by those outside schools in determining the structure and content of such courses. These concerns led a number of different groups who were interested in the quality of the in-service provision available to teachers to search for alternative strategies for professional development. These strategies tended to fall into one of two categories: school-based or school-focused.

School-based professional development

The school-based model was based on the view that the school, acting as a learning community,

> could identify and solve many of its problems including the INSET needs of its staff. The school would, if sufficiently motivated by a greater sense of control and direction over its own affairs, find the resources to provide INSET activities according to its own particular needs.
>
> (Hewton, 1988, p. 7)

Its advocates claimed that if professional development were school-based, i.e. occurring within the school itself, then the process of identifying needs would be easier, programmes could be more closely matched to those needs and the barriers to change would disappear. Choices about the content and delivery of such programmes would rest with the teachers in schools.

This approach, like the course-based model, has severe limitations. It tends to understate how sophisticated a task the identification of development needs is. It also fails to recognize that the management of change in schools is a complex process which often requires both external as well as internal support. At the same time there will be worries that the professional development of the school will take precedence over the personal development of individual teachers. Furthermore, if a school draws exclusively on its own resources for professional development purposes, there is a danger of parochialism since no school can ever have *nothing* to learn from those outside its own immediate confines. There are also resource implications since this approach to professional development is

> expensive in human resources and cash; and thus the potential effectiveness of the school-based model becomes a function of size; school-based INSET is likely to be richer in a large secondary school than in a small and relatively isolated primary school.
>
> (Henderson, 1979, p. 19)

School-focused professional development

The school-focused model of professional development emerged as an attempt to remedy the defects of the school-based model while retaining its essential school-based nature. The James Report on teacher education and training set out a clear rationale for this approach, with its emphasis on more teacher involvement in planning the INSET activities and each school adopting a planned approach to INSET as part of its general strategy of development and improvement:

> In-Service training should begin in the schools. It is here that learning and teaching take place, curricula and techniques are developed and needs and deficiencies revealed. Every school should regard the continued training of its teachers as an essential part of its task, for which all members of staff share responsibility. An active school is constantly reviewing and re-assessing its effectiveness and is ready to consider new methods, new forms of organisation and new ways of dealing with the problems that arise.
>
> (DES, 1972, p. 11)

Subsequently, Hoyle (1973) argued that INSET could best help in these areas if it was linked to the introduction and implementation of specific school innovations, focused on functioning groups (e.g. a departmental team or whole staff) and backed by external support, including consultancy services from advisers and teachers' centre wardens. He also proposed that schools should establish their own staff development programmes. This approach soon became known as the school-focused approach to professional development. Its emphasis was upon planning INSET activities in relation to specifically identified innovations, intended developments, tasks and needs in a particular school. These activities involve only a single teacher, a group of staff or the whole staff and might be conducted either at the school site itself (school-based) or at external centres such as colleges or teachers' centres. This approach has three main elements: the identification of professional development needs, the implementation of appropriate programmes to meet those needs; and the evaluation of the effectiveness of the programmes undertaken.

To some extent this model took its momentum from the debate about the entitlement of teachers to programmes of professional development which was rekindled by the discussion in the James Report (DES, 1972). It was suggested that all teachers should be given, as of right, regular, full-time access to programmes of professional development. The report also argued for the identification in schools of senior members of staff who would act as professional development tutors to their colleagues and who would contribute to the coherent and long-term planning of professional development in the school. Had these developments taken place, choice would indeed have been in the hands of the practitioners. In the event, access to full-time programmes of professional development has never been established in the way envisaged by James. Nor, until very recently, did many schools find the resources to undertake school-focused professional development or to identify a senior member of staff as professional development tutor or co-ordinator. Instead, the school-focused model of professional development has exhibited many of the weaknesses of other approaches.

It has sometimes degenerated into a 'tool-kit' form of development where immediate problems were identified and short-term remedies applied. It has also failed to reconcile satisfactorily the development needs of the different levels in the schools. In short, with a few notable exceptions, this approach to professional development was not firmly embedded in school policy and did not receive the resources that it required in order to be successful. Thus, again, it underestimated the complexities of initiating and sustaining change in schools. Such changes could not successfully be implemented by single individuals or small groups unless they were firmly rooted in the overall policies of the school. Yet this approach provided no effective means of achieving such an objective except on a random basis. To be effective, therefore, the professional development of teachers needs to be embedded in whole-school policy in a systematic way.

The main features of school-based and school-focused approaches to the development of teachers are summarized in Table 1.2.

School development and professional development

The need for teachers' professional development to be closely linked with the policies of the school emerge from the analysis of the school-based and school-focused models. This third approach to professional development is

Table 1.2 Group approaches to the professional development of teachers

School-based/school-focused model

Strengths	Weaknesses	Assumptions
Based on school needs	Requires ability to identify needs clearly	That all schools can identify own needs
Schools can provide own programme	Some schools may not have sufficient expertise or resources	That schools have sufficient resources to meet needs
Enables schools to use outside expertise		Professional development will be linked to whole school policies
May cope with different levels of professional development	May lead to parochialism	
Can use teacher expertise available in school	May lead to concentration on remedial or top-up approach leading to a lack of coherence	
	May ignore or undervalue individual needs while overemphasizing school needs	

based on the assumption that the development of teachers should be closely related to the overall planning and review processes of school management and should take account of the various characteristics of staff and staff roles, and the characteristics of groups of teachers. This is sometimes called the task-led approach to professional development; but the term implies a short-term, *ad hoc*, scheme with little coherent long-term planning when the reverse is, in fact, the case.

The policy-based professional approach to development first came to prominence in *Education in Schools* (DES, 1977) where we find it argued that every teacher will be expected to benefit from professional development throughout his or her career, 'in order to keep abreast of the subject, to extend and refine teaching techniques, to accommodate new patterns of school organisation, or to prepare for new responsibilities' (DES, 1977, p. 29). Did this mean that teachers were to be entitled to programmes of professional development? If so, what form would that entitlement take? Who would choose and what would be the available options?

In March 1983 the Department of Education and Science issued Circular 3/38, *The In-Service Training Grant Scheme*. Few people at the time, especially among in-service providers, recognized how seminal a document this was to be. Within four years the provision of in-service training for teachers was to be radically reorganized and the nature of its funding changed significantly. As we have seen, in-service training was the province of institutions of higher education who provided an annual programme of long and short courses both nationally and within their own regions, usually in consultation with LEAs. Successful courses – those that were well attended – were repeated. Others were dropped or changed. Alternatively, schools sought to develop their own programmes in relative isolation. Circular 3/38 was the first part of a process that was to change all this. Needham, in Chapter 2, and Lockwood in Chapter 5 examine the impact of these changes in detail.

By 1985 it was being made explicit to all teachers that they were:

> expected to carry out their professional tasks in accordance with their judgment, without bias, precisely because they are professionals. This professionalism requires not only appropriate training and experience but also the professional attitude which gives priority to the interests of those served and is constantly concerned to increase effectiveness through professional development. The Government believes that this concern should be fully taken into account in the policies for the staffing of schools and the training, deployment and management of teachers . . . the professionalism of teachers also involves playing a part in the corporate development of the school. HMI reports frequently refer to the importance of professional team work, where the teachers within a school agree together on the overall goals of the school, on the policies for the curriculum in the widest sense . . .
>
> (DES, 1985, p. 44)

However, the document *Better Schools* (DES, 1985) went on to point out that although annual expenditure on in-service training for teachers was £100 million, there was widespread agreement that these resources were not being used to the best advantage. LEAs and schools had little incentive to satisfy themselves that a particular form of professional development represented good value for money. Insufficient attention was given to evaluating the extent to which teachers and schools benefited from the training undertaken (DES, 1985).

In order to achieve a much more systematic approach to planning the professional development of teachers, the in-service training of teachers was, between April 1987 and September 1990, organized and financed under the local education authority training grant scheme (LEATGS). DES Circular 6/86 set out the new scheme: the Secretary of State would decide annually on national priority areas for in-service training, and indicate the level of funding available to local education authorities. LEAs would submit their INSET proposals and those approved by the DES would qualify for grants of 70 per cent towards the cost of national priority training and 50 per cent towards programmes defined as local but not national priorities.

From September 1990 funding for local priorities from central funds has been abolished and the DES contribution to expenditure on national priorities has been reduced to 60 per cent. It is still intended, however, that all professional development activity supported through this scheme should be monitored by the LEA in order to discover how far it contributes to more effective and efficient delivery of the education service. One specified area was the 'relevance of the training to expressed needs'. This has been a continuing emphasis of Circulars 9/87 and 5/88, as the DES stresses the need for systematic consultation with staff. Circular 6/86 explained that the Secretary of State's allocation of grant aid would take account of,

> the authority's current practice and future intentions for the planning and management of such training, including its arrangements for identifying the training needs of individuals (through appraisal procedures where these exist). The Secretary of State will wish to assure himself that these proposals are related to systematically assessed needs and priorities, are set within balanced and coherent overall policies and plans and build appropriately on the strengths of current arrangements.
>
> (DES, 1986, para. 17, I)

This scheme was intended to promote more systematic and purposeful planning of the professional development of all teachers. In most LEAs this was facilitated, in part, by the devolution of part of the professional development budget to schools, thus not only giving the power of choice to practitioners but also providing them with resources.

At the same time as schools were being provided with funds with which to organize at least some of their school-based in-service training, they were also being given time in which to train. The basic working year for teachers is deemed to consist of some 1,265 hours, of which some time could be set aside for working parties and meetings. LEAs were also allocated five training days when teachers could work together in the absence of children. Some of these days were used for national and local priorities but others were allocated to schools for the professional development of their own staff. The same (1987) DES Order also gave teachers an entitlement of sorts to professional development. The conditions of employment of all heads and deputy heads includes

7) Evaluating the standards of teaching and learning in the school, and ensuring that proper standards of professional performance are established and maintained.

8) b) Ensuring that all staff in the school have access to advice and training appropriate to their needs, in accordance with the policies of the maintaining authority for the development of staff.

(DES, 1987, p. 3)

That of all other teachers includes

5) a) Reviewing from time to time his methods of teaching and programmes of work,

b) Participating in arrangements for his further training and professional development as a teacher . . .

11) a) Contributing to the selection for appointment and professional development of other teachers and non-teaching staff, including

the induction and assessment of new and probationary teachers.

(DES, 1987, p. 5)

We find, therefore, that not only are teachers at all levels in the school expected to avail themselves of professional development opportunities; they are also expected to take part in helping to provide such opportunities for colleagues. Furthermore, the nature of the resourcing for professional development now makes it more likely that individual teachers, groups of teachers and teachers acting as a whole school, may have a direct part to play in formulating the professional development policy for their school. In the words of Circular 6/86,

> The Secretary of State will wish to assure himself that these proposals are related to systematically assessed needs and priorities are set within balanced and coherent overall policies and plans and built appropriately on the strength of current arrangements.

(DES, 1986, p. 7)

In order to achieve this, schools require a mechanism for establishing aims and a co-ordinating mechanism for ensuring that groups and individuals work together towards agreed objectives. The effect of this approach, however, is to shift the arena within which choices about professional development are made to the interface between the school and the LEAs. It also gives a much more proactive role to the practitioner in the school who may now do more than express preferences from a range of available options. The practitioner is now more able to determine the form of professional development that is offered to colleagues within one or a group of schools based on the time and money that is now available for that purpose. Teachers in schools can play a part in identifying their own professional development programmes, although tensions still remain between the legitimate demands of individuals for personal development and the policy needs of the school. Furthermore, the impact on the school and its teachers of making one choice rather than another becomes much more real. Thus if the choice in one school is for a full-term secondment for one teacher and a full-day's training for every teacher, the choice, while not easy, is clear.

This shifting of the arena within which choices are made has not been without difficulties. For example, there is still evidence to suggest that professional development programmes are managed in a relatively arbitrary way, and take little heed of the long term needs of the school and of individuals within the school (Cowan and Wright, 1990). The in-service days which are the major part of current professional development strategies of many schools and LEAs have undoubtedly enhanced the ability of practitioners to make choices and to meet their own needs. One recent investigation concluded that in-service days,

- encouraged better staff co-operation
- encouraged better use of facilities

- led to improved strategies for all school systems, discipline, reso
- helped to establish school appraisal scheme
- provided time to exchange ideas
- created opportunities to visit, liaise with colleagues in other de
  and institutions
- helped school develop policies
- raised staff awareness
- helped to highlight specific needs.

(Derived from Cowan and Wright, 1990, p. 117)

At the same time, however, the same training days,

- failed to match the needs of the school as a whole
- did not ensure that individual needs were met
- were not usually evaluated by staff to ensure both an avoidance of mistakes next time and continuing commitment from staff to any plans or policies formulated
- occurred at times which were inappropriate or unhelpful for immediate follow up
- were not based on long-term professional development plans
- had themes which often occurred in isolation and without regard for previous or subsequent activities.

(Derived from Cowan and Wright, 1990)

These criticisms remind us of the importance of locating professional development within an overall policy framework. This model is in its infancy in England and Wales and there is still some way to go before its success or failure

Table 1.3 The professional development model

Strengths	Weaknesses	Assumptions
Is part of an overall approach to school development	Insufficient resources may be available	That medium- and long-term planning is possible
Enables schools to choose appropriate methods of development	May be overtaken by LEA or DES policy priorities	Policy, once formulated, can be implemented in classrooms
Some resources are earmarked	Is subject to agreement of governors and to influence by LEAs	Resources will be made available
External support is available	May lead to emphasis on school needs rather than those of individual teachers	Whole school policies are the most effective approach to managing and improving schools
Is subject to agreement of governors		
Priorities have to be identified	Can be seen as a challenge to teachers' professional autonomy	
May be linked to appraisal	May be linked to appraisal	

can be established. It is based on the assumption that the professional development that forms an integral part of whole-school policy will be effective both as part of the continuing process of managing the school and as a contributory factor in initiating and supporting necessary changes. This is because such an approach allows professional development to be systematically planned and resourced as a part of an overall school development plan. This is the essence of the developmental model of teacher professional development. It is based on a coherent set of policies for school improvement and it places the professional development of the staff in the school at the centre of those policies as a crucial element in providing an even more worthwhile education for the children in the school. It also provides the practitioner with increased opportunities for choice and, at the same time, places upon the same practitioner burdensome responsibilities for managing the professional development process. Douglas in Chapter 7, examines how one school had coped successfully with just such a coherent programme of professional development. Table 1.3 summarizes the main strengths and weaknesses of the professional development model.

Some implications for schools

The Education Reform Act (1988) now makes it mandatory for every school with over 200 pupils to manage its own budget. This devolving of financial management to schools is based on the quaint Thatcherite assumption that all

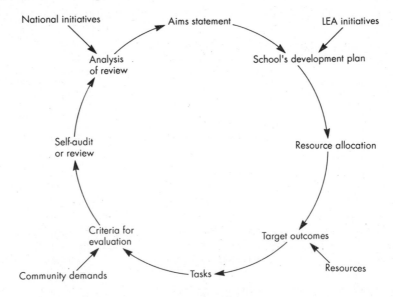

Figure 1.1 The school development plan

management is financial management. While the LEA remains in control of the professional development budget the school can now use its own resources to supplement what it receives from the LEA and may look at a wide range of alternative providers in order to meet its professional development needs. It also has to produce a school development plan which shows how it intends to implement the new national curriculum and how it will meet the many other challenges of the 1990s. This plan has, at its centre, the continued development of the teachers in the school.

In order to create a framework within which choices about the professional development of teachers can be located in the overall policy for the school, the school development plan must contain a clear view about how teacher development can contribute to the implementation of that plan. The implication of this is that the development plan is constructed in a particular way, with the aims of the school – in the form of an aims statement – as its main point of reference. We can see from Figure 1.1 opposite that the construction of a plan is a cyclical process involving eight stages. For practitioners to make informed choices about professional development for individual teachers, groups of teachers or for the whole school, the plan, and especially the resource allocation stage, must take full account of how staff resources need to be managed in order to achieve the target outcomes. All staff in the school must be aware of the key elements of the school's development plan and be able to recognize how they can make a contribution to it. What, then, is a school development plan and how is it produced?

A school development plan is a flexible instrument to support the management of the school. It is a cyclical process, not a finished product and operates over a three-year period with targets for the first year being very specific, those for the second year less so and only broad indications of intent given for year three. There are several essential features of the planning process:

- The school needs to have an aims statement which identifies the essential purpose of the school and guides all those in the school as they carry out their various duties. This will have to be a succinct, practical statement rooted in what the school is already doing rather than based on some vague philosophy or on some unattainable ideal.
- The school will have to know what it is already doing and how well it is functioning. It will require, therefore, a regular process of self-review or audit.
- As a result of this analysis priorities can be established for the next phase of development planning and, if necessary, the aims statement can be revised.
- The plan, when constructed, will identify a manageable number of development targets and establish a timescale for meeting them. It will also show how resources, including finance, time and the professional development of all the staff of the school will be organized to help achieve the targets in the development plan.

- These will be further subdivided into target outcomes or precise objectives together with a clear indication of how and by when they are to be achieved.
- The target outcomes will be expressed in terms of tasks to be performed by particular people within the school, perhaps working with colleagues from outside the school such as consultants, inspectors or advisers.
- Criteria for evaluating how far the tasks have been achieved, resources adequately and appropriately deployed and professional development programmes effectively carried out will be built in to the plan. These criteria and the evaluation which is based on them will then form the starting point for the next audit. One of the most significant features of this stage will be the evaluation of the teachers' professional development programme, since staff development is crucial if the plan is to be successful.

We can see from Figure 1.1 that the plan is not constructed within the school in isolation from other factors. Initiatives from elsewhere within the education system will impinge on the planning as will the availability of resources and demands of parents and other members of the school's wider community. This process is in its very early stages in schools, but it is already having a profound effect on the professional development choices that practitioners make and on the ways in which they make those choices. Professional development is now beginning to be seen as a major management responsibility in schools to the extent that all schools have at least one senior member of staff responsible for it and, in larger schools, often a team of teachers working together on identifying needs and organizing programmes. As a result of this, however, those with responsibility for the professional development of colleagues are recognizing the need for further training and support, especially in the areas of identifying professional development needs and in planning programmes. Thus one set of implications for giving practitioners the power of choice in professional development is that further professional development is required in order to ensure that choice is exercised for the benefit of the whole school within the framework of its development plan.

Conclusion

Practitioners in schools have always been able to make choices about their own professional development. These choices have been both constrained and informed by the context within which they have had to be made and by the perspectives that practitioners have adopted in making them. Teachers whose main perspective was derived from their own classroom practice and related to their own career progression would tend to have a perspective on development that was significantly different from somebody with the responsibility for managing and leading a team of teachers in a school. In a similar way the perspective adopted by senior management in a school, while recognizing the validity of the other two perspectives, would tend to reflect a concern for the whole school rather than only for isolated parts of it.

The choices that are made available to practitioners, in turn, are shaped by prevailing notions of what, legitimately, might be regarded as appropriate forms of professional development. Apprenticeship is a perfectly acceptable model under some circumstances but there are many things that cannot be achieved in this way. The course-based model provides valuable opportunities for individual professional development but there are considerable doubts as to whether this should be the only or even the predominant model for professional development if the intention is to improve and extend the quality of teaching and learning that is made available to children in our schools. School-based professional development can create an ethos within a school for the successful management of school-based change; but it can also prove to be restrictive and parochial in the longer term. In a similar way the school-focused model can lead to a series of short-term remedial activities or to a problem-solving approach that does not facilitate the long-term, planned development of the school. All of these models offer different opportunities for practitioner choice and practitioner control over professional development.

Development through learning is central to the purposes of everything that is done in schools in the name of education. This must be as true of the teachers as it is of the pupils, and it must also be true of the organization itself. The creation of an organization that can sustain its own growth and development must now become the single most important purpose of practitioner professional development. This does not necessarily mean that teachers will have no choice but to subjugate their individual professional development needs to those of the school, although it does mean that priorities have to be established.

The policy-based model of professional development that is now emerging offers an opportunity to practitioners to extend their control over their own development, albeit within a framework of provision and resourcing that is closely related to the needs of the school and to the development plan that formulates and expresses those needs. This plan can ensure that the most effective use is made of the expertise acquired by individuals as part of their professional development by linking the needs of individual teachers to those of the whole school. Only in this way can the competing choices of those at different levels in the organization be reconciled within a framework that allows practitioners to make informed choices about professional development programmes.

References

Bell, L. A. (1988). *Management Skills in Primary Schools*. London, Routledge.
Bell, L. A. (1991). *Managing Teams in Secondary Schools*. London, Routledge.
Billings, D. E. (1977). 'The nature and scope of staff development in institutions of

higher education', in T. Elton and K. Simmonds (eds.), *Staff Development in Higher Education*. Guildford, Society for Research into Higher Education.

Cowan, B. and Wright, N. (1990). 'Two million days lost', *Education*, 2 February.

Department of Education and Science (1972). *Teacher Education and Training (the James Report)*. London, HMSO.

Department of Education and Science (1977). *Education in Schools: A Consultative Document*. London, HMSO.

Department of Education and Science (1983). *The In-Service Training Grant Scheme*, London, HMSO. Circular 3/83.

Department of Education and Science (1985). *Better Schools*. London, HMSO.

Department of Education and Science (1986). *Local Authority Education Training Grant Scheme: Financial Year 1987–88*, Circular 6/86. London, HMSO.

Department of Education and Science (1987). *The Education (School Teachers' Pay and Conditions of Employment) Order*. London, HMSO.

Georgiades, N. J. and Phillimore L. (1975). 'The myth of the hero innovator and alternative strategies for organisational change', in C. C. Keirnan and F. P. Woodford, (eds.), *Behaviour Modification with Severely Retarded*. North-Holland, Elsevier Excerpta Medica.

Hall, J. (1988). 'Introduction', *Local Education Authorities' Project, Management in Education INSET Initiative*. Milton Keynes, BBC.

Henderson, E. S. (1979). 'The concept of school-focused in-service education and training', *The British Journal of Teacher Education*, 5, 1.

Hewton, E. (1988). *School Focused Staff Development*. Lewes, Falmer Press.

Hoyle, E. (1973). 'Strategies of curriculum change', in R. Watkins (ed.), *In-Service Training: Structure and Change*. London, Ward Lock.

Taylor, W. (1975). 'The universities and in-service education', *British Journal of In-Service Education and Training*, 1, 1.

Watson, L. (1976). 'A caring community: staff development in the school', *Secondary Education*, 6, 1, 20.

2

The management of professional development in a Local Education Authority

Eric Needham

The purpose of professional development

The education service depends for its success on professional leadership and teamwork, on the involvement of parents and on the support and advice of governors. The quality of relationships between all is of paramount importance as are the commitment, imagination and skill of the individual teacher'

(M. L. Ridger, then Chief Education Officer,
in Warwickshire County Council, 1988).

In writing these words Michael Ridger drew the attention of primary teachers in Warwickshire to the LEA's traditional philosophy – that all the educational work done is for, and can only be measured in terms of, its effect on children. Warwickshire, one of 104 local authorities, and about average in size, has always held firmly to that view.

A shire county of over 300 schools and colleges, Warwickshire is shaped like a boomerang with LEAs such as Solihull, Coventry and Birmingham to the west and the shire counties of Staffordshire, Leicestershire, Northamptonshire, Oxfordshire and Hereford and Worcester as its other neighbours. A county with no really large towns, much of Warwickshire is rural and underpopulated. Many of its primary schools are very small. Partial reorganization has left it with a variety of ages of transfer and types of school. For reasons of geography and administrative organization INSET has traditionally been planned in central terms on a county basis but delivered locally in teachers' centres, schools and other appropriate places. Residential courses have been developed. The advisory team has held annual planning meetings to co-ordinate monitoring of previous work, planning of priorities, devolution of available funds and to

make decisions on secondments. Local committees advise teachers' centres.
Networks of subjects, areas and phases have been created. Higher education
institutions have been much used, often with prior joint planning.

Thus it was that when national pressure to replan and manage effectively
began to be felt, this LEA already had a balanced plan for the (in-service training
of teachers). Within the present pressure for, and pace of, change it is of interest
to return to that moment in mid-1985 when change was imminent.

James Callaghan had made his national call for improvement several years
before, concentrating on the secret garden of the curriculum. People had
begun to look at effective systems of improving the quality of teaching in other
countries. The Conservative government, and in particular Sir Keith Joseph,
had declared a major policy of improving the quality of schools so that the
young people of the country would be qualified to work well in the new society
and to satisfy the demands of industry and commerce; would be square pegs in
square holes. There were, after all, many unemployed but still a great number
of vacancies. Skills needed teaching and enhancing and this, in turn, required
appropriate teaching. 'Better schools need better teachers.' With those
pressures and a government determination to get things done, it became
inevitable that serious, organized and swift steps would be taken to improve
the quality of the teaching force.

The initiatives – ESG/TRIST/TVEI

A series of initiatives therefore began. Three, in particular, affected Warwickshire – the technical and vocational initiative (TVEI), education support grants
(ESG) and the TVEI-related in-service training (TRIST). ESG was administered
by the DES, TVEI and TRIST being planned and organized by the Manpower
Services Commission (MSC) led by Lord Young. Thus, senior government
ministers, each with clear aims and machinery for action, offered LEAs the
possibility of money for carrying out agreed work. A pattern was about to
become established. The LEA would have the option of obtaining government
money for educational work; it would have to bid for the money against laid
down criteria and it would have to carry out the work (if its bid were successful)
in ways laid down by government departments. It would have to monitor and
evaluate the work done, firstly to ensure that the quality and quantity were
approved and secondly in order to establish a claim for later money from a
second round of bids.

This differed from the previous decision-making methods on the total
spending, type of quality of, and monitoring of money and time spent in INSET.
Formerly the LEA had appropriated money from its total rate-supported,
block-granted general educational fund. Now it had to offer to match government grants with money of its own and be accountable for planning, spending
and evaluation.

The Local Education Authority

LEAs ranged from those who had spent much money and planned to those who had spent much and not planned very well, to those who had spent too little relative to their number of children. Warwickshire was very much in the middle – not a high spender but not a low one; not overplanned yet not having no plan at all. By mid-1985 a variety of in-service training had emerged in the county. It was on that variety and on the quality of the personnel involved that Warwickshire was able to build in the next key year.

In mid-1985 in-service teacher training in Warwickshire was provided by a variety of means including short and long courses, the use of advisory teachers and teachers' centres, work in individual schools and LEA residential training. The whole rested upon an overloaded administrative system and the skills and background of an advisory team which felt that pastoral and professional support to schools and colleges was its major duty. There was an annual plan for INSET, worked out at an annual conference. There was some institutional INSET, where a school or college felt the need or benefit. There was a plan for secondments, both annual and termly. There were already strong links with HE providers for what was to come. However, it is easy to see with hindsight that, although at that stage much INSET was taking place and a great deal was of good quality and highly effective, there was no central LEA evaluation and monitoring and there was no coherent planning of the whole.

TRIST in Warwickshire

During the five terms that TRIST was in operation, a total of 154,631 teachers received training under the scheme. The outcomes of this training will take time to emerge but it is already clear that TRIST enabled Authorities to explore different ways of managing INSET; to try new and innovative approaches to the identification of teacher training needs and to the delivery of training; and to test various models for the monitoring and evaluation of training plans (MSC, 1987).

Warwickshire entered wholeheartedly into TRIST, setting up a management committee, establishing priorities for bids, appointing a co-ordinator and setting up a series of priorities of action. The following elements were important:

- work in active learning styles
- development of word processing and IT skills in teachers
- management skills in FE
- the use of advisory teachers for specific processes in schools and colleges
- whole-school/whole-college INSET (school-focused and planned)
- improving office/management systems

- linking with other LEAs
- establishing records of achievement/profiling
- economic and business awareness (understanding industry)
- work in electronics and technology
- school/college links to be encouraged.

This list shows the major area of concentration; but what farther emerged was that TRIST was a developing process. The LEA's plan changed and grew in the light of experience, so that when the planning for the first GRIST year (April 1987–March 1988) was under way it was realized that the LEA was planning a process rather than a mere list of events. For Warwickshire a new style of INSET (a residential course, follow up in schools with the professional help and commitment of advisory teachers and then further residential work) emerged as a way of ensuring change in the classroom. TRIST gave the time to experiment with this and build up a team of advisory teachers skilled in this style of work. Equally, school-based/school-focused INSET led to the planning of activities, the making of institutional bids, the carrying out of INSET, and its evaluation. It also led to experimental work such as the provision of extra funds and help to four secondary schools to take their work further and to work together (see Chapter 5). All this was done at what would previously have been seen as high speed. This brought problems but also produced action which in turn led to further action. In particular, as a result of TRIST the LEA knew more about the quality of its resources and was able to plan for and carry out the first GRIST year of 1987/88. Schools built up their own resources and skills.

Warwickshire, like other LEAs, was in the position of simultaneously carrying out the activities of one year while planning for the next. Evaluation of one year was in progress while the next year had already begun. This was to happen again at the end of the first GRIST year and there was to come a point when, at one and the same time, the LEA was

1 carrying out one year's work
2 evaluating the previous year's work
3 planning the next.

This cycle of planning was to emerge as the DES took over from the MSC the major control of INSET. Yet, in reality, TRIST represented only one-tenth of Warwickshire's spending for one age group (14–18). However, planning for TRIST was the catalyst for change in the whole of the county's INSET.

GRIST and the Thomas Report

During the first year of GRIST, (1987/88) the most important things to emerge in Warwickshire were;

- the appointment of school INSET co-ordinators

- the growth of the central administrative INSET machine
- the growth of LEA planning for FE colleges as a whole
- staff development groups
- the expansion of whole-school INSET into all secondary schools and over half the primary ones
- the beginning of the serious evaluation of activities.

This latter was to be done by the commissioning of a report from Norman Thomas (author of Chapter 9). He was to visit many schools with the help of a group of advisory teachers and to comment on what the LEA was doing and make recommendations about where it ought to be going. This would enable the LEA not just to plan for 1988/89 but to establish a pattern for the mid-term future.

Norman Thomas's investigations were in an LEA where changes had taken place. The number of secondments (particularly annual ones) had been much reduced (from 39 to about 6); correspondingly the number of termly secondments had been increased; but all secondments were part of a plan and were often in groups to a HE institution for a particular planned piece of work. Any school which had not at that stage made a bid for INSET funds had to have shown its reason for not doing so and was expected to make a plan/bid for 1988/89. The number of advisory teachers was increased. Advisers were spending more time in planning and encouraging INSET and leading teams and less in actual training. The LEA was making regular reports to the DES both of activities and of lists of spending and of training days.

The Thomas Report came at a time when the initiatives led by the DES, (Circulars 3/84, 4/85, 6/86), the TRIST initiative, the INSET implications of the ESG and the early work of TVEI) had coalesced with the styles and aims of the LEA into the first year of GRIST. The bringing together of these elements produced a whole that was exciting, innovative, leading to change and yet partly untried and not resting on a firm foundation of organizational practice. Thomas visited a great number of the LEA schools (ranging from the two-teacher rural primary to the large secondary) and four FE colleges and the College of Agriculture as well as special units, advisory teachers and parts of the youth and community service and teachers' centres.

The following gives the flavour of his findings:

What stands out from the evaluation as a whole is the sensitive flexibility of the local authority and its officers in responding to the expressed needs of schools and colleges, and the eagerness of so many teachers and lecturers to continue to improve the quality of the service they provide, their inventiveness in using the new opportunities that GRIST allows, and their persistence in carrying things through to a conclusion that will benefit their pupils and students.

(Thomas, 1988, p. 6)

The system of GRIST in Warwickshire has been conducted sensibly and sensitively by the County staff and eagerly and with an inventive flair by teachers for the benefit of pupils and students.

(Ibid., p. 6)

Thomas made a series of recommendations and a working party was set up to promote and carry out his suggestions. This evaluation was formative, summative and led to improvement. Among the key recommendations for future action by the LEA were the following points:

1 Consideration should be given to setting aside more funds for schools and colleges to bid for, so as to buy places on courses and employ advisory teachers.
2 All schools and colleges should operate a development plan, whether or not they currently require GRIST funding.
3 Further action should be taken by the advisory service to promote the formation of clusters of schools with the same INSET needs.
4 It was important to keep members of staff and governors informed about the GRIST programmes.
5 Schools and colleges should continue to be asked to say what consultation processes had been employed when making bids for GRIST funding.
6 Schools and colleges should make proposals for GRIST on a rolling three-year programme.
7 It was important to use a variety of topics and methods.
8 INSET manuals, handbooks and newsletters were proposed.
9 Adaptation of the FE staff development database should be considered.
10 In all but the smallest schools someone other than the head should be INSET co-ordinator.
11 The GRIST programme should be part of the general management of the institution.
12 Cross-phase, co-ordinated training should be encouraged.
13 Teachers' centres should be resource centres to help schools/colleges with staff development.
14 There was an urgent need to include ancillary workers in GRIST.
15 It was necessary to examine arrangements for supply cover, including INSET information for supply-cover teachers.
16 A series of evaluation questions and processes should be established.

As events were to prove, a key time in the whole development of GRIST, soon to become LEATGS (local education authority training grants scheme), was the period at the end of the first financial year – the first three months of 1988. At one and the same time the LEA was coming to grips with evaluating the first year of GRIST while it was still in progress, planning a second year in detail and monitoring the spending towards the end of the first year.

The issue of balancing the needs of individual teachers and institutions was still unresolved and the LEA had the additional problem of evaluation in terms of childrens' needs and the effects of INSET on children/students. Monitoring systems revealed a potential underspending as late as January 1988. Absorbing this took much time and thought. Dealing with this so that the extra INSET was in line with LEA plans and priorities was even harder. Yet again, ways of working evolved. Two aims emerged. The first was to achieve an accuracy of spending by March 1988, and in this there was virtual success. The second was to plan for 1988/89 so that such underspending did not happen again.

Planning for the future – January 1988

For Warwickshire a key planning stage (for the next year's work) was the annual advisers'/inspectors' planning conference of January 1988. This was a development of a traditional look at INSET. But the LEA now had to move further and lay down priorities for the next three years as well as the coming one. In teams colleagues examined how things had gone, what priorities had been and what they should be. As a result a document was produced for circulation to schools and colleges. Priorities were that equal opportunities (gender, race) be subsumed in everything; that cross-curricular themes should link separate aspects of learning; that staff development should affect the learning of children. These days were a learning experience for the team. One emergent problem was how to identify an ideal planning cycle spanning both the academic and the financial year. The concept that each school's three-year plan should be based on a curriculum plan leading to an INSET plan was accepted. From the general three-year plan, a detailed one-year plan would emerge. From this time on there has been no opposition to the general thinking of organized institutional planning. The only questions have been ones of refining the system and timescales. Norman Thomas's report underlined the effectiveness of such a system.

The changing nature of secondments

One major effect of GRIST/LEATGS referred to earlier has been the changing nature of secondments. Many LEAs would probably have difficulty in evaluating their secondments for the past ten years and showing the effects of some, let alone all, of them. The general purpose of a one-year secondment to an institution of higher education for refreshment and work towards a degree or advanced certificate was to rejuvenate individual teacher's careers and perspectives. How often, one wonders, did such teachers return eager and enhanced but back to the same situation they had left? Secondments given at the end of a teacher's working life should be discounted (that was never a Warwickshire method). Disillusion and frustration are not the ideal backgrounds to effective teaching and learning.

Under the new regime a secondary head was seconded for a term to examine modular curricular by investigating practices in other schools and LEAs; a primary head was seconded to a college to look at whole-school INSET and how it was conducted in other LEAs; a group of primary school teachers were seconded to write up materials for use in primary schools; a secondary deputy head was seconded to look at issues of women in management, to report on outcomes and run training sessions. All of these are examples of secondments leading to thought, action, dissemination and follow up. Significantly these and many other secondments have led to the growth of individuals who have then been able to lead teams in their own and other schools.

Where teachers have applied for secondment in the usual way, the procedure of prior evaluation of the putative benefit to the individual, the school or college and to the LEA, and then a negotiation with the provider, has been established. In some cases there has been secondment to the LEA itself and the establishment of a working group to monitor and support the secondment.

This has attacked the problem of 'the "disease of outside expertise" which has always challenged the school' (Anderson, Henning and Olsen, 1978, p. 5). The DES document 'The implementation of the local education authority training grant scheme – review of the first year and the future' (1988) refers to shorter periods of secondment which have 'equipped the teachers with the skills they needed to go back and put things into practice' (p. 6). This is borne out by experience of short-term planned secondments. However, it should be noted that some secondments may still be needed for individual study. This may be so particularly in the field of FE.

At this stage, the second year of LEATGS, it seems pertinent to point out some of the advantages and disadvantages to the LEA which emerged from this particular development of INSET.

The development of coherent planning

The great advantage, which was realized more and more, was that of coherent and cohesive planning. Although timescales are foreshortened, the ability to plan a whole LEA INSET year in detail and make sketch plans for future years gives a drive, impetus and sense of reality. A wider range of people is involved. No longer do teachers believe (in the majority of cases) that INSET is simply a list of courses on the staff notice-board. Rather, the vast majority of teachers are involved in planning, in the identification of the needs of thir own school, in the work of local teachers' centres, in the LEA INSET advisory committee. Each FE college has its own staff development group and involves all lectures through the use of the staff development management system (SDMS) of needs assessment, planning, monitoring and information banking. The youth and community service involves all of its full-time colleagues and many part-timers in the same work. Educational psychologists all meet in team planning of INSET.

It is now possible to begin to measure the effects of INSET. Significantly, INSET in Warwickshire, as in all LEAs, must be, and is, located firmly in the context of curriculum planning and thinking. This has been vital in work on GCSE, in TVEI, and in the changes in the primary curriculum. Whole-school (institutional) INSET has led to the emergence of new skills in schools and colleges. The need to produce a school/college plan, based on a three-year curriculum plan, a three-year staff development plan in outline and a one-year plan in detail, has given schools and colleges the opportunity of organized team thinking. Styles of INSET planning have followed the general trend in management planning and systems. INSET co-ordinators have been chosen in a variety of ways and are often not headteachers. Only one secondary head is now his own INSET co-ordinator; half the primary co-ordinators are not headteachers. This had spread thinking and responsibility. It has led to the growth of support groups of co-ordinators, and to training for them. The role of advisory teachers has been altered and extended as they work in schools and colleges in new ways. This has offered the opportunity of extended professionalism. Under the Warwickshire replanning of its advisoroy/inspectorate team this will lead to enhanced use of advisory teachers. Outside providers and trainers have been able to offer their help. Sometimes brought in by the LEA and sometimes by schools or colleges, they are always involved in a previously negotiated training initiative. The extended use of skills from within the LEA's own teaching force is clearly observable.

Whole-school INSET has brought increased co-operation between schools and between schools and colleges. There are happy and purposeful linking and clusterings. Warwickshire encourages this but does not put schools into clusters. So although most clusters are geographical this is not invariably the case. INSET in the smallest schools has been encouraged by their coming together. A further advantage of the new INSET has been the changed relationship of schools to HE. This has led to joint planning of courses and modules; purposeful secondments and reports; specific work in schools and colleges; and more effective use of money. Regional advantages of co-operation have been seen in the meetings of co-ordinators and their joint training activities. This was an outcome of co-operation begun during the five terms of TRIST.

From the point of view of the LEA, response to the developing nature of GRIST/LEATGS has been made more difficult for a variety of reasons.

Finance and monitoring

There has been a dichotomy of concern about spending. This emerged for the first time at the end of the first year of GRIST (spring 1988). If there is overspending the LEA is concerned. If there is underspending the DES (publicly) labels the LEA incompetent. Monitoring in an untried situation with developing but as yet not totally effective systems of financial control has led to great difficulties. This whole problem has caused time to be spent on readjustments to one year's programme while the LEA was simultaneously planning the next year in detail. This led to increased pressure on administrative staff, particularly those involved with finance. Monitoring of items and finance and training and producing the totals required by the DES in quarterly returns took time – amounting to about one to two weeks' work for a skilled person each quarter. The collation of information on schools'/colleges' in-service costs and the processing of institutional bids was a full-time job in itself. GCSE training added a deal of detail. The change from relatively few secondments to a whole range of smaller-scale INSET activities led to a vast amount of paper transactions. Planning the change to computer systems and the inputting of information again caused extra work. Although this was most serious in spring 1988 there is no reason to suppose that even with refinement of techniques and growing experience the problem will entirely disappear in future years.

The financial planning constraints imposed by the DES have led to the need to produce a plan by late September for approval by the DES in late December. The LEA then refines its own details for a start in the next April. The LEA committee cycle of financial planning and the academic year thus do not fit. This has serious implications for the management of whole-school INSET: it is difficult to plan without knowing how much money the LEA will actually put into the budget to back up DES grants.

Increased pressure on inspectors and advisers

The increased pressure on the working lives of advisers and inspectors needs comment. In addition to their other work priorities in schools/colleges and centrally, they have to play a more systematic role in INSET. A survey in Warwickshire revealed that about 40 per cent of advisers' and inspectors' time was spent on INSET-generated activities of one sort or another. These staff are also under pressure to update their own skills and plan their time to meet a growing range of targets.

The development of continuous planning has meant a skewing of resources of people and time into that area. The LEA is now involved in a continuous planning cycle, no longer just a few annual meetings and individual follow up.

The youth and community service

A further issue has been linking with the voluntary sector. The youth and community service highlights this. A full-time force of just over 40 people is extended by many hundreds of people – perhaps over a thousand. It was first necessary to discover just how many people, since all had a right to training under the LEATGS scheme. The regional co-operation mentioned earlier was immediately made more difficult by the disbanding of the DES regional planning committee of representatives of LEAs, HE and the HMI/DES. This has meant the spending of much time in the development of regional planning, built on TRIST and the group of LEA INSET co-ordinators.

The need for trainers

One great need, particularly as schools have developed their own INSET plans, has been for adequate and appropriate trainers. This has meant the training of the trainers; the use of outside trainers; and, most importantly, the extension of the skills of headteachers, deputies, INSET co-ordinators and others, not just in training techniques but also in appropriate philosophies and attitudes. War-wickshire has traditionally been an LEA which has encouraged good practice and developed policies from those good practices. An LEA which does not act in a prescriptive way has to adopt a correct stance to its training of trainers.

Supply cover

Supply cover, or its lack, has emerged as a key issue. Yet, on investigation, that is not an equal problem across the whole LEA. Variations depend on subject, phase and geographical distribution. Where there has been resentment at the discontinuity caused by absences through attendance on courses/meetings it has often been shown that it is the sum total of demand for cover that is the problem, not just INSET needs. A variety of ways of overcoming the problem have been developed. The extended use of part-timers, the use of Saturdays, evenings and residential experience has helped. The advent of the five training days has been important. Most of all, though, the view that INSET is not just something that happens out of school with supply cover has been reinforced.

Information flow

One significant effect of the last four years' developments in INSET has been the vastly increased information flow. Bidding forms, claim forms, information sheets, planning documents, handbooks and letters go to and from schools and colleges. Making telephone calls alone can be virtually a full-time job. LEA thinking, led by the Thomas Report and institutions' need to know, has led to a greater flow of information.

Planning documents require production, refining and distribution. Course requests require production, processing and record keeping. Course reports require circulation to key people, reading and recording. Handbooks need production, printing and updating: they must inform and help; they must tie in with LEA policies and work towards other initiatives. Documents to and from the DES require careful thinking, production and refining. All documents need printing and circulation.

In an LEA with about 4,000 teachers in schools and further education, the information flow has significantly increased. As a result the processing of information has required more effective management. The INSET office has acquired extra staff; word processors are increasingly used; a system of planning and recording has been established; and, most importantly, a clear look has been taken at the whole information-passing system.

Quality, evaluation and monitoring

Any LEA must be concerned that systems for managing INSET secure value for money and yet retain close personal contact with the people in schools and colleges actually carrying out the work. It is not enough to set up accurate paper and computer systems that should, in theory, work by themselves. The quality of what is achieved from in-service training is also affected by people's understanding of the tasks involved, by their previous experience of in-service work in schools, and by any training they may have had. In order to achieve effective systems and personal links and advice more central staff are needed, and their salaries and equipment use up a larger proportion of the whole budget.

In the LEA in the last four years much time has been devoted to the refining of paper and computer systems in order to facilitate planning, activity and recording. This will certainly continue. In-service training is developmental work. One inescapable conclusion is that systems will always need updating.

In December 1987 a DES letter to LEAs recorded that 'arrangements for monitoring and evaluation are generally at an early stage of development. They need to become more systematic, purposeful and comprehensive.' Evaluation had been required from LEAs, both by the MSC for TRIST and by the DES for GRIST, from the beginning. A later chapter will deal with the topic of evaluation in more detail; but from the LEA's point of view this has been a developing issue. It has gradually been realized that evaluation means more than notes on the outcomes of individual courses. There is the question of whether evaluation should be internal or external or a combination of both. It is of paramount importance that evaluation is built into the original plans, as opposed to being an addendum. Evaluation involves qualitative as well as quantitative judgements. By tradition and instinct LEAs have always veered towards the former. The DES at first placed a heavy requirement on the quantitative. Both methods require the establishment of aims and priorities as well as measurement techniques. Both methods also demand that an overview of events exists at the same time as responsibility is being devolved to schools and within schools. All in all a complex situation has emerged. As a result there have been great variations in LEAs' methods of evaluation. In Warwickshire developmental changes have occurred in response to shifting parameters.

Before TRIST evaluation was in terms of individual courses and of the work of individual people. It tended to be annual, summative and anecdotal. It was based firmly on a regularity of aims and of provision. With the establishment of TRIST and of TVEI there arose a need to evaluate the outcomes of particular initiatives. Although this was piecemeal, it led to serious evaluative thinking taking place across the whole educational spectrum, not just in the 14–18 age range. An outside evaluation of TRIST from Professor John Tomlinson and Martin Merson of Warwick University was based on observation of activities, interviews with teachers, officers and advisers, and a questionnaire. This was published and disseminated in March 1987. It was suggested that advisory teachers were effective and essential but needed closer links with the advisory service, better systems of reviewing their work and improved status. Whole-school INSET should be recognized as congruent with the school's develop-ment plan. Teachers should be involved in decision making. Consideration needed to be given to collection of appropriate data. Opportunities should be provided for reflection – much Warwickshire INSET was innovative and exploratory. Interestingly, there was to be a strong relationship between the findings of Tomlinson and Merson and Thomas's later, more detailed study. At the same time, people were being seconded and trained in evaluation aware-ness and in techniques for the training of others.

The first year of GRIST saw the work of Norman Thomas, referred to earlier. His summative and formative document, disseminated to all schools, led to the setting up of a working group to look at its findings and deal with its suggestions. At the same time, initial work was proceeding towards a future LEA evaluation plan. An LEA county evaluation strategy group was set up, consisting of the chief inspector, an FE college principal, heads of secondary and primary schools, a representative of the county teachers' advisory committee and the county INSET co-ordinator. This was to meet regularly and lay down the main lines of strategy and policy. Working to it would be an advisers'/inspectors' strategy group responsible for setting the actual tasks and establishing working parties. These would carry out the actual work and report back. Although working parties might represent phases they would also represent areas and initiatives such as youth and community or TVEI. The whole system would tie in with the LEA's general planning and policy groups.

In particular, the national curriculum, the Educational Reform Act and the local management of schools were to be tied in with the work of the various evaluation committees and working groups as all these innovations were issues of importance for INSET. An inspector has been appointed to bring this whole area together (a strategy being followed by many local authorities) and to collate work on it with a review of institutional development planning.

Other evaluation initiatives

The LEA is involved in three outside evaluation activities. With Dudley and Birmingham it is involved with Dr Neil Moreland of Wolverhampton

Polytechnic in a three-year DES evaluation project to look at the effects of INSET on teachers and children and to build up materials to help schools do better. With Professor Robert Burgess of Warwick University's Centre for Educational Development and Research, the project is also looking at the effects of INSET on children by observing the INSET activities of a number of schools, particularly those in clusters, and is working with several other LEAs. With the FE unit it is looking at staff needs by means of assessment in FE colleges and the evaluation of INSET there. These three activities together show how the LEATGS system has resulted in an LEA planning its thinking together with HE and other LEAs, to the benefit of the LEA's institutions.

The planning of future INSET is now actually involving the planning of evaluation. Yet from the LEA's point of view the timescale of activity imposed by the DES is not helpful. Work of this sort is not best done within the DES annual planning cycle. Authorities have to develop their own long-term continuous planning.

At this point it is significant to reflect that the 1988 DES document, collating the findings of HMI on the first year of GRIST across LEAs, in many ways emphasized the findings of Norman Thomas.

The DES document identified the following points:

- that a more systematic approach to INSET was emerging
- the emergence of explicit policies and designated people
- problems with appropriate (or any) supply cover
- significant numbers of new advisory teachers and advisers
- inspectors becoming managers of INSET, not providers
- notable devolution to schools and colleges
- a need for more efficient procedures of needs' identification
- a higher profile for training
- impacts on arising from the reduction in full-time secondments
- more attention to the impact of training on teaching and learning (a welcome point for Warwickshire).

From the LEA standpoint, the major development of GRIST/LEATGS has been the perpetual asking of sequential questions such as 'Where are we? Where are we going? How shall we get there? How shall we know we have arrived? What shall we then do?' Throughout this chapter it has been made evident that a system which had grown over the years to meet the needs of established thinking has been added to, refined and adjusted as a result of outside pressures and inside thinking. Each input of thought and activity has led to a series of further actions. Each has been followed, in some cases before its effects could be ascertained, by the next plan and process. The work of the LEA has been to make sense of all the initiatives, to translate them in terms of its own schools and colleges and to refine their language for the benefit of its children. In this way the established truisms and the developing methods can be merged to produce purposeful and balanced in-service training of teachers.

The children themselves are the living aim and end of our teaching. It is their thought, their knowledge, their character and development which make the purpose of our existence as schools and teachers. And it is the modes of their learning and understanding, their physical growth and social needs, which in the end determine the success or failure of our methods of teaching.

(Isaacs, 1932, p. 11)

References

Anderson, S., Henning, A., and Olsen, M. (1978). *Teachers' Further Education: A Danish Case Study*. Denmark Laererhojskole.

Department of Education and Science (1989). 'The implementation of the local education authority training grant scheme – review of the first year and the future', paper presented to an Invitation Conference at Buxton.

Her Majesty's Inspectors of Schools (1989). *Report of the Implementation of the Local Education Authority Training Grant Scheme (1978–88)*. London, Department of Education and Science.

Isaacs, S. (1932). *The Children We Teach*. London, University of London Press.

Manpower Services Commission (1987). *MSC Summative Report on TRIST*. Technical and Vocational Educational Initiative Unit.

Thomas, N. (1988). *Grant Related In-service Training in Warwickshire 1987/88*. Warwickshire Local Education Authority.

Warwickshire County Council (1988). *The Curriculum 5–12*. Education Department.

3

The role of an advisory service

David Wilkins

In the months leading up to and following the passage of the Education Reform Act of 1988, members of some LEAs – and in particular on their advisory services – had furrowed brows. Like the White Rabbit, they were to be seen hurrying down long passages, saying, 'Oh, my ears and whiskers, how late it's getting!' Big changes were round the corner, and there was little time to prepare. All the talk was of national curriculum monitoring and school inspections, or perhaps (for those who had heard the newspeak of the management consultants) of performance indicators and the setting up of quality assurance divisions.

But many LEAs had not so far asked their advisory services to engage significantly, or even at all, in monitoring activities. In some cases advisers' formal monitoring work in the 1980s was restricted to involvement with newly qualified teachers in their probationary year. Acting as friendly school visitors, they perhaps worked on an individual basis, offering curriculum advice and contacts to particular departments or teachers, giving support to the school in certain areas such as the interviewing of new staff and offering a range of external courses or help with in-school in-service days. Additionally they might well have been required to manage the work of other support groups, such as advisory teachers. But they might not have been asked to make formal comments on teachers' classroom work or to produce written reports evaluating what they had seen – practice varied a good deal from LEA to LEA. Some advisers would have argued vehemently that the need to take such a judgemental stance would have greatly damaged their positive developmental relationship with the schools.

Now it began to seem as if the 1988 Act would give them no choice. The Secretary of State needed local inspectors to carry out an in-depth monitoring of school performance since this would be quite beyond the resources of HMI. So the new emphasis for LEA advisers was presumably on evaluation. Perhaps (it was said with anxiety) their developmental function would have to go to the wall, or at least be very much diminished. Other groups – like advisory teachers – could, after all, offer support to schools in their developmental work. But who else would be qualified and available to say whether the schools were actually delivering the Secretary of State's new curriculum to their pupils?

The anxiety and even anguish apparent in a number of county and city halls in 1988 was not felt in Nottinghamshire. The advisory and inspection service (AIS) there was confident about the future. It believed, with much justice, that it had some time since found its way on to the new road and had indeed travelled a good way along it. Nottinghamshire advisers already had a new emphasis and balance in their work, a new way of operating which it was hoped would stand them in good stead in the 1990s.

This confidence came not just from considerable experience in handling formal monitoring procedures and writing evaluative reports but from the manner in which this experience had been acquired. The Nottinghamshire AIS believed that its approach to monitoring and evaluation did not separate it from developmental work but gave it increased chances of making an effective contribution to it.

Two fundamental beliefs underpin the position adopted by the AIS. The first of these is that most useful professional development takes place in the teacher's own school and classroom, not in professional or residential centres. The second is that the most powerful messages about how one's practice can be improved come from interaction with one's colleagues and from active, shared exploration of what is going on in each others' classrooms, not from theoretical lectures or from criticisms received from outsiders. The next sections try to show how these principles emerged from the way in which the AIS developed its formal inspection and review work in the late 1970s and the 1980s.

The developmental aspect of formal inspections

Nottinghamshire's advisers have been carrying out inspections and reviews since 1977, so they are well used to formal monitoring processes. Though at that time they were renamed inspectors, and the chief intention of some members of the education committee may have been that they should become watchdogs, sniffing out poor practice and inefficiency wherever it could be found, the advisers themselves took a broader and more positive view.

All inspectors claim that their work has a developmental purpose. Judgements that are not intended to secure some kind of improvement, it is argued, are hardly worth making and since no teacher or school is perfect there are always ways of suggesting change for the better. Nottinghamshire's AIS certainly argued this, with some passion. They had not been keen to be turned into inspectors and they feared a deterioration in their relationships with schools because of the change; but they were determined to turn the change to positive advantage. They knew that the novelty in their work was not the making of judgements itself – it is a commonplace of advisory work that one cannot give realistic and relevant advice without first observing and evaluating. The novelty was in the formality of reporting to governors and committee.

So the challenge was to make sure that this task of inspecting and reporting did not saddle them with a reputation as hostile destroyers, who told tales out of school, but rather that, while being objective and informative, it facilitated their support work. Inspections have to become a professional development tool. In the first years after 1977 the Nottinghamshire AIS relied on four, fairly commonplace approaches to achieve this.

The first was to associate the school's link inspector (who would always be a specialist in the appropriate primary, secondary or post-16 phase) with the inspection or review, usually by making her/him a member of the inspecting team. (Even the smallest rural primary school would merit a team of two. The other member of the team would probably not know the school well or at all; this would help to ensure objectivity.) The phase inspector would be able to set the inspection in the context of the school's past and its on-going development in order to make the final report seem as realistic and relevant to the school as possible.

The second device regarded as helpful was the recording of actual recommendations in the text of the report. Suggestions rather than instructions, these recommendations could be seen as a set of development proposals highlighting key areas for the school to consider when planning the next stages of internal change and progress. They would not necessarily be intended to cover every important aspect of the inspection or be targets for immediate achievement. They would be a selection of practical proposals related to the school's and the teachers' realizable developmental needs. One of the first tasks of the school after the inspection could then be to review the list of recommendations and consider ways of handling them, deciding which might be tackled immediately and in what way; which were urgent but needed resource support; which would have to be left for the time being; and which they might not wish to respond to at all. This kind of team debate, together with the subsequent establishment of action groups, would in itself be an important contribution to good professional development.

The third supportive aspect of this traditional mode of inspection is that of the follow up. The AIS work is not complete when the report is finally presented to governors and committee. The school will expect and be entitled to support in the months to come. The AIS will have a responsibility for seeing that support is available. Particular teachers or departments may want to debate practice or to be provided with in-service opportunities; the head of the senior management group may wish to examine how particular problems are handled by other schools. Depending on the need, the AIS will sometimes be able to meet it directly (often through the phase inspector linked with the school) or alternatively will be able to point to other groups from whom support is available. Either way, the support will relate to the real school situation and identified teacher needs.

To take an example, an inspection may have included an examination of the range of written work produced by a selection of pupils. A resulting recommendation may have been that:

> The school should build into its programme of professional development for all staff a consideration of the issues arising from this study of pupils' writing, including the giving of further attention to:
> - the importance of generative styles of writing
> - the value of opportunities to edit and reshape drafts
> - the link between audience and appropriateness of style; and
> - the learning opportunities available in good presentation of work.

Here is an obvious opportunity for the inspectors involved to work with the teachers, perhaps on a day-closure training event at the school, to illustrate their points more fully from the pupils' work concerned, and to consider practical ways of seeking improvement.

The fourth consideration goes closely along with the third. The AIS has always made every effort to report quickly. Many aspects of follow up are impossible until an actual written report is available to which the school can respond; the longer a printed report is delayed the more out of date and unhelpful it becomes. If development is a priority, then so also must be the reporting. The Nottinghamshire aim has therefore always been to draft, consult the school about the draft, revise, print and meet governors within three months of the inspection. If teachers, having seen the draft, are already responding to some of the recommendations (and this often happens) so much the better.

Changing the mode of operation

Streamlining the role

This fairly standard approach to inspections operated for some years before the two important changes were initiated in the mid-1980s. One of these was a redefinition of the role of the AIS, reducing its management and administrative functions. The other was the involvement of schools not just as passive recipients of the process but as actual participants in inspections.

Like most advisory services the AIS in Nottinghamshire has for a number of years wrestled with the dilemma of having more work on hand than – with the resources (particularly time) that it had available – it could complete to its satisfaction. This pressure sharpened its thinking and encouraged it to accept, or even to welcome, a streamlining of its functions. It was realized that some tasks on its current list could in fact be adequately performed by others and perhaps should be. The key question was becoming not 'What do our particular skills equip us to do well?', but 'What is it that no one else can be reasonably expected to attempt if we don't do it?'

The answer to this question had to lie in the area of external evaluation of classroom practice and the general management of schools, together with the resulting production of appropriate developmental advice both for the schools and for the LEA. It was, on the other hand, not necessary for the AIS to be ubiquitous in, say, the business of staff appointments. 'If we're not there, such terrible appointments are made, and we have to pick up the pieces later' is a conceited and misdirected argument. The proper role here is not to try to replace others but to support them where appropriate in evaluating and improving their practice. If a head is inexpert in shortlisting or in interview techniques, 'Here, let me do it' is not the appropriate response; it is better to arrange for supportive advice and, if possible, training.

It was equally not necessary for the AIS to manage the whole in-service programme for the authority or to run all the key courses themselves, even if this were practically possible. They could advise on the major issues and contribute in key areas; others could be responsible overall and other support groups could take the lion's share of work in organizing and presenting courses. Organizing county-wide festivals, conducting concerts, arranging swimming-bath timetables or the time of peripatetic teachers does not make the best use of advisers' skills. If they are doing these things they are not in schools supporting teachers and in-school development.

For these kinds of reasons Nottinghamshire introduced separate administrative sections to manage its various groups of advisory teachers (often working on time-limited secondments), its major projects such as TVEI extension and the development of records of achievement, training needs following the 1988 Act, the introduction of teacher appraisal and so on. The advisory and inspection service has been freed to advise and inspect. There is the additional advantage here that the AIS is able to evaluate and advise on developments such as TVEI without being accused of inspecting its own work and therefore of being inevitably blinkered or prejudiced.

Alongside this contraction of the range of its work went a simultaneous expansion. The variety of reviews and inspections being attempted was considerably increased and methods were refined. Sometimes the focus was on increasing the volume of activity by finding more economical approaches. For instance, a small team of three inspectors was given four days to inspect a fair-sized comprehensive school. Their task was to see whether – within the time allocated – they could get beyond surface perceptions to a depth of view of important aspects of the school so that the head and staff felt that the exercise had been of some real use to them and the inspectors felt they had increased the range and quality of their perceptions of the school.

The experiment was a success. A good deal was able to be said (in a helpful way) about the school's management systems, its overall planning, its handling of professional development issues and its thinking about the curriculum. No portrait of individual subject departments emerged or was expected, but advice was able to be given, based on a range of lesson observations, examination of pupils' work and interviews with teachers and pupils, about prevalent teaching styles, the diet received by the children, and general attitudes and expectations. Short though this inspection was, the normal follow-up response, as already described, was also available. In sum, this kind of very short inspection was felt to be both effective and efficient and it was added to the AIS's developmental armoury.

Partnership in inspections

At other times the focus was on sharing the process of inspection with the school, so that the teachers could feel greater ownership of the resulting recommendations. No immediate economy in the use of inspectors' time followed from this approach; indeed, it was found to take longer, because of the teachers' comparative inexperience in handling observation and assessment techniques. But it was based on the sound principle that the best way of securing lasting change in schools is to secure the active involvement and motivation of the teachers. If a position can be reached where the teachers' own investigations lead them to recommend, say, that 'a consistent school policy on homework should be produced', they are likely to produce a consistent homework policy. They will want to take notice of what they have said to themselves.

In the longer run this will mean that inspectors will act more as validators than evaluators. They will be assessing the quality of the school's own system of evaluation of the emerging judgements, and of the effectiveness of the resulting development. They will be setting all this against what is happening elsewhere, so that comparative standards are maintained, and they will be giving appropriate advice. They will be catalysts, rather than the main deliverers of programmes for good teacher development. Steps towards this desirable goal are likely to be small, and have certainly been so in Nottinghamshire. However, the direction of travel has been established, and real progress has been made along the road. It is one of the most encouraging journeys on which the inspectors have been able to embark in recent years.

The first tentative partnership was established in 1985. A short general inspection of a comprehensive school was planned. One of the school's deputy heads was invited to join the inspecting team of five, to participate in some of the lesson observation, the related aspects of the planning and the subsequent discussion of emerging conclusions. This worked well. Although lack of experience of the co-operative process caused both partners to be too cautious and circumspect, the final report was improved by the perspectives that the deputy added, the school's commitment to the report was probably increased and the follow-up work seemed to be more intensive.

Another incidental aspect of this particular partnership was that the school's senior managers felt bold enough to ask for a significantly critical part of the final report to be substantially changed. They explained that they fully accepted its truth and validity but felt that it would be so unpalatable to the department in question that developments already in progress to improve matters there would be jeopardized. An alternative commentary was therefore found, which allowed the inspectors to feel that their legitimate criticism had been firmly and properly made, while the school's senior managers felt that they had a platform on which to build. In the longer run the best interests of the school's pupils were probably served by this agreement.

Other partnerships have followed, in primary as well as in secondary schools. The extent of teacher involvement has been different in each one, particularly because of variations in the present experience of the school in evaluative techniques. (If, for example, teachers have never had the chance to observe each other teach and are uncomfortable with another adult in their room, only a limited partnership is likely to be attempted.) The following picture is intended to illustrate these partnerships. It shows inspectors and teachers working side by side in an inspection. While it is not a description of any single piece of work in Nottinghamshire, none of it is invented. All the kinds of activity suggested here have actually been tried, in schools, at one time or another, with some success.

Outline of a cooperative inspection

The school is an 11-to-18 comprehensive with a staff of 60. When the short inspection is announced to the headteacher, he sighs; the time of year will be very inconvenient (it always is). Then he becomes more positive. There will be ways in which it will fit in with his development plan and it may be useful. The head is offered the choice of a traditional (HMI-type) inspection or one that involves the school in partnership. This is no choice at all and he goes away to talk to his staff about the kind of involvement they want.

A committee of a dozen is set up to represent the school. It ranges from a teacher just into his second year of teaching through to two deputies (but not the head). The five AIS inspectors have two or three joint meetings with the committee. The general purposes and style of inspections are discussed. The committee proposes a long list of certain areas that it would like this short, and therefore restricted, inspection to include; the inspectors reduce the long list to a short one that has one or two of their own suggestions added and after debate with the teachers make a final decision that includes on the list an examination of the place of group work in class teaching, the provision for pupils with special educational needs and perceptions of the school held by parents and members of the local community. Three small working groups (each with teachers and inspectors as members) are established to work out details of processes to be used, including schedules for use in classroom observation and questions for use in a variety of interview situations.

The breadth of experience that the inspectors have and the forms they have used successfully in previous situations are found helpful by the teachers. (Some of the forms and the ideas will be useful not now but when the inspection is over and normality has returned.) Two information-giving and consultative meetings are held by the complete joint planning team with the whole staff during this preparation period.

The inspection is carried out in two parts. The first part includes some interviews but concentrates on classroom observations. These are often made through pupil pursuits, where a class or an individual pupil are followed for a day (or more), so that the observer gets a view of what the pupils' learning experiences are over this period. Selected members of the teachers' committee produce their own collection of these observations, to set alongside those of the inspectors for each of the year groups concerned. It turns out that the teachers are rather harder on their colleagues than are the inspectors, focusing less on their strengths and more on their weaknesses. Plenty of material for future in-service work emerges, including ideas that will help the school's developing approach to its self-appraisal techniques.

There is general agreement that the observers have seen a good deal more group work than is normally likely to be typical in the school. Teachers have in some cases evidently prepared special events so that the observers can find what they are thought to be looking for. No one is deceived; the pupils have revealed that what is going on is outside their normal experience and that of their teachers'. Special event or normal, there is overall much material for future developmental work.

The second part of the inspection is shaped in detail when the first part is reviewed. One or two gaps that are found to exist in the information so far collected can be filled. Discussions and interviews tend to dominate, often carried out by an inspector and a teacher working in tandem. The questions about management style, asked of the head by one of his MPG (main professional grade) teachers, are particularly pertinent and powerful. Parents and local residents show some misunderstandings about school policy that need to be set right but make some helpful suggestions about how to make the school's public relations policy more vigorous and imaginative.

When the information gathering is over the evaluation and writing begin. The final report will be from the inspectors, who will accept responsibility for all the conclusions and recommendations. But the teachers' committee is fully involved in the debating and weighing and drafting and shaping that come first. There will be an appreciation and a sense of ownership of the final report that is never achieved by the purely external inspection. Next year's action plan for the school will effectively be already enshrined in the recommendations.

Quis Custodiet?

In all of this description of developments in Nottinghamshire, much use has been made of words like monitoring and judgement. Even the partnership just described, it will have been noticed, is not an equal partnership; the AIS has a heavy judgemental role and retains final responsibility. It is proper, therefore, to ask: who evaluates the evaluators? What guarantee is there of the quality of an inspectorate's actions and opinions?

The most satisfactory answer is likely to be found in a good appraisal system. Inspectors, at least as much as any other group, should have their performance regularly appraised, and a key role in this should be played by headteachers and other professionals from within the education service. At present, most LEAs do not have such a system in place. Until they do, inspectors need to be particularly scrupulous in seeking the highest standards in their work, as much of which as possible should be done openly and be available for scrutiny. The Nottinghamshire AIS has these needs very much in mind, and it may be helpful to draw from the account so far given one or two aspects of its normal practice that are felt to be relevant in this respect.

1 In any review or inspection activity the inspectors make available for comment both the criteria against which they will measure what they see and the methods and schedules they will use for the measuring.
2 Specific opinions formed during an inspection – say about a particular lesson that has been seen – will be described to and discussed with the teacher concerned. (Schedules completed about particular lessons seen during an inspection are not, however, retained or filed, on the grounds that individual teachers are not the focus of attention and what has been seen may well not have been a fair sample of their work. Where outside inspections, reports are written about particular teaching sessions seen, this will normally be after the discussion with the teacher, who will receive a copy of the report and have the opportunity to comment in writing on it.)
3 Any resulting general report, with its recommendations, will be made available to the school for comment and there is a genuine willingness in the inspectorate to respond positively to these comments. In practice two measures of the general acceptability of the judgements made by the inspectors may be seen in, firstly, the level of comments normally made by the schools (they tend to be concerned with small detail rather than big issues) and, secondly, the normal willingness of schools to proceed to implementation of the recommendations that have been made. (On those rare occasions when a suggestion is rejected by a school or a department, it is open to them to find an alternative way of moving forward. The recommendations are not compulsory.)
4 Reports of formal inspections are debated by the governors, who have their own perceptions of the school and who receive comment from head and

teachers as well as inspectors. They are free to make critical resolutions if they wish. In practice nearly all reports are welcomed and fully accepted.
5 Reports and comments from governors go on to the education committee, which has equal rights – as rarely exercised – to be critical of the report.

The essence of all these points is that they involve openness. Inspectors must have the confidence and the courage to make themselves, their tenets and their methods available for inspection. Short of a proper system of inspectorate appraisal this is probably the best safeguard available to the schools. The more that criticism of an advisory service is made possible and easy, the less, perhaps, it will be necessary.

The prospect for the future

Supported by this kind of open and co-operative practice, the Nottinghamshire AIS will move with confidence into the era of national monitoring. Schools will be accumulating the results of a variety of tests and assessments of their pupils, completing tick lists that certify a proper coverage of the national curriculum and appraising the work of their teachers. The local advisory monitors will be issuing the schools with clean bills of health, to certify that all is as it seems.

However for advisory services the 1990s will be characterized by more novelties than the requirement to monitor the delivery of an imposed national curriculum. In the first place LEAs, shorn of some of their former powers and recognizing the greater freedom of schools in the era of formula funding and LMS, will be likely to attempt to reassert themselves through influence instead of control and to develop a working partnership with governors and schools where the LEA is the senior partner. There will be an (overdue) emphasis on development planning at all levels, to be accompanied by regular audits that will give an indication of progress. It will doubtless be stressed to the junior partners that greater freedom brings greater responsibility and that their accountability is not only to the parents but also to the LEA. In this context the LEA is likely to depend on its advisers (or its inspectors) to provide, through their fieldwork, evidence that validates and interprets information obtained from schools' own appraisal processes, from public examination results and national testing, and from the various other sources that will certainly be available. That advisory services will in this way have a more central place in LEAs' thinking is already evident (in the year following the passage of the 1988 Act).

But the schools, too, may well be looking at advisers in a new light. Many headteachers will be facing substantial new challenges and problems in the management of resources – Can we afford to continue with three deputy heads? How can we maximize the use of school premises out of school hours? – and all of them will be involved with such issues as teacher appraisal, the changing role of governors or the effects of greater parental choice, as well as coping with the national curriculum. These larger responsibilities will, however, bring certain greater freedoms, one of which will be in deciding where to seek advice and support. The question posed by those in schools to advisers is likely to be, what skills can you offer that will help my school survive and progress in this new era?

The overlap between LEA and school needs is not immediately clear and some LEAs are approaching the apparent dilemma by creating a team of inspectors separate from the advisory service. This suggests, at least to the outsider, on the one hand a group of judges with the 'vocabulary' and the best available answers, and on the other a team of helpers who have time to support good professional development and are not tainted with the stigma of making judgements.

In my view, this is an error; the argument against such a separation of powers seems as overwhelming now as it has ever been. Even when they are in the middle of their 'evaluation of quality' role, inspectors or advisers are not really engaged in the task of seeking out inadequate teaching. Of course, incompetence or underperformance, where it is found, must be addressed, not (as has too often happened in the past) ignored. But the wider purpose, even of formal inspections, is a much more positive one – and just the same as that of all advisory work: to improve the quality of the child's experience by improving the quality of the education offered. Everyone involved in the privileged work of education should be seeking to improve their performance, assessors – be they HMI, LEA advisers, headteachers or even prime ministers.– just as much as the assessed. There are not two competing sides helping children to make the most of their lives; there is only one.

For advisers, then, the focus should be on the school and the classroom and monitoring, where it occurs, will be simply one more tool in their armoury, all of which is designed to help the development of teachers. It is to be hoped that, before the turn of the century, schools will be doing much of their own evaluation and appraisal work. Advisers, bringing with them a wider view of other schools than many teachers or even heads can hope to have acquired, skilled in planning, data collection, classroom observation and analysis, will be validating the school's work, offering constructive comment and debating the next stages and targets the school should set. Monitoring on the one hand and supporting on the other will be inseparable parts of the same process.

Authority-wide, formal in-service programmes serve a useful function. But they can never do more than skim the surface of need. Most professional development for teachers will occur in the school and the classroom and this is where good advisory services are likely to continue to focus their activity.

This chapter is for the most part concerned with aspects of the work of Nottinghamshire's advisory service, which is responsible for monitoring and supporting the work of teachers in colleges as well as in schools. Where appropriate in this section, the word school should be taken also to refer to college. The views expressed in this section are the author's and not necessarily those of the LEA.

4

The role of the advisory teacher in staff development

Shirley Andrews

Staff development has been an important educational issue for many years and encompasses a wide variety of different topics, methods, forms and modes of delivery. Recent changes and developments in education and the 'plethora of legislative and cross curricular initiatives' (Stillman, 1988, p. 14) – new technology, subject matter, forms of assessment, multicultural education, special needs, equal opportunities, and gender, DES special project, TVEI, GCSE, computer-assisted learning, national curriculum, etc. – have, however, brought the issue of staff development to the forefront thus serving to highlight the need for the formulation of coherent policies. Government arrangements for GRIST, introduced in April 1987, together with the identification of priority areas for funding to ensure the allocation of resources where they are most needed, have further emphasized this need. The extent to which an LEA can mount a successful staff development programme is, however, dependent upon the organization, expertise and delivery of those agents appointed to oversee such schemes, be they members of the LEA advisory service, teachers' centre wardens, school heads or teachers with responsibility for a specific subject area. The purpose of this chapter is to focus upon the role of one specific group of agents, advisers, and in particular on the contribution made by advisory teachers.

The writer herself was directly involved in the organization and implementation of staff development programmes having been seconded to a specific curriculum project on a 0.5 basis over a period of two years. Her brief was to 'encourage and develop the use of electronic technology in music throughout the LEA's secondary schools'. A parallel appointment was also made in the area of pop music. The work and development taking place, together with the knowledge, expertise and skills of the two teachers, within these specific areas of music was well known throughout the LEA. The calibre of those appointed was thus ensured. Both projects were funded by the LEA as a response to pressure from external agencies, HMI, DES, pupils, etc. The advisory teachers were directly accountable to the music adviser and director of the Centre for Performing Arts (CPA). More specific reference will be made to the role of the advisory teacher in relation to staff development later. Before this is done, however, a brief survey of the development and role of the LEA advisory service will help to put those developments into context.

Development of the advisory service

The LEA advisory services 'have had a long history and form part of the development of the education service since the end of the 19th Century', (DES Welsh Office, 1982, p. 33), being originally 'established and maintained in order to provide some assurance for the taxpayer that his money is being properly spent' (Blackie, 1970, p. 1). During this time education and the demands made upon it have changed. The role of the adviser has had to change in order to 'reflect the changing nature and growing complexity of the education service with which it is closely related'. (DES, 1982, p. 4). The context in which advisers have fulfilled this role has tended over the years to alternate between inspection and advice. The tradition established by Dr Kay Shuttle-worth in 1840 stressed an advisory rather than inspectoral role. 'Inspection is not intended as a means of ensuring control but of affording assistance' (Bolam et al., 1978, p. 10). The post-war period signalled a change of emphasis in the adviser's role. Indeed, the 1944 Education Act required that 'inspections be made of every educational establishment maintained by an LEA at appropriate intervals' (DES, 1982, p. 7). More recently 'the press of events' has been to make 'the evaluative role of Advisers more discernible'. This arose from an 'emphasis on accountability which has been gathering steam since the mid 1970s as the economy declined and the education service found itself in a climate where its prevailing position of self-evident justification came to be questioned more and more' (Wilcox, 1985). Past history has shown, then, that 'the work of the Advisory Service is sensitive to changes in its context' (Walker, 1981, p. 13), both in the way it performs its duties and in the demands made upon it. This is as true today with the Education Reform Act (ERA) and local management of schools (LMS), both of which 'will affect the balance of monitoring and evaluation activities in LEAs' (Birnbaum, 1989, p. 156). But what *is* the role of an LEA adviser?

The role/functions of an LEA Adviser

Results obtained from research have confirmed that 'advisers have many roles and many aspects to their work' (Bolam et al., 1978, p. 2).

A major responsibility of LEAs is the quality of education. The responsibility lies both at the LEA centre and in individual schools and colleges. At the centre, the part of an LEA's organisation primarily concerned with the quality of pupils' education is the local Inspection and Advisory Service.
(AUDIT Commission, 1989, p. 3)

'Job specifications and functions of LEA Advisers were found to be varied, differing considerably from one LEA to another' (Bolam *et al.*, 1978, p. 221). According to Howarth (1985, p. 94), these tasks could include

the development of the curriculum, commissioning, planning and producing materials, implementing local/national policies, exchanging information, maintaining standards, formulating guidelines, translating guidelines into effective practice, advising colleagues, planning/offering INSET, supporting/encouraging staff, assisting with professional development, staff selection/appointment, appraisal/monitoring/discipline of staff, help with problem solving, advising on the management of contraction, fighting for resources, links between LEA and schools, promoting links between related agencies, providing information for policy makers including the formulation of reports which influence policy.

It was found, however (Bolam *et al.*, 1978), that in spite of the wide diversity of duties, certain tasks appertained to all advisers. The firstly was inspection – evaluating the performance of both schools and teachers and 'informing teachers and schools about decisions taken by policy makers and administrators', (Bolam *et al.*, 1978, p. 221). The second, was administrative – clerical work dealing with a multitude of requests, queries, etc. and the writing of testimonials, reports, submissions seeking finance, etc. The third aspect was advisory – to improve educational standards through advice to teachers and schools, provision of INSET, advising heads and LEA on staffing, teaching accommodation, etc. The fourth task was professional – responsibility for the pastoral care of staff under the adviser's jurisdiction, guiding staff in career development and providing appropriate opportunities for them to develop further.
Advisers are, then, faced with a

range of functions relating partly to teachers and schools and partly to the administrative officers of the authority. In their administrative or inspectoral role they inform teachers and schools about decisions taken by policy makers and administrators and evaluate their performance. In their professional or advisory role they try to improve educational standards through their advice to teachers and schools.
(Bolam *et al.*, 1978, p. 221)

Research has shown, (Bolam *et al.*, 1978; Dean, 1984) that most advisers would prefer greater emphasis to be placed on the advisory function of their role, particularly where it appertains to staff development and innovation.

Recruitment of advisers

It would appear, then, that advisers consider staff development to be a significant feature of their work. In order for this function to be carried out successfully, however, the advisory service must essentially remain sensitive to the changes and developments and demands made upon it at all times in order that the 'changing nature and growing complexity of the education service with which it is closely related can be reflected' (Dean, 1984). This is particularly important today in the light of the many changes such as the move towards a national curriculum with its associated attainment targets and testing, and core and foundation subjects; local financial management; and ... government recognition in 1986 of the need for appropriate staff development packages to be implemented with the foundation of the LEA training grants scheme. The aims of this are:

> to promote the professional development of teachers; to promote more systematic and purposeful planning of INSET; to encourage more effect-ive management of the teaching force and to encourage training in selected areas which are accorded national priority.
>
> (Letch, 1988, p. 10)

It is therefore imperative that

> as central influence ... grows, each LEA should have a voice which interprets national policy in a local context ... schools need access to an influence which is not politically distorted by either the DES–HMI–MSC nexus or by transient extremism in Local Government.
>
> (Matthews, 1985)

> Local Authority Advisers operating as individual local services relating to the needs of those individual LEA's fulfil this criteria.
>
> (DES, 1982, p. 35)

The calibre of those appointed to this position is, then, of utmost importance. It is for this reason that it has been suggested that 'Local Authority Advisers must be drawn from the ranks of experienced teachers and Heads since they must be first and foremost professional educationalists rather than Local Government Administrators' (Fiske, 1969).

The majority of advisers are, in fact, 'appointed from the ranks of teachers, lecturers and Heads' many of whom have had at least six years' experience. Over half had taught for eleven years or more, while 76 per cent had held some form of graded or senior posts in schools and 20 per cent had been Heads (Bolam *et al.*, 1978). It would seem logical to assume, therefore, that those applying to the LEA advisory service have had relevant experience of several levels within the school system. This is particularly appropriate for, as Dean (1985, pp. 11–12) has pointed out,

> the teacher brings with him first hand and recent experience of children in and out of the classroom and usually also experience as a manager of colleagues in school. He also brings knowledge and expertise in some aspects of the school curriculum. This knowledge and skill will be of great value to him as an Adviser.

It also means that 'advisers have experienced the teaching/learning situation as a significant responsibility, not as an abstract generalised notion . . . quality of insight and observation will therefore grow from such experience because it is based on personal understanding and observation'. (Gentle, 1976, p. 16). The credibility of those appointed to the LEA advisory service appears, then, to be 'established on the basis of the experience brought to the job' (Dean, 1985, p. 11). Nevertheless, a newly appointed adviser will have 'new knowledge to acquire and new skills to develop . . . knowledge of how Local Government works from the inside . . . the procedures used in his own office and the expectations of the staff there' (Dean, 1985, pp. 11–12).

> All Advisers need a great deal of knowledge about different forms of school and classroom organisation, the advantages and disadvantages of each, the snags and problems likely to be encountered and some of the solutions.
>
> 　　　　　　　　　　　　　　　　　　　　　　　　　(Dean, 1985, pp. 11–13)

Training

It would seem logical to assume that once recruited all advisers participate in a basic training programme. Research has found, however (Bolam *et al.*, 1978; Dean, 1975, 1984, 1985; Lewis, 1984), that 'Advisers receive very little training for the tasks they have to perform' (Lewis, 1984). 'Advisers, like heads, have usually had to learn their job from bitter experience, without very much by way of training for it and often with only a minimum amount of help from others' (Dean, 1975, p. 11). It has even been suggested (Dean, 1985) that because "many of those who have spent some time in the Advisory Service have become highly skilled at the job" that it is "tempting to use this fact as evidence that Advisers don't need training"' (Dean, 1975, p. 12).

Results of a questionnaire survey distributed to advisers (Bolam *et al.*, 1978, p. 235), showed that '82% of respondents had received no specific training for Advisory work'. The majority did indeed feel that there was a need for some form of training in both the 'general aspects of Advisory work including personnel management, job evaluation and organisation as well as in areas which were specifically related to subject specialisms'. It was also felt that 'some form of general induction course for new entrants' to the profession needed to be provided' (Bolam et al., 1978, p. 235). The training for evaluation programme (at the Centre for Adviser and Inspector Development), set up in the last year as a direct response to the Education Reform Act, is recognition of the fact that advisers need help and training to carry out their role successfully.

The success of the LEA advisory service seems, therefore, to be largely dependent upon the personal experience and expertise of its individual advisers. This will have far reaching effects as far as the adviser's role in staff development is concerned. It is therefore essential that advisers keep up to date with their subject or other specialisms. 'One significant function the Adviser has is as talent spotter of those teachers who are doing original or inspiring work in the classroom' (Collins, 1976, p. 15). An adviser needs to be constantly 'aware of the strengths and weaknesses of work in his subject area across the schools of the LEA . . . identifying possible areas of development in individual schools and groups of schools' which will in turn enable them to 'foster a range of activities' which will assist them in the formulation of their staff development programmes (Dean, 1985, p. 14).

The investigation into LEA advisers and educational innovation in 1978 showed, however, that advisers were in danger of being 'pushed away from direct participation in INSET towards an evaluative, administrative and organisational role' due to the increased emphasis given to 'inspection, accountability and value for money' (Bolam et al., 1978, p. 228). 'Improvements in education sought by the Government . . . will make extra demands of LEA Advisers. They will need to spend more time evaluating the quality of education' (Kirkman, 1985). It was becoming clear that advisers were increasingly being made to take on board two additional functions, a generalist role in one specific subject and, the adoption of a pastoral role to a group of schools. To the advisers it seemed as if the nature of the job has changed very fundamentally within the last few years. It is likely that the increasing complexity and technicality of LEA administrative processes and of school organization and curriculum processes have lessened the need for and reduced the scope of the individual adviser. But what effect has all this had on the role of the adviser?

Due to the pressure of the changes outlined earlier, the LEA advisory service is finding itself increasingly confronted with one particular dilemma. At a time when 'greater flexibility is being demanded of them' its members are 'growing older' (NAIEA, 1983). The result is that advisers are being 'asked to make teachers familiar with ideas they are not necessarily familiar with themselves' (NAIEA, 1983, p. 19). Credibility with teachers could therefore be diminished; innovation after all 'should be a specialist function. People should innovate in what they are most knowledgeable about, most experienced in' (Bolam et al., 1978, p. 153). To compensate for this it was noted that 'new positions and roles' were being created in the form of advisory teachers, thus resulting in a 'substantial growth in the number of staff carrying out jobs similar to those of Advisers' (Bolam *et al.*, 1978, p. 229). This expansion of LEA advisory services', has meant that 'in England and Wales many LEAs have appointed Advisory Teachers on the teachers salary scale, (Burnham), which is quite separate from that of Advisers, (Soulbury), to give direct support to teachers in their classrooms' (Open University 1976, p. 55). This has enabled them

> to deploy resources far more flexibly, not least because Advisory Teachers are already employed on Burnham scales; no special approach to the Education Committee is therefore needed as is the case when a new Adviser is appointed on Soulbury scales'.
>
> (Bolam *et al.*, 1978, p. 232)

The role of advisory teachers

The post of advisory teacher is a recent phenomenon in the history of the LEA advisory service. Advisory teachers tend to be appointed from within an LEA, the general pattern being for them to be 'seconded temporarily from their schools on part or full time to give additional professional support to schools' in order to 'augment the work of local authority Advisers particularly in School Based INSET and particularly within schools in curriculum and Staff Development' (DES, 1982, p. 341). Advisory teachers are appointed from the ranks of successful teachers and it is usual for a post to be filled by invitation rather than by open advertisement. The quality and expertise of those appointed is thus ensured because the knowledge, skills and personal development are known to the LEA. Appointment from the ranks of practising teachers also ensures that advisory teachers have 'high credibility' among other teachers 'since their classroom and school experience is unquestioned; this is not the case with permanent Advisers, whom teachers tend to see as drawing on an ever decreasing share of their 'experience capital' (Bolam *et al.*, 1978, p. 232).

The main function of the advisory teacher appears to be to provide support for schools by advising teachers and offering help and training in the particular area of development to which they are appointed. Advisory teachers tend therefore to be 'placed in specific jobs with highly specialised roles as well as individual subjects that would not otherwise receive the individual attention of an Adviser' (Whittle, 1983, p. 63). This has been further substantiated by the DES who in several policy statements (DES, 1983, 1985), proposed that there should be an 'increase in the number of short term attachments for specific tasks particularly in areas of rapid obsolescence – information technology – or to match an initial spurt or development or to tackle an acute problem' (DES, 1983, p. 9). But what effect does this have on the main function of the advisory teacher and what help does he or she receive in terms of training and support?

Reference was made earlier to the lack of specific training for advisers and to the fact that their credibility appears to be 'established on the basis of the experience brought to the job'. (Dean, 1985, p. 11). Advisory teachers have a distinct advantage here over their full-time counterparts since they bring with them recent knowledge and expertise in the particular field of education or subject discipline to which they have been appointed. Like other members of the advisory service, they do require help/training in certain aspects of the job, particularly those tasks which appertain to the role of advisers described earlier, such as implementing local and national policies, planning and offering INSET.

Advisory teachers do not share all of the responsibilities of the LEA adviser. They do not, for example, perform the inspectoral or professional tasks of advisers, nor do they carry out all of the administrative and advisory tasks of their full-time counterparts. Advisory teachers do not, for example, have any part to play in the appointment of staff nor do they have direct access to LEA finance. This means that although the advisory teacher is able to supply support in terms of help, expertise and training, he or she may not always be able to supply the necessary resources in terms of finance for equipment, staffing or training that a full-time member of the LEA advisory service can. The main function of an advisory teacher is, however, to advise other teachers on a particular aspect of education. What strategies are available to help him or her to fulfil this aspect of the role?

Strategies for innovation and staff development for advisory teachers

Much work has been done over the years on the different strategies adopted by advisers in the fulfilment of their role in staff development (Bolam *et al.*, 1978; Dean, 1975, 1984; Lewis, 1984). During one study into LEA advisers and innovation (Bolam *et al.*, 1978) advisers were asked to indicate which strategies 'most accurately described their role in bringing about change' (p. 155). The following alternatives, based on the knowledge linkage roles identified by Havelock (1969), were given.

- conveyer: to transfer knowledge from producers to users and between users
- consultant: to assist users in the identification of problems and resources; to assist in linkage to appropriate resources; to assist in adaptation to use
- trainer: to transfer knowledge by instilling in the user an understanding of knowledge or practice
- leader: to effect linkage through power or influence in ones own group; to transfer by example or direction
- innovator: to transfer by initiating diffusion in the user system
- defender: to sensitize the user to the pitfalls of innovation.

Results obtained found that all of the roles identified above were adopted by LEA advisers at some time or another. The roles of trainer, leader and innovator were identified as being particularly relevant where staff development and curriculum innovation were concerned. It was suggested, however, that moves towards 'greater emphasis on inspection, accountability and value for money' were 'pushing the Advisory Service away from direct involvement in change and Staff Development' and that those aspects of the role associated with this were 'likely to be carried out by others' i.e. advisory teachers (Bolam *et al.*, 1978, p. 225; AUDIT Commission 1989, p. 15). Advisory teachers are responsible for researching, developing and disseminating the area of development to which they are appointed; the roles of trainer, leader and innovator are particularly relevant within this context and that of providing staff development programmes within schools.

The advisory teacher is, by the very nature of the duties which he or she performs, 'in a unique position' within the LEA in that he or she is 'in close touch with schools and thus knows where teachers are using new methods and materials successfully' (Holmes, 1971, p. 68). This means that the advisory teacher is able to 'identify possible areas of development in individual schools or groups of schools' which in turn enables him/her to provide the appropriate help, training and support by 'fostering a range of activities' which lead to staff development (Dean, 1979, p. 14).

Reference was made earlier to the fact that staff development

incorporates a wide range of activities which may appropriately be undertaken by teachers as part of their personal and professional development . . . and consists of a profusion of activities, ranging from loosely structured discussion groups to the highest levels of formal postgraduate studies.

(Bush *et al.*, 1981, pp. 417–18)

Staff development programmes organized by the advisory teacher could therefore incorporate a wide variety of activities ranging from the provision of peripatetic support, working alongside teachers in the classroom, to the organization and running of short courses, workshop sessions, seminars, discussion groups and school-based INSET. The mode of delivery will to a large extent be determined by the subject matter.

The results of a questionnaire distributed by the author, the advisory teacher in question, for the purpose of determining the training needs of teachers within the LEA with regard to electro/acoustic music (Andrews, 1986), showed that workshop sessions were considered by 82 per cent of the respondents to be the most appropriate form of training. The provision of peripatetic support where the advisory teacher works alongside teachers and pupils in the classroom was identified as being the next most popular mode of staff development – (70 per cent). The third most popular form of training was identified as the demonstration of equipment (58 per cent). The main consensus of opinion was, then, that workshop sessions would provide the most appropriate form of staff development in this instance.

It was suggested earlier that advisory teachers have 'high credibility' with practising teachers as a result of their recent classroom experience and knowledge and expertise in the subject area to which they have been appointed. On the other hand, however, this standing could be diminished by the adviser's perceived status; the advisory teacher is not after all involved in all of the tasks and responsibilities of a full-time adviser, particularly where direct access to LEA finance for equipment, staffing and training is concerned. If the advisory teacher is to successfully fulfil his or her role as far as staff development is concerned the appropriate help/support in terms of finance and resources must be provided. Only then will the advisory teacher have 'the opportunity to mount a programme of appropriate courses and other In Service activities' (Dean, 1979, p. 15).

Role of an advisory teacher in staff development

The concern so far has been to describe and define in general terms the functions of the advisory teacher as they relate to staff development. The following section will seek to examine this role more specifically by focusing on the role of one particular advisory teacher. The advisory teacher in question was one of a team of two music teachers seconded on a 0.5 advisory/teacher basis. Reference was made earlier to the fact that advisory teachers are generally appointed in order to

> augment the work of Local Authority Advisers particularly in contributing to School Based INSET . . . particularly in areas of rapid obsolescence – information technology – or to match an initial spurt of development or to tackle an acute problem.

> (DES, 1983, p. 9)

These are areas which might not otherwise receive the support of the advisory service. It was against this background that the two advisory teachers were appointed, one to oversee the development of pop music, the other to 'encourage and develop the use of electronic technology in music'. The latter had been running courses in electro/acoustic music for several years within the LEA up to and including examination level and had thus acquired the knowledge and skills of how to use the technology available. Her 'classroom and school experience' was therefore 'unquestioned' thus 'affording high credibility with practising teachers'.

The responsibilities of the advisory teacher included the development of a course/courses in electro/acoustic music; the setting up of two studios within the LEA for this purpose; the running of both studios and courses and the provision of INSET for other music teachers in the LEA. In order to fulfil these responsibilities it was necessary for the advisory teacher to adopt the following roles, based on Havelock (1969), described earlier:

- innovator: inventing new ideas and courses in the area of specialism and transferring these ideas to others through various means – INSET, workshop sessions, and demonstrations;
- leader: the advisory teacher must be capable of leading others by providing example or direction by working alongside pupils or teachers in the classroom or in the provision of advice and support;
- trainer: the advisory teacher is expected to 'instil in the user an understanding of an area of knowledge or practice'; he or she is therefore required to offer/provide appropriate training for teachers;
- consultant: the advisory teacher is required to give advice on his area of specialism in terms of equipment requirements, resources available, courses and staff development requirements.

Factors affecting the advisory teacher's role in staff development

The initial responsibility for the two innovations lay with the director of the CPA who consulted with the LEA to see if funds could be made available for the appointment of two specialist change agents in the form of advisory teachers. The choice of appointments were obvious since the work and specialist skills of the teachers concerned were known throughout the LEA. As far as electro/acoustic music was concerned equipment was readily available at the school where the advisory teacher had taught for several years and it was decided that this was an obvious site for one of the studios. The CPA was chosen as the second site due to its location on the opposite boundary of the LEA and the fact that a room was readily available. The involvement of the advisory teacher up to this stage was extremely limited. From here on, however, she was expected to take an active role.

The first year was fraught with problems some of which could have been overcome had the advisory teacher had the same influence/status as an LEA adviser. Firstly, there was lack of adequate communication between the different levels involved in the setting up of the studios – education officers, director of CPA, music adviser, technician, electrical liaison officer, city engineers, health and safety officer, advisory teacher. Secondly, insufficient funding was available for essential work to be carried out at the studio – electrical supply, benching, sound proofing, security and for equipment to be purchased. Thirdly, because the advisory teacher had no direct access to LEA finance, any orders for resources had to be channelled through the director of CPA or music adviser. This often resulted in orders either going completely astray or in them not being processed properly. Fourthly, all forms of INSET were curtailed, due to the action taken by teachers in support of their pay claim. Many of the problems outlined above are not uncommon in education, however, for, as Hoyle found, there is often 'a lag between new materials and methods and the organisational changes – finance, equipment and training facilities – to support them' (Hoyle, 1975, p. 343).

The second year got off to a better start. Reference was made earlier to the fact that the advisory teacher distributed a questionnaire throughout the LEA's secondary schools so that an overview of the training needs identified by teachers could be obtained and an adequate staff development programme formulated in readiness for when industrial action ceased. Workshop sessions were identified as the most appropriate form of training and two courses – electro/acoustic music in schools, stages 1 and 2 – were submitted for inclusion in the LEA's INSET programme. The courses were organized on an eight-week basis during the autumn and spring terms and took place outside normal school hours (4.00 p.m.–6.00 p.m.). Very nearly all the LEA's secondary schools had identified a need for INSET in the area of electro/acoustic music. Attendance at both of the courses was, however, disappointing. From a total of 19 schools only 5 were represented (26 per cent). Two demonstration/exhibition sessions, organized during school hours, also took place at this time. Attendance at these was substantially better, 15 schools being represented (77 per cent). The effects of industrial action among teachers had left many feeling disillusioned and although they acknowledged that there was a need for staff development in the area of electro/acoustic music they were not willing to participate in any courses which occurred outside normal school hours. For the same reason (industrial action), schools were not prepared to release staff from lessons on a regular basis in order to attend INSET.

Management implications

The management implications associated with the formulation of staff development programmes are extremely diverse, not only for the advisory teacher but also the LEA, school and individual teacher. The main purpose is to ensure that the overall aims of the programme are successfully carried out by bringing together the appropriate resources, both material and human, at the right time and in the right place using the most appropriate mode of delivery/training. Staff development and the role of the advisory teacher are 'intimately connected' (Sanday and Birch, 1974, p. 8). Staff development should, however, be viewed as 'a means not an end and should be seen in the perspective of a proper educational management programme and structure' (Lambert, 1981, p. 21). It is essential that the advisory teacher is able 'to offer to teachers a range of opportunities matching their needs' (Dean, 1979, p. 15). 'For some teachers participation . . . may be the most effective form of INSET' (Sanday and Birch, 1974, p. 8). Indeed, the teachers in the example LEA did in fact request development programmes where they could be participants, i.e. workshop sessions and peripatetic support. It was clear, however, that even intensive training prior to implementing a particular curriculum innovation was not very effective. One-off workshops prior to and even during implementation are not very helpful. This is because most INSET is not designed to provide the on-going, interactive, cumulative learning necessary to develop new concepts, skills and behaviours. Failure to realize that there is a need for INSET is a common problem. No matter how much advance staff development occurs, it is only when people actually try to implement new approaches that they realize the problems and need support and training. This is where the skills and knowledge of the advisory teacher come to the fore. It is therefore up to the LEA to provide the appropriate funding for resources and training and a realistic framework within which the advisory teacher can work which allows him or her to mount the most appropriate form of training necessary for successful staff development.

Summary and conclusion

This chapter has examined the role of the advisory teacher in staff development, focusing on the role of the LEA advisory service, the duties, functions, recruitment and training of advisers and strategies for innovation and staff development. Specific reference was given to the role of advisory teachers paying particular attention to one advisory teacher, the factors which affected her role and the management implications associated with the formulation of staff development programmes.

It was suggested that the role of advisers is determined by the context in which they are required to operate. The consequences of the enormous changes and developments currently rife in our education services have meant that the advisory service has had to modify the way in which it operates; indeed the emphasis now appears to be on 'adaption' of role. National curriculum, ESG and LMS, to give but three examples, have all had far reaching effects on the duties and functions of advisers. Greater emphasis is being placed on the supportive, monitoring and evaluative functions of an adviser's role and while advisers are still involved in LEA training programmes the main focus of their attention is likely to be on the management of INSET rather than on its delivery. These changes in role have resulted in some LEA's reorganizing their advisory teams shifting the emphasis away from subject advisers to general curriculum advisers and

> reassigning some of their responsibilities to Advisory Teachers particularly in the area of In Service education. This reassignment has been made possible by the availability of Central Government grants to support the appointment of Advisory Teachers.
>
> (AUDIT Commission, 1989, p. 15)

The main function of an advisory teacher is to provide support for teachers in the classroom 'particularly to match an initial spurt or development' (DES, 1983, p. 9). If national curriculum requirements are to be implemented, teachers will need proper support in terms of training and help in the classroom. The recent DES national curriculum document states that:

LEAs and their inspectors and advisers have a key role in preparing for implementation both in supporting schools in their planning and particularly in providing early INSET for the teachers most immediately concerned.

(DES, 1989, 9.10)

One of the outcomes of this document and ESG arrangements has been

the appointment across the curriculum of Advisory Teachers in the core subjects. These Advisory Teachers will support classroom teachers to help them deliver the new National Curriculum requirements from September 1989 onwards.

(Soulbury Committee, 1989, p. 6)

This would seem to suggest that we may be about to witness a surge in the number of advisory teacher appointments. Before LEAs jump on this bandwagon, however, careful consideration must be given to the duties/functions which the advisory teachers are to perform, the support required in terms of funding for resources and the framework in which they will be required to operate. Unless these factors are resolved the advisory teacher will be unable to operate effectively and the skills and expertise which she or he possesses will not be sufficiently utilized for the good of the LEA, other teachers and the education service in general.

References

Andrews, S. E. (1986). *The Role of the Part Time Advisory Teacher in Curriculum Development*. MEd thesis, Warwick University.

AUDIT Commission (1989). *Assuring Quality in Education. The Role of Local Authority Advisers and Inspectors*. London, HMSO.

Blackie, J. (1970). *Inspecting and the Inspectorate*. London, Routledge and Kegan Paul.

Birnbaum, I. (1989). 'Advisers: Monitoring and evaluation in the new era', *Education*, 25 August.

Bolam, R., Smith, G. and Cantor, H. (1978). *LEA Advisers and the Mechanisms of Innovation*. NFER, Slough.

Bush, T., Glatter, R., Goody, J. and Riches, C. (1980). *Approaches to School Management*. London, Harper and Row.

Collins, G. (1976). 'The role of the adviser', in *Dialogue*. London, Schools Council Publications.

Dean, J. (1975). 'Training advisers', *National Association of Inspectors and Educational Advisers Journal*, 1, Pt 3.

Dean, J. (1979). 'Inset and the advisory service', in *National Association of Inspectors and Educational Advisers Occasional Paper No. 2*, September.

Dean, J. (1984). 'The LEA adviser: developing roles', in P. Harling (ed.), *New Directions in Educational Leadership*. London, Falmer.

Dean, J. (1985). *Managing the Secondary School*. London, Croom Helm.

Department of Education and Science/Welsh Office (1982). *Study of HM Inspectorate in England and Wales*. London, HMSO.

Department of Education and Science (1983). *Work of HM Inspectorate in England and Wales: Policy Statement by Secretary of State for Education*. London. HMSO.

Department of Education and Science (1985). 'Draft statement on the role of LEA advisory bodies, *Times Educational Supplement*, 13 September.

Department of Education and Science (1989). *National Curriculum. From Policy to Practice*. London, HMSO.

Fiske, P. A. (1969). 'The local inspectors in Redcliffe-Maude's England. 'Address to NAIEA'.

Gentle, K. (1976). 'The significance of advisors' work', *NAIEA Journal*, 1, Pt 4.

Havelock, R. G. (1969). *Planning for Innovation through Dissemination and Utilization of Knowledge*. University of Michigan Press.

Holmes, B. (1971). 'Leicestershire UK', in Centre for Educational Research and Innovation, *Case Study of Educational Innovation II at the Regional Level*. Paris, OECD.

Howarth, G. (1985). *The Role and Relationships of the LEA Secondary Adviser Examined by Reference to Theories of Role*. MSc educational management thesis, Sheffield City Polytechnic.

Hoyle, E. (1975). 'The creativity of the school', in A. Harris, M. Lawn and W. Prescott, *Curriculum Innovation*. London, Croom Helm.

Kirkman. (1985). *Times Educational Supplement*, 13 September.

Lambert, K. (1981). 'Staff development: theory and practice', *School Organisation*, 1, 1.

Letch, R. (1988). 'Grist to the mill' *Perspective*, January.

Lewis, J. A. (1984). *The Education Advisory Service in Cheshire with Emphasis on the Degree to which Advisers Operate as Change Agents*. MSc thesis, Crewe and Alsager College of Higher Education.

Matthews, P. (1985). 'Extra advisers needed urgently', in Lodge, B , *Times Educational Supplement*, 27 September.

NAIEA (1983). *National Association of Inspectors and Educational Advisers Journal*, 19.

Open University (1976). 'Innovation: problems and possibilities', in *Curriculum Design and Development*, E203 Unit 22–25, Milton Keynes, Open University.

Sanday, A. P. and Birch, P. A. (1974). 'Curriculum development: in service education and the role of the adviser', *NAIEA Journal*, 1, 1.

Soulbury Committee (1989). *Soulbury Officers Panel Claim – 1989*, unpublished.

Stillman, A. (1988). 'LEA adviser: change and management', *Educational Research*, 30, 3.

Walker, R. (1981). *The Observational Work of LEA Advisers and Inspectors*, Centre for Applied Research in Educational Social Science Research Council, University of East Anglia.

Whittle, J. (1983). *Size and Structure of Advisory Teams in England and Wales*. MEd thesis, University of Warwick.

Wilcox, B. (1985). 'Revolution or rosewater?', *Times Educational Supplement*, 20 September.

Part II

Professional development in schools

5

The management of the GRIST initiative

Beryl Lockwood

On the 29 August 1986 the Department of Education and Science published a Circular (6/86) setting out the Secretary of State for Education's plans to:

> improve the quality of teaching and further the professional develop-
> ment of teachers through support for local authorities in the training of
> teachers ... The scheme is intended to help local authorities to organise
> inservice training more systematically so as to meet both national and
> local training needs and priorities.
>
> (DES, 1986)

As was explained in Chapters 1 and 2, this initiative would replace all previous financing schemes for in-service training and was to be known as the local education authority training grants scheme (LEATGS) – but is more commonly known as grant related in-service training (GRIST).

The main aim of the research which informs this chapter was to consider the effects the introduction of this new form of in-service training had on a local education authority as reflected in a small sample of schools. In considering the effects of this new initiative the following were the main areas of concern:

- the perceptions of the introduction of the initiative based on the DES Circular 6/86
- the different approaches adopted by four schools to the management of the initiative.

Structured interviews were conducted with a county in-service co-ordinator, a county in-service evaluator and the in-service co-ordinators in four schools. (The questions within the interview schedules were based on the aims and objectives set out in DES Circular 6/86.) Conclusions regarding the effect of the new initiative upon a local education authority and four schools, especially in terms of the way education is managed, were formulated.

In Chapter 1 it was argued that views on what in-service training is have changed dramatically in the last forty years, and continue to do so. The arguments range over issues such as who it is for – the institution, the teacher or the pupil; whether there should be a formal qualification; and what and when is the best time for the training to take place. The James Report (1972), entitled *Teacher Education and Training*, recommended in its third section that training should continue throughout a teacher's working life with increased provision of short courses plus a sabbatical term every seven years initially and eventually every five years. This training should be carried out in existing education departments as well as new professional centres which should be set up. While there was widespread support for the recommendations (Watkins 1973; Henderson 1978) the economic state of the country meant that recommendations were not initiated; but the need for in-service training took on a higher profile in educators' minds. Reports following the James Report continued to mention the need for in-service training (DES, 1977; ACSTT, 1978) leading to the introduction in 1985 of TVEI-related in-service training (TRIST). This was seen by some (Saunders 1987) as an interim measure, a programme that would last for only two years. Questions were asked as to what would follow on at the end of the project. But *Better Schools* (DES, 1985) had indicated that a government-sponsored in-service training scheme would be needed to train staff for government thinking and initiatives. Sensible, forward thinking LEAs and schools should have used TRIST time to prepare for what would follow. TRIST was followed by GRIST (DES, 1986).

According to the circular the main aims of the scheme were to support expenditure on in-service training so as:

to promote the professional development of teachers
to promote more systematic and purposeful planning of in-service training . . .
to encourage more effective management of the teacher force
to encourage training in selected areas, which are to be accorded national priority.

(DES, 1986)

The training support grant would fall into two categories. If the training was based on one of the identified national priority areas then the grant would be at the rate of 70 per cent. If the training was based on a priority identified by a local education authority then the grant would be at the rate of 50 per cent. Local education authorities still had to finance the training of teachers but the DES would assist. Local education authorities were asked to submit their in-service proposals to the DES for consideration and as a result each authority would receive a grant indicating how much should be spent on each of the priority areas. In the first year of the scheme the DES was allocating £200 million of which £70 million was for training identified as national priorities. Requests had to be submitted to the DES by 17 October 1986 and authorities would know if their bid had been successful by 19 December 1986. The grant would then be paid to local authorities quarterly.

The DES also specified what the money could be spent on. This included tuition fees, residential fees, examination fees, travelling expenses, supply cover for staff on training and evaluation costs. One of the major conditions of receiving money for training was that all training must be monitored and evaluated by local authorities to assess ... 'how far it has contributed to more effective and efficient delivery of the education service and to the objectives and policies set out in the authorities proposal for grant aid' (DES, 1986). The DES would require from local authorities details of how training was undertaken within the authority, how many staff had been involved in the training, how long training lasted, how expenditure was incurred, what improvements had been made to planning, how relevant training was to staff, the results of evaluation, and how effective the training was. The GRIST initiative meant that LEAs had to decide upon a structure for managing in-service work at a time when the roles of the LEA, further and higher education institutes and schools were changing. It became essential to have a structure that facilitated the identification of needs, planning and designing work, implementation and evaluation and review. A suggested structure is set out in a handbook by Oldroyd and Hall (1988) and is reproduced as Figure 5.1.

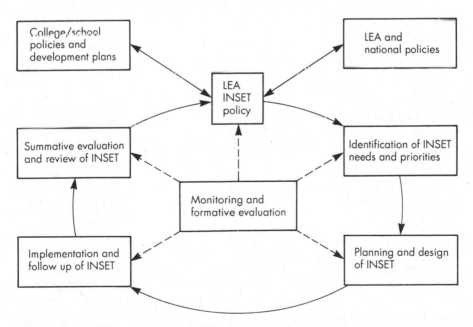

Figure 5.1 A cycle for managing INSET at LEA level

A similar structure should be adopted by schools which should:

- have a school policy
- identify needs
- prioritize needs
- plan INSET
- implement INSET
- evaluate and review.

Monitoring and evaluation should be continuous. It is necessary to be flexible and to review after each stage of the cycle to check if set objectives are being met. Whenever a change process is taking place within an LEA or school a similar cycle should be adopted to ensure proper management. Short cuts could lead to disaster.

Although many LEAs and schools had structures before GRIST one of the major effects of the initiative has been to ensure that a management system becomes an essential part of every LEA and institute; this was one of the aims set out in the GRIST proposals.

Methodology

It was decided to carry out the investigation by interviewing a representative of the LEA and either the headteacher or INSET co-ordinator in four schools (see choice of population). The reasons for using the interview technique were as follows:

1 The investigation is an exploratory piece of research and the interview technique is suitable for this type of investigation.
2 An interview allows the interviewer to clarify points if necessary.
3 An interview allows the interviewer to pursue emergent themes.

Other methods that were rejected were:

1 Questionnaire, because it is impersonal, response rate is usually low and the investigation does not involve sufficiently large numbers.
2 Telephone interviews, which are impersonal and expensive. Eye contact and body language are lost.
3 A blank tape for interviewees to talk to; this is impersonal and follow up work is impossible.

Development of interview schedule

The questions that formed the interview schedule were designed to elicit comments that would allow a comparison to be made between the reasons for the establishment of GRIST and the focus of it, as described in Circular 6/86 (DES, 1986), and the perceptions of the interviewees. Therefore in the schedule each question was related to an area of Circular 6/86. The following were considered:

1 the reasons for GRIST, according to Circular 6/86
2 the main areas of focus according to Circular 6/86
3 the questions to be used and the reasons for their inclusion in relation to (1) and (2).

According to Circular 6/86 the aims of GRIST were to:

- improve the quality of teaching through promoting the professional development of teachers
- help LEAs organize INSET more systematically
- replace all other previous financing schemes
- support the expenditure of LEAs
- encourage more effective management of the teaching force
- encourage training in selected areas.

The main requirements of a GRIST bid, according to Circular 6/86, are:

- that INSET should be for the whole school, should be school-based, and should be based on expressed need
- that LEAs must indicate that they have taken all expressed needs into account, collaborated with other authorities and consulted universities, institutes of higher education and other experts
- that LEAs must monitor and evaluate GRIST programmes
- that the DES would require information on numbers trained, duration and form of training, how money has been spent, planned improvements of training, effectiveness of training, whether objectives have been achieved, relevance of training to staff and results of evaluation.

It was also clear that the 19 DES national priority areas would receive a higher support grant (70 per cent) than LEA and school priorities, which would attract 50 per cent funding from the DES.

Findings

Once the interviews had been conducted the analysis was evaluated. The responses are compared to the expectations of Circular 6/86.

Promoting the professional development of teachers

In answering the questions all the interviewees mentioned the professional development of teachers. Not all used the phrase 'professional development': 'to encourage development of staff and schools' (school 1). The evaluator suggested that there was a need to look at teachers as individuals as well as the needs of the whole school. Teachers should ask questions such as 'Is there a need arising from the problems I am currently facing? Where is my career going? What developments do I need?' (county evaluator).

Some schools ensured that the individual needs of their staff were met by attending county courses 'if they [the courses] fell in with the general aims of whole-school INSET' (school 1). 'Individual needs [are] reconciled by teachers going on county courses either in their own time, or in school time if the school will benefit' (school 2). 'Agencies other than the school provide for the needs of some individuals . . . for example, county courses, courses at University and the DES' (school 4).

One of the problems of GRIST identified in the literature and in the interviews is that although the DES claims that GRIST is for the professional development of teachers, the main emphasis of the document is towards whole-school INSET. It is vital that the needs of the individual are not lost. There is almost a conflict developing between the two needs. The headteacher and/or the school co-ordinator must ensure that a proper balance is kept: 'if we are not careful the needs of the individual are forgotten' (school 4). Schools 1, 3 and 4 regretted the lack of support for higher degrees as this meant that development and stimulus for individuals had been removed, unless, as the county co-ordinator said, individuals themselves financed a part-time higher degree. Obviously if whole-school development is taking place then individuals are benefiting as well. Many staff members in schools have also been involved in GCSE training and this has direct relevance to their classroom teaching.

Promoting more systematic planning of INSET

All the interviewees (except at school 2) mentioned this aspect of GRIST in a roundabout way. No one actually said that this was one of the aims of GRIST, but answers showed that the LEA and three of the four schools were either developing, or had developed, systems of planning to ensure that the INSET was relevant and part of the school policy: 'Next year's INSET is a continuation of this year's as it is a continual process' (school 3). 'GRIST has made the school think about training in a more systematic way' (school 1).

Planning is essential if schemes are to function efficiently. But not all schools have systems to cope with planning: 'some schools are not organised for the system . . . incoherent planning can be disastrous' (county co-ordinator). The DES is saying that more systematic planning is needed and LEAs and schools are trying to do this; but systems take time to set up. Good planning is long-term as well as immediate. For the second year of GRIST and DES initially said that it would require LEAs to submit proposals and plans for three years. This would be to their advantage because LEAs and schools could plan for the future knowing that financial assistance would be available. Obviously the second and third years' plans would only be in an outline form. The county co-ordinator and evaluator and school 4 said that this would be to everyone's advantage.

Having said that initially they would require three-year plans from LEAs the DES changed their instructions and required submissions for one-year's plan only. Systematic planning cannot be undertaken when there is no guarantee that financial assistance will be available in subsequent years. It is also difficult for the LEA to plan when indicative grant allocations and final circulars are late arriving from the DES, giving LEAs little time to compile their submissions (Warwickshire 1987).

Encouraging more effective management of teachers

Four of the interviewees mentioned more effective management as a consequence of the introduction of GRIST. School 2 and the county evaluator did not mention this aspect of the initiative. 'GRIST is money to bid for, to do training as the school wishes to meet management and staff needs' (school 3). 'GRIST was introduced as some parts of the other system was not working on the delivery of education to children' (county evaluator). 'GRIST is seen as a whole thing – as one coherent plan philosophically and financially' (county co-ordinator). 'Every term the management team sets its objectives for the term and then evaluates them at the end. The term's objectives leads to the INSET needs and evaluating them assesses INSET and its priorities' (school 4).

For GRIST or any initiative to be successful it must be managed at LEA and school level. Therefore co-ordinators and headteachers need to have management skills. Many do, although their styles of management will vary. The county co-ordinator and evaluator were concerned as to whether all teachers had the necessary management skills: 'some heads are not capable of managing the exercise' (county co-ordinator). Therefore training is needed for the headteachers as well as the school co-ordinators.

Encouraging training in selected (national priority) areas

The DES originally identified 19 areas as training priorities. LEAs were made aware of these in Circular 6/86. In the second year of GRIST the 19 priority areas remained with 4 additions bringing the total to 23. Most schools saw GRIST money as being available to meet the needs of the school: it was a 'system of financing for schools and colleges to use for conducting school based in-service training according to the needs of the school' (school 1), and 'resources to do what is required in the school' (school 3). 'GRIST is money to bid for to do training as a school wishes to meet management and staff needs' (school 4). School 3 did say that at the beginning of TRIST they were aware of priorities, but more recently had become concerned with the needs of the school and therefore did not pay much attention to national priority areas. The county evaluator said that the scheme involved 'the government having a say as to what the money is to be spent on, that is, intended topics' (county evaluator).

Awareness of the national priorities

The county co-ordinator saw the scheme as a 'system centralised on schools – organising, planning and delivery plus evaluation of staff development for teachers, . . . in the employment of LEAs with the government body known as the DES attempting to keep control of everything'. The higher rate of grant (70 per cent) for training within the national priority areas encouraged LEAs to bid for these areas, rather than local priorities.

Whole-school and school-based INSET

For school policies to be implemented, the training needs to be school-based and involve all staff. Therefore most senior staff in school welcomed the initiative. Some staff initially resented the imposition of the scheme, but many now realize its value. 'GRIST is for the whole school rather than just enhancing certain areas' (school 3). [It] provides time and quality environment for INSET and has made it possible to give INSET a more professional approach (school 3). 'The school never got together as a whole for in-service training before TRIST' (school 3). 'GRIST has led to changes in school practices' (county evaluator). 'All staff are involved . . . although some still rather reluctantly' (school 1). 'It is for the whole school and it is good that all should be involved' (school 2). 'Everyone is involved and therefore all staff know what is being talked about. Staff are now used to in-service training and it forms a natural part of their job' (school 4). 'It is for all teachers . . . [they] can learn from each other . . . look at problems together . . . schools should get the benefit directly' (county co-ordinator). 'Too much or too little of it can be disastrous as it will become fragmented' (county evaluator). 'The danger is that too little can be done in developing the individual teachers and departments when training is based on the whole school approach' (county evaluator). 'The needs of the individual may be lost and therefore a better balance needs to be arrived at' (county evaluator). While accepting the many benefits to the school the needs of the individual must not be lost.

Monitoring and evaluation

Monitoring and evaluation must be built into any process. No one mentioned evaluation in their general description of GRIST. But all mentioned evaluation in their answers. The county co-ordinator evaluates training by:

● receiving reports from the county evaluator

- receiving reports from schools (termly reports were requested in the first year of GRIST)
- advisory team meetings.

The county evaluator visited schools and asked a series of informal questions, which included:

- how the GRIST bid was prepared
- what the implications of the bid were for the school
- how staff training could be improved
- what was good and should be preserved
- how events worked (e.g. methodology and implications)
- what evaluation processes the school had carried out
- what effect GRIST had had on the administration load for teachers and secretarial staff
- what extra help was needed.

Schools used differing techniques to carry out their evaluations. Schools 1 and 4 used formal questionnaires and informal discussions with individuals and groups to identify needs and ways of improving implementation. School 2 had *ad hoc* discussions with staff. School 3 saw evaluation 'as an ongoing state with the Headteacher and co-ordinator asking pertinent questions of the curriculum parties . . . see evaluation as a process that results in a product'.

The areas of interest to the DES are how effective training has been, whether its objectives have been achieved, the relevance of it to the staff and how training could be improved. The LEA asks schools to address themselves to these questions in their termly reports. The financial year and the school year are different. Plans for the second phase of GRIST have therefore to be started before the first phase really begins. Recommendations arising from evaluation will therefore be difficult to implement immediately but may help in the planning for phase 3.

Taking account of expressed needs and collaborating with other authorities

Expressed needs have been discussed above. On collaboration with other authorities the county co-ordinator said that 'regional planning bodies . . . were abandoned under GRIST; yet areas are expected to co-operate!' 'West Midlands set up a self-help group for co-ordination under TRIST with some funding from the MSC'. It would appear that systems for facilitating co-operation and collaboration have been disbanded. On the other hand Warwickshire LEA has close links with Warwick University.

Reporting back to the DES

The DES requires information on numbers trained, duration and forms of training, how money has been spent, planned improvements of training, the effectiveness of training, whether objectives have been achieved, the relevance of training to staff and the results of all evaluation. The reports that schools send to the LEA are expected to address all these questions.

Most studies of this kind have limitations, and this study is no exception. The particular limitations affecting this study were that:

- The views of only four schools were canvassed and this number was too small to allow any major conclusions to be drawn.
- Only one LEA was used.
- The views of teachers were not requested, only those of the headteacher or co-ordinator. The original intention had been to ask teachers similar questions but it was decided that the task would be too big for the scope of the original study. But teachers are being affected by GRIST and by the whole-school approach to INSET. Their views and perceptions are therefore important.
- Little has been written about the major impact GRIST is having on the teaching profession.

Implications for the future

Before TRIST and GRIST there had been many providers of in-service training. One of the problems faced by course organizers was forecasting what would be needed. Universities attempted to predict interaction through consultations with teachers, schools and LEAs but a criticism of courses made by teachers was that they were often not relevant to teaching (Henderson, 1978). Planning was difficult because of the problem of predictability and because of the varying types of groups requiring training.

But GRIST has brought about major changes. It has meant a move towards centralization, with schools and LEAs having to meet the requirements of the DES. Many of the new initiatives have been linked to extra financing for LEAs and schools provided by the DES on the understanding that certain criteria are met. Different arguments are put forward as to why this is happening. Some would argue that the DES is trying to bring order out of chaos (Graham, 1986) and that money is being used to entice LEAs to respond to government criteria. 'The stage is being set for the exercise of far reaching power over the education system by centrally determined decision making.'

The present government has clearly adopted a highly interventionist strategy with regard to education. Nevertheless it is certainly true that until recently many LEAs have welcomed the new innovations and the extra finance that government initiatives have brought into schools. Some LEAs have not adopted all the schemes and have therefore not received the finances.

One of the major changes brought about by GRIST is the change of emphasis away from the LEA and universities as providers of training to a situation where the LEAs and schools are its main providers. The reduction in university involvement is causing problems for the universities with fewer students and changing roles for university staff. With schools now major providers they must ensure that their management structures are sound and that the management process involves needs identification.

Another major change brought about by GRIST had been the change from INSET for the individual to INSET for the institution. The 1972 James Report stressed the development of the individual but by 1974 the ACSTT was recommending that the needs of the school were of the greatest importance; this was supported by the 1977 DES document. There are those who feel that the school's needs should be met first: 'INSET, especially school-focused INSET, can make a significant contribution to the improvement of education' (Bolam, 1982).

There are others who stress the needs of the individual:

> Inservice education does not often bring about change in the classroom unless the activity relates to a specific objective, unless activities are connected with the individuals personal professional development profile they are of little value, and, frequently, informal links established during activities are often more important than the activities themselves.
>
> (Routledge, 1987)

> [T]he hierarchial needs of the individual – basic psychological necessities, safety and security, love and affection, a sense of belonging and a sense of approval, esteem, knowledge, understanding and the attainment of self naturalisation.
>
> (Owen, 1970)

> 'Non award bearing courses have risen from 1049 to 1191 . . . for example two days to train for GCSE – rising from 38,442 to 42,597 and the number of hours increasing by 68%. This is incredible because the DES is saying to teachers that they can prepare themselves for all sorts of major changes in just two days. In fact the proposals for strengthening inservice provision have robbed teachers of any sustained study and professional development opportunities.
>
> (Santinelli, 1987)

It is important that headteachers and INSET co-ordinators try to ensure that the needs of the individual and the needs of the school are met: 'The school must get its balance right' (county evaluator).

The main advantages of the introduction of GRIST have been:

- in-service training for all staff
- schools having to develop policies
- in-service training becoming part of the whole school and not an addition
- the development of structures to manage the process in schools
- resourcing for the initiative
- training being directly relevant to the classroom situation.

For GRIST to develop further in schools the following problems need to be addressed:

- training for senior staff to manage the process effectively
- the disruption to pupils' education caused by supply cover taking lessons
- how to meet the needs of the school and the needs of the individual; the issue of further qualifications and the academic satisfaction of staff needs to be reconsidered
- the further development of the accreditation of school-based training.

The main recommendation of the James Report was that staff should all have regular secondment (at least every seven years) for training, to develop themselves and to assist in their schoolwork; GRIST is recommending that the emphasis should be on school-based training. GRIST is probably meeting the needs of the school and pupils at a time when great change is taking place and schools are expected to have development policies, but the James Report recommendations were meeting the needs of the individual teacher.

In the future in-service programmes in school have to address themselves to the needs of the school, pupils and individuals. Many staff have enjoyed short- and long-term secondment in the recent past and this has fulfilled their needs for further study and 'recharged batteries'. There is a place for this type of work within the in-service programme, but perhaps the training of the individual has to be channelled towards DES and LEA priority areas so that schools and individuals can both benefit. The introduction of GRIST and whole school in-service programmes has proved to be beneficial in the short time of its existence; but there is still much developmental work to be done.

References

Advisory Committee on the Supply and Training of Teachers (1978). *Making INSET Work*. London, HMSO.

Bolam, R. (1982). *School Focused Inservice Training*. London, Heinemann.

Department of Education and Science (1972). *Teacher Education and Training* (the James Report). London, HMSO.

Department of Education and Science (1977). *Education in Schools: A Consultative Document*. London, HMSO.

Department of Education and Science (1985). *Better Schools*. London, HMSO.

Department of Education and Science (1986). *Local Education Authority Training Grant Scheme: Financial Year 1987–88*, Circular 6/86. London, HMSO.

Graham, J. (1986). 'Centralisation of power and the new Inset funding', *British Journal of Inservice Education*, 13.

Henderson, E. S. (1978). *The Evaluation of In-service Teacher Training*. London, Croom Helm.

Oldroyd, D. and Hall, V. (eds) (1988). *Managing Professional Development and Inset – A Handbook for Schools and Colleges*. National Development Centre for School Management Training, School of Education, University of Bristol.

Owen, R. G. (1981). *Organisational behaviour in schools.* Englewood Cliffs, NJ, Prentice-Hall.

Routledge, M. D., 'Identifying inservice needs in a northern LEA', *British Journal of Inservice Education,* Autumn.

Santinelli, P. (1987). 'Schools out for teachers' *Times Higher Educational Supplement,* 13 November.

Saunders, M. (1987). 'Perceptions on TRIST: implications for inset', *Research Papers in Education,* 2, 2.

Warwickshire Education Department (1987). Part of a planning document circulated to schools in Spring 1987 setting out plans for 1988–1991.

Watkins, R. (ed.) (1973). *Inservice Training: Structure and content.* London, Ward Lock Educational.

6

INSET in primary schools

Julie Moore

Financially supported primary INSET has been with us officially for a relatively short period of time. Unofficially, most good primary schools have had a system of looking at their current practice, evaluating it and moving on at a pace and in a direction best suited to their circumstances. Their starting point has been their perceived need in their own school. This is by far and away the most effective way of addressing INSET in the primary sector. The advent of extra local education authority training grants scheme (LEATGS) funding has meant that primary schools now have the flexibility to identify specific curriculum areas and the means of targeting money to provide additional support. It has also enabled LEAs to develop strategies to encourage schools to look at the whole-school curriculum and to prioritize areas of identified need in relation to the whole-school need and linked to local and national criteria.

A wide range of INSET activities is going on in our primary classrooms. Successful primary teachers have always had to have a degree of professional flexibility, teaching all aspects of the primary curriculum. School-focused INSET has not changed this; rather it has encouraged primary teachers to extend outwards and be more aware of their classroom-based work in relation to the whole-school curriculum. It has provided opportunities for staff development both inside and outside the context of the school, enabling all teachers to be actively involved both at an individual professional level and at collective group level.

I spent one term on secondment to study school-focused INSET in depth. During this study I visited eight LEAs and my objectives were:

1 to discover good practice and methods of approaching school-focused INSET

Table 6.1 LEAs visited

Local authority	Category	Local authority	Category
A	Large city	F	Small urban authority
B	Large shire county	G	Small metropolitan authority
C	Large rural authority	H	Small urban authority
D	Small urban authority	I	Large shire county
E	Average-sized urban authority		

2 to concentrate on how schools establish INSET needs and how they evaluate their INSET programme
3 to produce materials to assist school teachers
4 to make increased skills and knowledge available to Warwickshire LEA.

I approached key people in different roles to give me a wide range of perceptions about INSET from the differing viewpoints of providers, enablers and consumers. I particularly focused on how schools identified their INSET needs and how they evaluated their INSET programme. Table 6.1 identifies the types of LEA visited.

INSET needs and programmes

Funding

Differential allocation in the INSET funding received by schools inevitably means there are differences in the range of INSET activities schools can provide. LEAs have significant variations in their direct and indirect allocation to schools of INSET funds. One LEA (E) gives every primary school an annual sum of £1,000 plus an extra INSET staffing allowance of two teachers. At the opposite end of the spectrum, LEA (I) gives every primary school £30 per teacher so that a primary school with six teachers would receive £180. Other LEAs have a range of methods for allocating INSET funds. A common one, in the majority of LEAs I visited, is to give all primary schools a set amount of money based on criteria linked to their size. Schools can then use this money for their individual school-focused INSET activities. They can also bid for a further amount of money which is held centrally by the LEA and is distributed according to identified need, usually supported by short- and long-term INSET planning. This enables schools to top up their original allowance. The proportion of money directly devolved to schools, and monitoring how it is used, are crucial elements in the range quality of INSET provision that schools are able to provide for themselves. Most LEAs also have a third category of funds which is used for secondments, residential courses, etc. This type of provision is usually extremely specialized and is invariably linked to LEA or national criteria.

All LEAs have a monitoring process built into their INSET planning. In some authorities the allocation of funds follows clear guidelines; these are drawn up and followed by advisers/inspectors. In other authorities it is not always clear to the various recipients how decisions about allocation are made. Primary schools have varying degrees of independence and flexibility in planning and resourcing their INSET, depending on the policy of their LEA. Inspectors and advisers usually have direct control of a proportion of primary INSET funding and indirect control of the remainder.

All the LEAs in this study have introduced a range of strategies and support for school-focused INSET. Common to all LEAs is the provision of advisory and/or curriculum support teachers and educational development centres and/or teachers' centres. These centres have permanent staff, are used as a base by advisory teachers and are resource centres for teachers. Courses are held, both inside and outside the school day, which are matched to the identified needs of teachers and schools.

Identifying needs

To assist schools in the identification of their needs LEAs have encouraged the use of strategies ranging from a fairly complex grid system to very informal discussion at school level. Identification is a complex process and time spent collectively by all the staff in school on identifying their INSET needs is time well spent. LEA (C) had a particularly effective system for identifying needs in that various curriculum areas and issues were considered across the educational phases. Schools completed a grid with an order of priority for each area; this enabled LEA planning to be matched more readily to the identified needs of particular schools and groups of schools and encouraged cohesive strategies between educational phases. LEAs (C) and (E) had given direct support to schools to develop strategies for identification of needs. This was achieved by specific training for school INSET co-ordinators. Other LEAs had a somewhat *ad hoc* approach and the range of identification processes varied from the superficial to the extensive.

Identification of needs is crucial to school and curriculum development, but is only one part of the cyclical process of identification, implementation and evaluation and cannot be considered in total isolation. For identification to be successful, it has to be a whole-school process, with everyone making a contribution, being involved in decision making, planning and evaluating. A good starting point is to brainstorm ideas, either in year groups or as a whole school, and then begin to focus down and prioritize. This process takes time, but it is worth it because everyone is involved at each stage. Some issues are obviously long term and will need a great deal of involvement over a

Table 6.2   Overall framework for planning

Identified area	Teacher(s) responsible	Staff involvement	External support	Feedback	Timescale	Evaluation
Maths	Mary/Jo	All staff	Maths advisory team	Staff governors, pastoral adviser	Sept 1989– July 1990	Half-termly All staff–orally May 1990–all staff written

prolonged period of time; others will be relatively short term and could possibly be considered by a small working party which would report back to the full staff at an agreed time. It is a good idea for the INSET co ordinator to have an overall framework for planning; Table 6.2 is an example.

Everyone on the staff could have a copy, evaluation being the basis for future identification. Whichever way the school's needs have been identified, the implementation of a programme to meet those needs is the next stage. All schools are at a different stage and their INSET provision must be matched to their developmental programme.

Modes of delivery of INSET

Any INSET event includes a variety of experiences which are intended to develop the skills, knowledge and understanding of the teacher. These are co-ordinated in school by the INSET co-ordinator; in some cases this role is undertaken by the headteacher, in others by a teacher.

A wide range of INSET provision is based in schools. At an early stage most primary schools organized visits to other schools to observe good practice. Teachers have been encouraged to extend their professional horizons and branch out from their own schools into the wider world. The world of the primary teacher can be somewhat insular, working with his or her own class and classroom with little professional interaction with colleagues. Fortunately this is changing and most schools have used some INSET funds to buy in supply cover to teach classes while staff visit other schools or classes in their own school. Most schools devise a schedule, or visit checklist, to enable teachers to observe specific aspects of the curriculum. These can then be used as a starting point for further discussion back in their own schools.

Staff workshops led by colleagues and/or advisory teachers have also been extensively used by schools. These range from one-off after-school sessions to workshops which can be the starting point for a specific aspect of curriculum development which embraces the whole school.

Advisory teachers/curriculum support teachers have played an important role in the development of school-focused INSET. One LEA has a team of curriculum development teachers who work in school one or two days a week for a minimum period of one term. Headteachers can bid for a period of one term for curriculum support teachers to work in a curricular area with particular teachers and a contract is drawn up between the school and the team. Objectives are decided and a programme is planned between the support teachers and class teachers. At the end of the term both groups evaluate the programme so that schools have a clear idea of its effectiveness.

In LEA (H) advisory teachers work alongisde colleagues for a fixed number of days each term. Schools can bid for advisory support as part of their planning bid. If successful, advisory teachers then plan with class and headteachers how they are going to work in the classroom. Their role is wide and varied, depending on the needs of the schools, and they work individually or in pairs within school.

Teachers working cooperatively alongside each other are being used as an INSET strategy in some authorities. A teacher with a particular skill or particular curriculum responsibility is released to work alongside colleagues in their classroom. Supply cover is brought in to teach the class of the supporting teacher, thus enabling good practice to be extended and developed throughout the primary school and making the best use of the school's own teaching resources.

Teacher exchange is an aspect of INSET that appears to be underused by most LEAs. This is a development of co-operative teaching within a school extending between schools. Teachers with a particular skill can extend their professional experience by working in another school for a year, thereby giving both donor and recipient schools professional expertise in areas which they might otherwise not have.

Another strategy of school-focused INSET is the clustering of small schools to share INSET experiences and resources. A number of LEAs with small schools of two or three teachers have adopted clusterings and generally this is proving very successful. Schools jointly identify an area of INSET need and plan its implementation and evaluation. By pooling their resources small schools are able to achieve a wider range of INSET provision and the benefits of shared experiences and a cross-fertilization of ideas enhance the quality of both teaching and learning. Clustering is a further example of INSET provision that can be extended across the range of primary schools to the benefit of all, and it is cost effective.

Providers of INSET

Primary INSET has a range of providers. LEAs provide courses at educational development centres and teachers' centres. Colleges and universities have active primary INSET programmes, and subject and other professional organizations also provide primary INSET. LEA provision is usually matched to the identified needs of schools. LEA (A) has a very complex system of INSET provision provided by the INSET team, and schools bid for places on courses which are held during the day. In this instance the INSET team identifies and decides the content and delivery of the courses. LEA (E) asks schools to identify their needs and INSET co-ordinators link their needs to the provision of courses based at educational development centres. The task of the LEA is to correlate all the information from schools and enable suitable linked provision to be made. Yet another LEA, (I), asks all schools to submit a three-year plan for their INSET needs and then the advisers and co-ordinators match identified need to provision.

One college of education has primary-focused INSET courses, based both in college and school, with practical school-based work being an integral part of the course. LEAs provide the funding for this type of course and targeted schools are invited to send along a member of staff. Schools can also bid, through their LEA, for a place on the course. In another LEA, a course was based at an educational development centre but planned and organized by a college lecturer. Fees were paid by the LEA to the college. This course had open access within the LEA and schools bid for a place. The focus of this course was a practical language programme for primary schools. Subject organizations like the United Kingdom Reading Association and the Association for Science Education also provide specialist courses and these are usually held after school. Journals like *Primary Science Review*, published by the Association for Science Education, provide material which schools can use as a basis for INSET activities.

LEAs are successfully addressing the issue of school-focused INSET. Methods vary between authorities, but the implementation of a rolling programme of school-focused INSET which addresses the needs of the schools is gathering momentum. Schools are having to analytically consider all aspects of their role in the educational process and plan their own development. LEAs provide the support for this to be done successfully through advisers, inspectors, advisory teachers and INSET co-ordinators.

Evaluation of INSET

The aim of INSET is to improve the quality of learning experiences for children in our schools. Unless schools have an in-built system of evaluation it is impossible to know if they are achieving their aim. Evaluation emphasizes the importance of a structured approach to meeting the identified needs of schools and the setting of clear objectives is essential. If schools formulate clear objectives as part of their identification process, then evaluation becomes easier and is an integral part of the INSET programme. The cyclical nature of INSET (Figure 6.1) indicates that evaluation is the key to guiding the whole process, because it leads to identification of further needs.

There are three ways of evaluating INSET: at the level of the individual

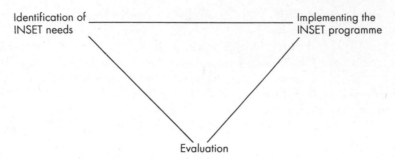

Figure 6.1 INSET as a cyclical process

teachers; the school; and the LEA. At an individual level self-evaluation heightens the awareness of teachers to analyse the learning experiences they are providing within the framework of school-focused INSET. By co-operatively planning their INSET objectives within a timescale teachers are able to develop classroom strategies to achieve these objectives and, as a result, can evaluate themselves much more effectively.

Whole-school evaluation is a natural progression from the processes discussed earlier in the chapter. It is complementary to individual self-evaluation and is based on the cyclical nature of school-focused INSET. Oral evaluation is on-going at various levels within school. Colleagues working co-operatively, sharing ideas and strategies, modify and adapt as their INSET programmes develop. This flexibility of approach develops as primary teachers work together on a whole-school basis within their INSET programme and within their identified timescale. Alongside oral evaluation, written evaluation can also give teachers an opportunity to share their perceptions of INSET at an individual and collective level. These written evaluations can then be used as a basis for future planning and identification of needs. The setting of clear objectives within a timescale makes constructive analysis and evaluation so much easier.

An LEA needs to address evaluation in two distinct areas:

1 monitoring and assessing the INSET programmes in its schools
2 monitoring and assessing its own role as provider.

Again, these strands are inextricably linked and relate to LEA planning and organization of resources (human, physical and financial). LEAs will need to know how schools are identifying their INSET needs, how they are planning to implement their INSET programme to meet those needs and how they intend to evaluate. They need this information from schools if they in turn are to be able to organize and plan effectively as INSET providers and enables. LEAs also need to be aware of schools' forward planning and their school development plans if they are to effectively fulfil their role under the terms of the Education Reform Act and the national curriculum. Like schools, LEAs will need to have an on-going system of monitoring and evaluation and clearly defined strategies for supporting schools.

Schools and LEAs are working together to improve the quality of education for the children in their care. It is evident that some LEAs are much further ahead in their INSET planning and provision than others; but all the LEAs I visited were adopting a coherent approach to primary in-service and staff development. The best examples of good practice I discerned were in authorities which were developing coherent systems for identification of needs, implementation and evaluation across all educational phases. The emphasis in these authorities was in providing specialist training for head-teachers and INSET co-ordinators, providing a range of matched courses to school-focused INSET needs and having a clear framework for local and national priorities within school-based INSET planning. They had also adopted a system of cross-phase clustering for INSET.

The implementation of the national curriculum is dominating INSET provision at the present time and is likely to do so for several years to come. Schools are having to address their own curriculum and examine the degree of match between their present curricular provision and the requirements of the national curriculum. The processes described in this chapter are particularly relevant when addressing national curriculum issues.

LEAs are currently involved in massive INSET activities centred around the requirements of the national curriculum. They are having to provide training for thousands of teachers within a closely defined timescale. However, schools will also have identified other INSET areas which are relevant to themselves and their particular stage of development.

The challenge for headteachers, teachers and governors, is to meet the requirements of the national curriculum while continuing to maintain the identified school-focused INSET initiatives which are relevant to their own school. The way forward over the next few years will be challenging for primary schools and LEAs. Never before in our primary educational system has so much centralized direction been mandatory. Primary teachers have to have a broad base of skills, knowledge, experience and flexibility. It remains with them to maintain the tradition of excellence in primary education.

7

'Teachers as experts': a case study of school-based staff development

Bruce Douglas

The Branston approach

The 'teachers as experts' tag is significant not so much because it was a better motto for school-based activity than any other we could have chosen but because of its nakedness. What strikes me most when I look back at what has happened at Branston School and Community College is how overt the rhetoric was right from the start, how openly determined we were to place the process at the top of the agenda, ahead of even the tasks or product outcomes. Our motto, 'teachers as experts', unclothed by any reference to specific developments, reflects that determination.

Branston School and Community College is an 11–18 school and community college in Lincolnshire. When I took up post as principal in January 1986 it had about 1,200 students and 74 teachers. It was a time of turbulence. National withdrawal of goodwill was in force, a fact worth bearing in mind when evaluating the degree of responsiveness of teachers to our school-based approach. I am convinced of the need for professional research and development to be seen as a natural part of every school teacher's role, within his or her own institution; but I certainly claim neither any originality for the ideas expressed in this chapter nor for anything at all we may have done. This chapter is merely an account of some real happenings in a school and an accompanying view on professional and school development.

Underlying this view is the belief that professional development and school development are two sides of the same coin and that both are advanced, not compromised, by being brought together. Real professional development is fostered when teachers reflect on real-school data. Therefore the actual process of teacher research/development should be an aim. At Branston we salute those British educators who have for years been showing the way, whether through action research, through the school improvement movement, or just by instinctively acting in this way. What we have proved is that the appetite of teachers for professional development is immense, and we have demonstrated at least one way of minimizing the disruption to teaching (our prime task) that the spending of INSET money can traditionally cause to schools. In both respects our experience leads to a demand for a far greater *delegation* of INSET resources to schools than, at the time of writing, is envisaged within the country's new LMS legislation.

Two key features of the Branston approach were:

- that as far as possible INSET resources should be largely delegated to participants *within* the school
- that activity should be built into the academic year timetable, so that teaching class disruption (that black cloud shrouding the silver lining of traditional off-site course-centred INSET) could be minimized.

Considering that over one-third of the teachers at Branston have been involved in school-based work in *each* of the three past years the level of disruption has been very low. That is why the prize of achieving academic year planning, within a setting where INSET funds are granted on a financial year, is one that is worth fighting furiously for. There are ways, and educators in schools, LEAs and training institutes together must find them.

Having found funding (a different story) I went to the staff in April 1986. In a year of national industrial action it was the first full meeting since my appointment in January. I invited the staff to share my belief in the process, at least to the extent of agreeing that over Easter I should write a launch pack outlining some definite projects and procedures and containing an invitation to respond. Colleagues agreed. Five separate projects were suggested: on the role of tutor; the modular curriculum; curriculum descriptions; classroom phenomena; and prevocational education (though in truth, this last project was already in progress).

What cannot be doubted is the openness of the claims for the process. The launch pack ran to more than a dozen A4 pages and from the front page with its title ('Teachers as experts') and its health warning ('contents may seriously damage the status quo'), to the final rationale it was littered with almost naively clear statements about a particular kind of professional development. For example (p. 11):

Rationale
The key feature of the Branston proposal . . . is that teachers themselves can be active in promoting changes of style or content which will lead to significant developments across the curriculum . . . activity should be used precisely to develop this model of teachers, and groups of teachers . . .

and on the same page within the listing of project criteria, was the reminder that:

> projects should be collaborative. Participation in them, the process, should be regarded as an important outcome in itself, as a way of supporting the view that school self-analysis and self-renewal are key aspects of a teacher's professionality . . .

and 'Every effort should be made to relate projects to other aspects of school development, including other school INSET, secondments, departmental curriculum-development etc.', and again among the statements of criteria:

> The stimulation of direct consideration of, or research into, what happens at the point of learning should be an aim. Teachers should be encouraged to become their own researchers into classroom phenomena.

The pack's introductory remarks and descriptions of the individual project briefs were similarly frank in their commitment to teachers as experts, and to an implied definition of what constitutes a professional. The projects themselves implied an enlarged professionality (groups were to define for colleagues the role of the tutor, find a way of communicating the whole curriculum experience to fellow teachers in the school, investigate classroom happenings) and the invitation to share that view was unabashed and open.

> Are you tired of being told by 'experts' what teaching and learning is like? Wouldn't *you* be the best placed, most fully aware, most professionally skilled person to find out – by noticing, or designing situations, or collecting statistics, or timing happenings, or interviewing, or tape-recording, or filming, or mutual observation or . . . or . . . (Launch pack on classroom phenomena, p. 9)

The next page almost claimed this research role as a professional entitlement (p. 10).

> How long will it be before teachers are given the chance to reflect, grow, be changed, feed back, in a sympathetic environment? Classrooms are where we have decided to spend our lives – can't we find ways of studying them?'

These extracts may by now have induced knowing smiles among the cognoscenti of school-based, teacher-centred staff development. Indeed I smile, too, at the unrelenting fervour of the appeal to my new colleagues (from which I retract not a word, retreat not an inch). The point is that this was how the appeal *was* first framed, wearing its professional philosophy on its sleeve.

Attached to the launch pack, which went to each member of staff individually, was a response sheet (pp. 12–13). On one side were described possible levels of involvement, and on the other the possible study areas. The sheet is exactly reproduced below.

BRANSTON TRIST ('TEACHERS AS EXPERTS') LAUNCH PACK

RESPONSE SHEET

This sheet is to indicate your present feelings about getting involved, at what level and in what area(s). Please tick one box in A, and one or more in B. No final commitment is implied. Feel free to make joint or group returns. The extra INSET resources are for you to use. Please don't feel you have to, though – somebody else will if you don't. Please return to Dg by June 3rd at the latest.

A   LEVEL OF INVOLVEMENT (tick the box nearest to your present wishes)

1. *No* involvement – on reflection the scheme is unsound.
2. No involvement in 1986/7. Too many priorities this year, but count me a sympathetic non-participant.
3. *Some* involvement – (am interested in hearing speakers, whether colleagues or outsiders, and in reading reports, etc., but not in group membership, discussing, writing or visiting other institutions.)
4. *Significant* involvement (interested in hearing speakers, considering reports and issues, exploring issues as a member of a group, possibly helping write brief reports, possibly suggesting INSET activities, possibly visiting other institutions. Prepared to set work for supply teacher on one or more occasions next year if the group requests me to undertake a task for them, so I can take time out.)
5. *Major* involvement (interested in co-ordinating the work or findings of a group, and playing a leading role in the tasks listed in 4. above, possibly organising outside visits, speakers in, ensuring colleagues' work is co-ordinated, written up and disseminated to colleagues. Prepared to report on behalf of project group to bodies such as Adcom, academic board, Heads of House, staff meetings, etc.) Willing to accept 1–2 periods reduction in class-contact (if timetabler can manage) in order to undertake research or team-leadership role.
6. *Ultimate* involvement (willing to eat, drink and sleep research and development, freely to give up the hours between 4–10 p.m. each night, if necessary, marking books before breakfast in order to keep up. Able to vow, as the Good Lord is my witness that I will earn the professional staff at Branston a national reputation for pioneering work in school-based INSET, willing to sacrifice . . .

B   AREAS OF INVOLVEMENT (if more than one tick, show order of preference; if involvement in more than one area is wanted, say so)

(1) None – Box A 1. or A 2. already ticked
(2) Tutorial role/style/content etc.
(3) Curriculum

     (a) descriptions (designing a curriculum communication system)
     (b) modular
     (c) CPVE (for CPVE teachers)
(4) Classroom phenomena (if you have a partner or partners please indicate names below. If you have an idea or area for a project please state. If you want to first join a research group then find a topic with them please tick here
Research partner(s) (if any at this stage)

_____

_____

Suggested topic (if any at this stage)

_____

_____

. . . .

Any other comments you wish to make about anything at all in this launch pack

Remember: The *worst* that can happen is not that bad, and probably won't! The best that can happen is a change in how you see your professional life, and possibly a change, caused by *you*, in your school.

The response was huge and hugely encouraging. Excluding those who already knew they were leaving the school, 80 per cent of full-time staff responded positively (levels 3–6). There was one openly negative response and twelve teachers made no return. Although level 2 was worded so that non-participants did not have to describe themselves as hostile, and the level 3 descriptions allowed colleagues an avenue of positive 'involvement' without demanding too much activity, 35 responses (not counting those of the senior management team of five) volunteered to go beyond that to level 4 or 5, i.e. significant or major involvement. This was wonderful.

The first year of the Branston approach

From the start it was possible to match the individual levels and areas of involvement with the responses. Those opting for major involvement were approached and signed up as team leaders. These were given a slightly reduced teaching timetable (2 × 35 minute periods per week). An overall co-ordinator was named (a senior teacher who was a member of the senior management team) and was given four periods. These allocations immediately disposed of about 40 per cent of the (joint TRIST/LEA) funding.

The staff were informed of the names of the names of the seven team leaders (two of the five projects had joint leadership) but 'Needless to say, the title "team-leader" implies nothing about where the ideas, plans for development come from. He/she is simply the focus/co-ordinator of the team effort' (staff bulletin, June 1986). Staff were also informed that the total lists of responders would now go to team leaders, so anyone who expressed an interest could expect to be approached by (or could approach) the relevant project leader. In other words, groups would form themselves.

The same bulletin described the co-ordinators' role:

> to liaise with the teams and leaders, facilitate whatever they plan to do, promote the feedback from each project to everybody else, and keep an eye on the submission criteria, reporting back to me so I can account to the MSC and LEA.

Despite my own enthusiasm for teacher-centred research, or perhaps because of it, I felt I should make two decisions – one easy and one difficult. The easy one was to try to follow the logic of the argument I had made to outside agencies, that the delegation of INSET to school level was a virtuous deed in itself (because it would ultimately stimulate the growth of school-level INSET management, and self-renewing schools).

Accordingly, the rest of the resources were simply given to the project groups (expressed as a bundle of supply teacher days each) to use as they saw fit. Accounts would have to be kept, minutes of meetings and reports would be expected, but those involved in the activity would be in control and decide how and when to meet and spend, as well as deciding exactly what to study or research. For me that was the easy decision.

The difficult one was to decide not to become involved as a team member. Although as an individual I was extremely frustrated at being left out, I felt I needed to demonstrate, by keeping my distance, a faith that those who had responded could develop projects by themselves and also to demonstrate that what was happening was something different from a line management plan'. I am still unsure whether this was a necessary self-denial but it felt right at the time.

The team leaders recruited group members from among other responders, and the scheme was off the ground. At the same time the final launch target was achieved when pleas for funding for external evaluation was agreed with the LEA, and I was able to make a successful approach to Chris Day, the head of teacher INSET at the University of Nottingham.

I had always presented to colleagues my belief that external evaluation would be a boost, not a threat, to our activities. Evaluation has important psychological, or political, benefits. Both participants and non-participants are made aware that their activities are valued enough to be studied seriously, and the final report, published a year later, did help validate the process (which is not to say it found nothing but success) both for us an insiders, with future intentions for school-based activity, and also for outsiders whom we needed, and need, to convince. Finally, the process of evaluation employed, which was for the evaluator to get inside the project as it progressed, by listening, interviewing and helping us reflect, was helpful, as was the final report. We were perhaps fortunate in having the right kind of evaluator. He had the appropriate expertise and personality and was independent both of the LEA and of the school management structure. The benefits to organizations of truly external evaluation are rather often overlooked by the people within them. Just now, as schools and LEAs, under the impulse of ERA, move into a somewhat more inspectorally dominated system, it seems paradoxical to urge that schools also find their own independent evaluators of professional development; but perhaps it is worth considering (and not just in the area of INSET).

It is not easy to quickly describe the outcomes of the projects nor to categorize them as successes or otherwise. Chris Day's evaluation was certainly challenging, yet one thing it did confirm was the sheer quantity of professional activity generated. Virtually all who responded positively did in fact participate and the very fact that so many Branston teachers became involved in the process of teacher-centred professional research and development was perhaps more important to me than any other single outcome.

Certainly in terms of value for money I had no difficulty in justifying school control (and within the school, teacher control) of INSET resources. The team leaders clearly gave more time to their project activities than the timetable relief they were paid, and so did group members. For example both the curriculum descriptions group and the learning for learning group (signi-ficantly, almost the first act of the classroom phenomena group was to choose its own name for itself) often met after school in order to plan activities, questionnaires, strategy, thus reserving most of their allocated resource (about twenty supply day equivalents each group) for when supply cover was essential (e.g. when group members followed a student or a class for a day, or undertook other classroom observation). The modular curriculum group wanted to maximize the number of visits out to other schools. Groups did sometimes feel the need to meet together in school time, for perhaps half a day, for example to organize report writing, but in general the unsurprising but important mes-sage was that if teachers control INSET resources, or are granted timetable release, then they will give excellent value in terms of time and quality of attention.

Some other outcomes were equally easy to see. The curriculum descriptions group produced a 50-page report for staff colleagues containing a number of pictures of the first-year curriculum. (The group had come to concentrate on this cohort, and to focus more and more on the class pursuit as a method.) Five of the team took a day each in one week to experience the curriculum as it was presented (i.e. the *real* curriculum) to class 1G. This was backed up with an elaborate questionnaire to all departments about their perceptions of the elements of learning (as HMI defined) that were involved in their part of the curriculum. The results were published in the form of pie charts, bar charts, schematic diagrams and typed up lesson observation sheets. Again there was perhaps nothing new here for experienced classroom analysts (but it is different when it is your school studied by your colleagues).

Even more complicated classroom behaviour analysis was attempted by the learning about learning group (in fact there was some cross-membership between those two groups, showing just how much interest and stamina some people have). But again, *that* it happened, and the insights it gave to those who undertook the research were as important as the product. This group began by deciding to focus on teacher questions as an aspect of teacher–student interaction, on interaction between students in groups and finally on what motivates students to work. They, too, became engaged in student pursuits as a major exercise and although they made some observations on group work, ran out of time before dealing with their large final question.

One of my strongest feelings about the outcomes of such work is that they are concerned with the building up of long-term questioning of our own perceptions of what it is we are creating together at the school. It is very difficult to estimate the direct impact, for example, of the Baker day display produced by the curriculum descriptions group of colourful versions of their statistics. It seems to me that my colleagues here are – must be – gradually creating, from within, an inexorable commitment to the consideration of what the total learning environment is that we are jointly providing.

Paul Laycock (learning about learning leader) summed this up in his seminar paper for a Classroom Action Research Network (CARN) conference we were asked to attend:

> The strongest impression formed by the group was of the sheer number of questions generated by teachers. This surprised both the observers and the observed. The most startling case involved a teacher who had been happy to have a lesson of hers observed though rather apologetic that the lesson would not involve many questions; in fact, 110 were recorded in 35 minutes.
>
> (CARN conference paper spring 1987)

This observation, along with others the group made on the relative scarcity of thought-provoking questions (compared with the number of those de-signed for class management purposes) could no doubt have been gleaned from many a study; but the transforming potential for this school resides significantly in its home-grown nature. It is now in our own data bank so this potential will be available for tapping in the future, too.

As another example, the curriculum descriptions team found a discrepancy between the amount of classroom discussion time forecast by departments and the much lower figure actually observed. We have not suddenly been transformed as an institution by this apparently small detail of curriculum description but our entry into the business of looking at what we are doing *will* change the school, because it will change us. Fred Williams (curriculum descriptions team leader) ended his CARN conference seminar paper with the comment that

> Finally, the more staff can observe other staff teaching, and students learning, the more will be the general awareness of what the curriculum really is, and less the need for a description.
>
> (Seminar paper, Newnham College, 1987)

Of course it could be said that these two projects were very much process centred; but so in a sense were they all, even where overtly task centred. The prevocational group met, trained itself, and the Certificate of Pre-Vocational Education was delivered more effectively as a result. Process or product? The modular curriculum group met, explored, visited and reported. I cannot say that our modular GCSE balanced science course, or the recent introduction of modular community arts to the fourth and fifth years, or preparations for modular delivery of humanities subjects, were the result. Indeed I cannot even prove a connection; but I believe that the awareness raising the group generated among themselves and others helped pave the way.

In fact this group paved the way in a second respect, because its co-leader, Dave Rickaby, was about to start a one-term teacher fellowship at Leicester University. He was prepared to use this to carry out a study of the modular curriculum, on behalf of the group, rather than to pursue an independent topic of research. Thus he and the group gave us our first example of an off-site secondment formally tied to a school-focused development.

The tutorial group was similarly beneficial, both to its participants and as a result of its work but of course it is difficult, as with the modular group, to disentangle its effect from the effect of whole-school policy, because it is true that we embarked upon a large whole-school change in the pastoral system at the time when the groups were meeting.

Professional development and school policy

The relationship between our 'teachers as experts' groups (or any school-based professional development and whole-school policy-making is worth consideration at this point. There are two main issues here. The first concerns the relationship between individual professional development needs and the development needs of the school as a whole, and the second the relationship between the policy makers and the researchers or developers. There is a great deal of coherence between individual and school development, because each is the best vehicle for the other. Of course, there are tensions. It might, for example, be that the 'best' professional development for, and as perceived by, an individual teacher is not centred on something that the school has as a top priority. There is no way of avoiding this tension entirely, though I must say that as someone involved in appointing staff I know just how much weight *I* attach to participation in real-school development, and so for candidates applying to Branston there is no huge discrepancy (if individual teacher needs equals, as they often do, career profile needs).

If more award-bearing courses could be aligned to school-based work that would bring twin benefits: the first, formal professional recognition of teachers as experts, and the second the validation of school-based research and development as a normal aspect of professionality. The ending of the DES pooling arrangements reduced at a stroke the opportunities for teachers as individuals to gain award-bearing course secondment. This was a bitter pill for many at Branston to swallow.

However, there is no reason at all why schools and award-giving institutions should not collaborate on this. In fact they have been doing so for years, though in a relatively minor way which now needs to become mainstream. At Branston in the second and third years of our teachers as experts scheme, participants were invited to consider this possibility of award linkage, and so far three have become engaged in studies centred on school-based issues – two leading towards diplomas in educational enquiry and one towards an MPhil – all validated by our closest (but not very close) university. Indeed, although once again no direct link can be established with a climate encouraged by teachers as experts, it was interesting that when the LEA promoted a scheme for a Saturday morning BPhil course, four Branston teachers responded – the biggest take up from any school in the county. Was this climate or chance?

As far as school-initiated award linkage is concerned, funding for the fees and secondment time has come from a variety of sources both within the LEA and from our own resources. (We choose, naturally, those courses which have least off-site, most on-site, school-focused activity.)

Three years on, as we in Lincolnshire come to the end of the first financial year of the county's pre-statutory scheme of local management, it is clear that many schools have had difficulty in spending their delegated INSET money (equivalent to about two supply days per teacher per year). It is important to say, with statutory LMS impending, that this is in my view an entirely temporary phenomenon, arising only because schools have not been in the habit of managing their own INSET resources. Some obvious patterns have not yet been established. This is a criticism of previous history, not of our schools.

At Branston we have simply used the delegated funds to further the existing teachers as experts approach and we could happily have spent a multiple of the sum delegated. For example, we code the appropriate percentage of third year participants' salary to INSET (i.e. that number of periods they are timetabled for INSET/development) and pay from our own funds university fees and travel.

Two further points on this. Firstly, because the projects in the third year form part of a school plan for professional and school development there has been no problem at all in justifying, as we rightly have to, this LEA-earmarked part of our delegated school budget.

Secondly, because we have extended the idea of granting timetabled non-contact teacher time to virtually all participants, the disruption to our students has been relatively slight. In effect, professional development and school development have been built into the timetable. Significantly, across the county schools have reported the hesitation they naturally feel to disrupt the classes of teachers involved as one major reason for their reluctance to spend newly delegated INSET resources.

It is vitally important to appreciate the importance of this idea of building in professional development time so as to avoid disruption. The third supplementary Task Group on Assessment and Testing report has recently argued (Section 46) that there is no need for more INSET resources to cope with national curriculum and assessment developments because if those resources were provided schools would go beyond the limits of acceptable disruption to teaching. It is not only the curiously bad logic of this assertion that must be challenged but also its ignorance of what is practically possible given *more* INSET resources and the control of them by schools.

It does seem that there is a great opportunity to be taken. If the argument for statutory delegation is that schools, as front line creators of education, should be given control of something like 90 per cent of all educational spending, then it is clear that this must also include 90 per cent of all available INSET resources. Not to delegate that part of the service would be rather like removing Rolls-Royce's research and development budget and transferring it to the Department of Trade and Industry. (Rolls-Royce might not think this the best way to achieve success.)

What experience confirms as practical, and LMS principles suggest as logical, is not necessarily envisaged in the DES delegation Circular 7/88. The door is not entirely closed, however, and there are opportunities for truly imaginative LEAs to pass direct to schools a great deal of LEATGS money – if strings are attached, fine, let schools know the parameters and bid for accountable resources on that basis, with school bids and reports in turn providing the basis for LEA bids and reports to the DES.

If LMS is about levering up quality in schools, then schools and all who care about them really must fight for school control of this most powerful lever of all, which connects directly to the engine of genuinely professional, and real curriculum, development.

For what is said about the importance of ownership by teachers of the role of researchers into the curriculum process at the point of learning (the real curriculum), also applies to curriculum content and overall curriculum patterning. If teachers become convinced that they really are conveyors of prepackaged curriculum units, prepared for and sanctioned only by successive secretaries of state or their national committees, rather than believing that they are joint creators of education through their thinking provision of learning opportunities, then slowly but surely our system will cease to breed the kind of entrepreneurial, lively, morally engaged teachers who alone are fit to teach the new generations. Professionally stunted educators can no more produce compassionate, lively, enquiring minds than mere messengers can write poetry, and no secretary of state should want increased control over a dying body. What drives the organism (and professional development) is professional commitment and a sense of vocation. Every teacher knows that children's perceptions about themselves as masters of their learning is even more important to their progress than the important matter of studying a worthwhile and specific topic. What is true of our students is also true of ourselves.

Of course I immediately acknowledge the importance of a national framework and authority-wide initiatives – but even for those legitimately externally identified training and curriculum development targets, I back *institutionally* controlled professional and school development to score more bull's-eyes than any other system. What I did find truly remarkable from the start of the debate about local management of schools is how the rhetoric of school control over resources, a concept justified because schools were front line managers of the service, failed to lead naturally to a delegation of the majority of INSET resources.

Did nobody else find it amazing to read Appendix B of the original report on local management of schools, commissioned from Coopers and Lybrand? There, in attempting to list over fifty 'factors relevant to performance indicators' there is no mention whatsoever of a school's efforts at professional development of its teachers. (Mrs Rumbold's list of school indicators, published after this chapter was first written, is little better.) We *must* change this perception and we must not be faint hearted. Of course schools will need to learn how to do it – but if the system has never given them power over INSET resources it can hardly expect either sophisticated managerial strategies to have evolved or a sophisticated customer relationship with providers. Of course the preferred outcome is the expansion of professional development resources in absolute terms, because LEAs, for example, have never had anything like enough for authority-wide initiatives. But given a hard choice, let professional development resources go to schools. This would create a sea change.

Nor is it true to say that school control of the bulk of professional development resources would lead simply to in-house activity and to the reinvention of a thousand not quite circular wheels. LEA personnel should be in a key position to identify and provide relevant training and if they did, schools would buy it. Witness Branston's willingness to spend resources on fees for university courses, as well as bringing visiting lecturers in, and sending visiting teachers out. Moreover our experience shows that our colleagues in higher education are already geared up for the revolution. In 1986 when, although the pool was already evaporating, LMS was on few people's agenda, I visited our two nearest institutions, uninvited, to sound them out on the possibility of direct links with schools adopting a teachers as experts approach. Chris Day, as head of teacher INSET at Nottingham University, and Len Watson, head of the Centre for Education Management at Sheffield Polytechnic, were in common with others in higher education, willing to talk and capable of understanding the needs of the school in this area. They were perfectly willing to suggest possibilities for bringing about school-centred professional development into which they could input theoretical and practical expertise and award-bearing validation. In fact their minds were working very hard on making flexibility a key feature of post-pool professional development. As principal I had no INSET money of my own at the time, but their instinctive reactions, indicative of the readiness of our closest institutions of higher education, has much to do with the fact that we are currently spending INSET money on award-bearing courses for our staff, linked to school-focused work. This seems to be so natural that the old INSET mechanisms perhaps have to be regarded as an historical obstacle to (as well as a grand, lost support for) real professional and institutional development.

The Branston approach – year two

At Branston, in year two, another invitation went out to all staff. There was much of the same rhetoric and the whole idea of a school control over professional development was as self-consciously presented as before. The interest that outsiders had shown in the first year of the scheme was seen as evidence that we were offering 'an example of the way resources for INSET/development can be channelled to teachers themselves rather than outside training agencies' (Staff Bulletin, summer 1987).

Yet outside training agencies, if freely chosen by us, were seen as a professional resource. This was the bulletin where award-linkage was formally presented as an opportunity.

> Further, and especially since full-time secondments to award bearing courses will, as we thought, become much rarer under GRIST, I would like to see if Branston teachers could take a lead in gaining professional qualifications by 'writing up' school-based developments. It seems only fair that school-based professional work should get validation ... Of course part-time study involves sacrificing personal time, too, but I would be interested in supporting anyone who wanted to give this a go. If several Branston staff managed to gain diplomas from school-focused work, that could be an important model for teachers and officers in Lincolnshire and beyond.
>
> (Staff bulletin 6/87, p. 1)

After acknowledging that the choice of project areas in year one had been my own as incoming Principal, the bulletin went on (p. 2):

This year, although I refer below to current curriculum development issues, I also invite bids for development time from individuals, groups or departments on any area. Whole school research/developments, or at least whole departmental ones, remain likely to get preference over individual, self-contained ones, but individual projects or pieces of research are certainly possible.

These are difficult times in many ways, and we need to seize whatever positive professional developments we can see. I still think this is one of the best, for us as teachers, and for our students, because it develops us and the schools we are creating. Despite the importance of today's national events (I write on election day) it is not governments, but we who control the quality of schooling.

If you wish to make a bid, please do so by . . .

At this time our area of Lincolnshire was beginning to suffer the first significant effects of falling rolls, and we knew the authority had an enlightened policy of 50 per cent abatement of teacher loss. The bulletin made clear that we would seek to cover the curriculum close to Pupil–Teacher Ratio staffing and use abatement to fund teacher time for INSET/development.

When the list of successful bids was published to staff shortly afterwards, it showed that about half of our teachers were involved in some way, either through individual projects/developments or through departments. The initial list is shown below.

Branston research/development time 1987/8

Staff	PPW	Area of research development
Pr	2	Mapping Health Education (in pastoral and subject curricula Yrs 1–7).
Lh	4	Library (whole school needs assessment and initiation of computerisation of catalogue/information retrieval).
HM*	6	The pastoral curriculum and delivery.* (+ Diploma)
Sd	2	Profiling in HE and across the curriculum
Lt	2	Special needs in Geography ⎱
Wn	2	Special needs in PE ⎰ in conjunction
Nf	4	Special needs in Maths with An
An	3	Special needs in mainstream classes.
He	4	Managing student-interaction and group work in tutorial time.
Ba	2	Creative performing arts cross-curricular modules.
Wh	2	
Dy	4	Research/development of broad-based integrated or
Ht	2	co-ordinated modular science 14–16 examination
Ct	2	course for 1988–90 and associated Lower school
To	2	developments (e.g. 1st, 2nd year syllabus –
Py	2	third year graded assessment modules).

Lg   2
Wl   4   Gender and equal opportunities in the curriculum.
Cp*   6   The pastoral curriculum and its delivery.* (+ Diploma)
Eng. Dept. 10–15 days supply
(Wm,Lk,Sp,Hs,Tu,Ro,Be,Mn,Ms) Departmental teaching workshops for
                    trialling, observation and team analysis of teaching
                    techniques.

Lang. Dept. 6 days supply
(Ry,Mv,Se,Wd,Ch,Wl) Departmental review of the place of languages
                    in the whole curriculum with reference to student need
                    and curriculum structures.
*Assuming applications for two-year Diploma in Educational Enquiry
accepted by Nottingham University. Precise areas of research-
development by negotiation between applicants, the school and the
University, within the context of whole school tutorial development.
                    (Extract from Staff Bulletin, summer term 1987)

There were some minor later alterations, and, unfortunately, a (few) reduc-
tions in the spring term as a result of an exceptional mid-year staffing reduction
imposed by the LEA. As before there was a mixture of process- and product-
oriented activity. For example, the 10–15 days given to the English department
was really a way of giving time to teachers to discuss teaching, whereas the
science department also had a deadline for the introduction of a change to
balanced science GCSE. Of course my argument is that the process of aiming at
the science product, and the professional insights produced by the English
analysis of process would turn out to be as potentially valuable. Process and
product are in fact simply words we use to show what we happen to be focusing
on. There is no clear objective distinction – after all professional development
itself is only a product in the terms of this chapter and this book. If we chose to
see the accumulated learning gain of school leavers as education's product
then we would see professional development as merely one small part of the
process leading to school-leavers as output.

During year two we tried to keep staff informed of events, for example by
way of an INSET newsletter in which participants/groups could write a
paragraph outlining what they were doing. There was an end-of-year presenta-
tion at a staff meeting from some of the participants, too. These were strategies
to remind ourselves that, among other things, teachers are researchers and
developers.

The problem of dissemination is a difficult one and we are still working on it.
We tried to build a dissemination in various ways from year one, partly by the
high profile of the whole approach and by publication of written or verbal
reports from participants at staff meetings. I also took the view that with so
many people involved in so many projects, two things would happen. Firstly
some of the projects would lead to, or tie in with, fairly short-term develop-

ments (e.g. the new tutorial system, CPVE, and the new science and community arts courses), and secondly over time a very significant proportion of teachers at Branston would have had the opportunity to self-develop by participation.

Into year three at Branston

Happily for everyone, by the time year three was due for launch, the invitations to participate were now becoming briefer, and in summer of 1988 the year three 'Teachers as experts' bulletin was only two sides, plus two response sheets (one to department heads and heads of year, asking for departmental/ pastoral team needs, and another to individuals asking them to list individual, pastoral, departmental or whole school needs).

That bulletin gave a clear indication that the highest priority for funding would be to follow up the recommendations of the curriculum descriptions and learning about learning groups of 1987, which both concluded that collaborative, classroom-focused teacher research was worth pursuing. The bulletin again advanced that process as 'a key way for teachers to gain insight into the curriculum we are jointly creating for our students, and the learning situation as experienced by them' (Staff Bulletin, spring 1988).

It was suggested that the techniques we had learned should be used to look at a particular time slice of a year group (say one term of the third year – the group who had been pursued as first years previously).

> Within this framework, however, it remains very important, I believe, that the control of the research (what *exactly* to look at, *how* to analyse) should be with the teachers-as-researchers, as it was before. Therefore ... we shall delegate the budget to the groups, who can decide for themselves how to spend it. Mostly, of course, the money will go on *time* to pursue, discuss or write up experiences for the rest of us.

> We cannot accept that academics, administrators, politicians can tell us all we need to know about education (though we need their help, of course, and they have legitimate powers over schooling). We must be educational thinkers ourselves, not just teaching machines. We'll teach better as a result, anyway.

> (Staff Bulletin, spring 1988)

In other words, the same (sincere) rhetoric as before. The responses came in and in that year 25–30 staff received some timetable remission for INSET/ development.

Again there was a mixture of projects, though fewer free-standing individual ones than in year two. The science department received a second year of timetable relief (they had met their deadline for new course introduction but had a case for further development time). The humanities faculty have been looking at modularization in years 3–5 and records of achievement, and all staff in the special needs departments have received time for a major review (we have a Moderate Learning Difficulty unit on site as part of the school and a whole curriculum rewriting is in progress). The staff who introduced community arts GCSE into the fourth year had, like science, a case for further development time and the two joint librarians were involved in implementing a reorganization and reappraisal linked to a development plan which they had successfully submitted to an LEA competitive matched funding scheme.

Nine individual members of staff joined a classroom curriculum team, who named themselves the curriculum of learning group in recognition of their relationship to two previous Branston research groups. The leader was given (a little) extra time in order to allow him to make their work, under his team leadership, the focus of an MPhil degree, again at Nottingham University. He became the third to take that route. We also funded from delegated INSET the second year of our two diplomates. This time we have been able to give all members of the curriculum of learning group 2 (× 35 minute) periods per week, costed (as 5 per cent of salary, including on costs) to the delegated school INSET budget. In both years two and three teachers as experts has continued with the idea of an INSET co-ordinator, who is given 3–4 periods a week for the task of facilitating and monitoring, which can mean stimulating and receiving reports or actively connecting in-house groups to outside agencies.

Teachers as experts at Branston

Naturally the projects described in this chapter are not happening in isolation, and nor is the teachers as experts philosophy confined to them. For example, we have instituted the idea of team days or half days in the summer term post-exam weeks, when release is least disruptive. This has grown from somewhat smaller beginnings three years ago until now we have 20 or 30 of these meetings on the calendar. Typically they are year tutorial teams or departmental teams working on self-selected tasks, but we have also managed to give cross-curricular teams some time. Every member of staff is therefore involved at least two days or half days. A professional agenda for the day and a report is requested. Such meetings can be on- or off-site and sometimes involve other agencies. (When I think of all this valuable INSET time, tied into current school developments, I dread those who would tidy up the school year into four terms, in order to gain from the supposed post-examination slack. Whatever the other benefits, we at Branston rather deny that they can be gained at the low cost of ending slack. Professional development surely rates higher than that.)

There were no such things as Baker days when we began, but of course my instant reaction, leaving aside (as if one could) the thought of the imposed loss of five holiday days from teaching staff, was that here was yet another INSET resource, equal in size to what we had previously regarded as very major funding, whether from outside or from internal resource allocation. If the introduction of Baker days is resulting in far greater awareness of, and expertise in, the school-level management of professional development, then that simply confirms the point made earlier about school expertise growing in response to delegated INSET responsibility and resources. Naturally we try to incorporate these into a school development plan, too, and as the reader might by now expect, my own anxiety is that schools themselves should retain control over the timing and the content of such days.

The clear anxiety of central or local government to retain INSET control is misplaced, illogical and at odds with the rhetoric of LMS. In any case there is no *need* for anyone outside the school to specify professional training content, for the real imperatives, whether of the national curriculum or of other local/ national policy, are necessarily ones schools know they need to meet. Let schools and teachers find their own ways to hit the targets. Criticize culpable misses but do not try to steady our arms as we take aim, any more than the PE department holds the elbows of aspiring netball points scorers. Give us targets and opportunity, and the right to call on whatever expertise we want, from wherever in the system we want. No good offer of help is going to be spurned, if it is of high quality.

Finally, to the issue of who controls professional development within a school. This is important, because there is no ducking the accusation that people are both extolling the virtues of teachers as experts, and speaking the rhetoric of ownership, and yet at the same time using position power and resource power to exercise hierarchical or managerial control. Going back three years to one of the original five groups, on the role of the tutor, there is some evidence (our evaluator thought so) that the early days of its operations were compromised by my decision as principal to move from the historical house pastoral groups towards a horizontal year- and tutor-based system, with a weekly extended tutorial lesson. Some members of the group and some outside it felt that their brief should have allowed them to decide on recom- mendations about the whole-school structure, as well as to explore the professional role of the tutor within any given pastoral system. Most of the ex-heads of house were involved in the tutorial group (two were leading it) and although they were and are a superbly committed set of professional col- leagues, they did, quite naturally, feel the tension of the position. They were, as always, willing to commit themselves personally to the success rather than the downfall of the enterprise, but did not want the INSET group to be seen by other colleagues as the agent of the structural change, or their own mem- bership on it to be interpreted as a middle management initiative backing the new structural system. This was fair enough, I thought, and after discussion with them I wrote a paper on our move to a horizontal tutorial structure, designed not only to show again its rationale but also to demonstrate that the structural change, within which the tutorial role would in future be exercised, was a policy decision divorced from the studies of the INSET group on tutorial role.

The fact that now, three years on, the same set of people, along with their tutorial teams, have made successful strides towards creating an educational reality of the pastoral five-year plan, is not the point. The point is that there was tension between teachers as experts and traditional policy making by the school leadership.

My response is partly simply to accept the situation and to point out that everyone in schools is permanently aware of it. After all there is always a tension inherent in the fact that no headteacher can be an expert with respect to his subject departmental colleagues, who therefore have proper professional control of their curriculum areas. That is why, for example, departments create capitation spending plans, and not me. On the other hand, although they may not think I get it right, my colleagues do expect me to have views, and promote initiatives in curriculum or organizational development, and although it is perfectly possible to decide to run a school on the basis of a moot (assuming for a wild moment that governors, parents, the LEA and the government are happy) that is not the way we are at Branston. We are fairly typical.

Of course, the tension runs both ways. Not all school decisions made by INSET participants are as they would be if I made them but the merits of delegation to fellow professionals far outweigh the supposed benefits of a system where I overruled and so withdrew ownership in every case that came to my notice (and of course that begs the question of whose decision would be the 'correct' one. I guess my colleagues rightly reckon to know more about many aspects of the curriculum than I do.) Besides which I reject all simple calculations of the cost–benefits of delegation within a profession if they rely on the idea of a fixed quantum of control. There is such a thing as a net overall increase in control or power. Rather than focus entirely on the legitimate question of whether teacher ownership and school management team control of professional development can co-exist, I prefer to recount the advantages for all of our professional development philosophy. I will then have justified a fairly robust (I would say idealistic) determination to implement the approach.

Perhaps that apologia satisfies no critics. The fact remains that I do reject the alternative extremist view. Yes I have deliberately and consistently used my position to find and make available resources for professional INSET and school development, and have tried to influence, by persuasion and by the power of allocation, the ways in which these resources are spent. I simply deny that this necessarily contradicts the essential idea and merits of teachers as experts.

Standing back, the questions are whether the approach has strengthened the school and whether it has been true to its motto. I think the answer to both is yes. We can point to a number of measurable products (reports, specific courses introduced, course-trained staff and, soon, awards gained). I want to point again and again to the not so easily measurable products. There is an element of faith in this, which some will find irritatingly subjective, but I cannot but believe that professional discussion by on-site colleagues of real data found by themselves is anything other than transforming, both of morale and of professional awareness. This applies whether the investigation is into how many minutes a day a student spends reading (i.e. a piece of data not yet connected to action) or how many extra moisture-meters the department needs if it is to implement balanced science syllabus X, rather than single science syllabuses ABC (i.e. what one might term a 'near-market' piece of research rather than a 'fundamental atomic particle' type of basic investigation).

It is, of course, quite possible simply to demand that new courses are introduced, new ways of working are tried, coherent collections of curriculum data are produced. Indeed as I write we are entering a phase where a certain kind of curriculum mapping will surely be imposed, nationally or locally. ('Identify where in years 1–5 the following cross-curricular aspects of health education/European understanding, etc. etc., are being delivered.') When I look at the curriculum map of one term of the third year that the curriculum of learning group has produced, I can see behind its apparent simplicity to the potentially transforming processes that went into it – including the experiencing of that curriculum by a number of colleagues in classrooms about the school, including interviews with children and teachers about what they felt was happening.

When, as I guess we will have to, we come to fill in our national curriculum cross-curricular theme grids, we can at least remember at Branston that we were doing this as professionals, from the inside, before we had to, and therefore will perhaps not be doing it in future just because we have to. This is important for our future professional development. For even if pleas that whole-curriculum patterns and content should to a real degree remain with teachers and schools are rejected, and even if a testing regime becomes so prescriptive and so closely tied to measurable, content-heavy programmes of study that the educational environment is in danger of being reduced and dimished for students, and the professional creativity of teachers correspondingly denied – then above all, we will need a strongly self-confident profession, capable of attracting those who just will be creative and non-mechanical, within whatever limits are imposed. I am not, in fact, entirely pessimistic about the ultimate centralization of control, but I shall be much happier if INSET/development resources are finally delegated to school control (even if almost the same kind of off-site courses and secondments as now are the freely paid for result).

In conclusion, I am unrepentant of promoting what has happened at Branston; but I have played my part very stumblingly, and yet it *has* happened. For three years an appeal for volunteers has been met with a fairly massive response. A transcript of an old interview with our evaluator shows that my own feelings at the time of the first year's appeal were ones of considerable vulnerability and exposure. Here was a naked question asked of colleagues, and an act of faith, which need not have met with the response it did. It is my colleagues, not I, who have been writing the script.

Therefore the Branston case history has nothing to do with me and everything to do with the professionalism of so called 'ordinary teachers'. I have met very few teachers who are not extraordinary. Just when a centralizing of curriculum power and the need for school-level management of imposed change to tight deadlines is tending to divorce educational managers from their colleagues (who see them more and more as system managers and accountants, not fellow professionals) the teachers as experts philosophy has perhaps some value in showing the commitment of senior management to chalk face professionalism. It is anti-hierarchical. It is also, for teachers who participate, anti-isolationist and anti-depressant at a time of threatened morale.

Yes, of course those who have responded have received some free time in which to do the work; but that is not the point. That time needs to be seen not only as an incentive to participants, but also as a *recognition*, both of teachers as professionals engaged in professional activity, and of that activity itself as of high enough institutional priority to be allocated a share in our most precious, most inelastic resource. All those involved are working harder than if they had not had the extra time; but at least not only they, but also the school is showing some commitment.

For that commitment is essential. There is no point in a school taking this route if it is not believed in. Naturally, I am aware that many schools across the country have been following this philosophy for years, and I will end as I began, disclaiming any originality for Branston School and Community College. We are just another example of how widely British educators interpret their professionalism.

But the unoriginal message is worth restating. For if as a headteacher I say to my staff that the sin against the Holy Ghost for teachers is not to believe in young people, I say also to my fellow headteachers that the corresponding sin for those running schools is not to believe in teachers. This chapter is dedicated to my colleagues at Branston, with thanks and admiration.

References

Coopers & Lybrand (1987). *Local Management of Schools: A Report to the DES*.
Day, C. (1988). *Teachers as Experts 1986–7 – an evaluation report*. University of Nottingham School of Education.
Department of Education and Science (1988). *Education Reform Act: Local Management of Schools*, Circular 7/88. London, HMSO.
Department of Education and Science (1988). *Task Group on Assessment and Testing: Third supplementary report*. London, HMSO.
Douglas, B. W. (1984). *Quality Control and the Management of Schools*. Centre for Education Management, Sheffield Polytechnic.

Douglas, B. W. (1989). *Local Management of Schools – a Headteacher's Perspective*. Centre for Education Management, Sheffield Polytechnic.

Laycock, P. (1988). 'Learning about Learning', unpublished workshop paper presented to CARN International Conference at Newnham College, Cambridge, 26 March 1988.

School Management Task Force (1990). *Developing School Management: the way forward*. London, HMSO.

Williams, F. (1988). 'Curriculum Descriptions', unpublished workshop paper presented to CARN International Conference at Newnham College, Cambridge, 26 March 1988.

8

Staff development in further education

Maureen Woodward

The 1950s and 1960s were halcyon years in terms of funding and growth in the education system. During those decades staff development did not attract a great deal of attention. This situation altered in the 1970s and 1980s. Staff development, assessment and appraisal became issues which were, and still are, hotly debated. This period has been marked by financial restrictions in expenditure on education and changes in the nature of education itself, particularly in further education.

The changes faced by further education have necessitated government, local authority and college management action to enable staff to adapt to the new demands made upon them so that the service offered in more effective and efficient. Sir Keith Joseph, the former secretary of state for education, clearly spelt out his expectations in a speech made in January 1985: 'we must get better value for money' and 'build on good practice and get rid of extravagance and inefficiency'. One response to this was the emergence of staff development policies in many colleges and the implementation of staff development programmes, funded by the then new grant related in-service training money which had replaced the previous funding arrangements for in-service training.

But what exactly is this panacea for all ills, this catch all and much latched on to phrase which seems to have broad descriptive meaning and a distinct evaluative dimension? What is staff development? In 1973 the Association of Colleges of Further and Higher Education and the Association of Principals of Technical Institutions established a joint working party to report on staff development in further education. The ACFHE/APTI working party report (1973) was influential; it was 'something of a milestone' according to Dr Tolley (1981). The joint report produced a working definition of the prime aims of staff development, and made a number of practical recommendations about

how colleges might implement schemes using the guidelines suggested
therein.

The emphasis in the report was for the need for staff to broaden their
individual experience in terms of research, consultancy and professional/
industrial experience. This was an acknowledgement that the fundamental
changes which were taking place in further education at the time and were to
take place in the future had to be met by changes in what was expected of the
staff; such changes were also affecting the colleges themselves and how they
were managed.

Between 1975 and 1978 the Advisory Committee on the supply and training
of teachers published three documents which also help to define what is meant
by staff development in further education. ACSTT I (the Haycock Report) 1975
reported on the training of FE teachers; this was followed in March 1978 by a
discussion paper, ACSTT II, which dealt with the training of adult education and
part-time FE teachers, whose numbers had been increasing dramatically over
this period. A few months later another discussion paper entitled *Training
Teachers for Educational Management in Further and Adult Education*
(ACSTT III) appeared. It suggested that there should be an element of
educational management incorporated into initial FE teacher training and that
emphasis should be placed on this area in post-initial in-service training to
improve the quality and quantity of educational management.

The strong emphasis on training in the three reports, over and above other
aspects of what might be considered to be important for teachers' development
and the fact that this was the one area where the DES made concerted efforts to
encourage action, was not surprising, for a number of reasons. The rather *ad
hoc* provision made for further education teacher training was giving cause for
concern not only at initial training level but also in-service level, given the need
for retraining and redeployment of staff into the new FE growth areas. Further
education colleges had their roots in the old mechanics' institutes and they
initially grew out of the need to provide training for 'the practical man',
responding primarily to the needs of industry and commerce.

The creation of the Industrial Training Boards in 1964 and later the
Manpower Services Commission in 1973 under the aegis of the Department of
Employment separated off many of the traditional training initiatives from the
further education sector. The result of this was that the demands made on FE
for vocational education shifted from the manufacturing/industrial nexus to
the service industry. These demands were in line with changes in the job
market. Unskilled jobs were rapidly disappearing and youth unemployment
among those with no skills or training was high. The main increase in jobs in
the 1970s had been in the service industries, and required different skills from
those needed in manufacturing industries.

New skills were required of students by employers and this affected the
nature of FE teaching itself. Traditional information delivery techniques
rapidly became outmoded; a more progressive, student-centred style was

necessary, incorporating student profiling and self-assessment, which would supposedly act as incentives for student learning, since many of the new 16–19-year-old students were reluctant learners. Exam boards were responding, incorporating more internal and continuous assessment and new 'student friendly' exam modes. Computer-based learning programmes and open learning packages were also increasingly seen as cost-effective ways of enabling students to learn at their own rate.

Added to this were other factors which brought changes to traditional further education: the demand for 'O' and 'A' level packages increased from adults who had 'missed the boat' first time around and from school students wanting a second chance in the relative freedom of a college rather than school environment. Other groups for whom courses were required included many who had in the past been ignored by this sector: the adult unemployed, those with disabilities, ethnic minorities, the disadvantaged, girls and women, and students without basic literacy and numeracy skills.

In many colleges greater efforts were also being made to move from non-advanced to advanced grades of work, thus providing greater promotional opportunities for staff and greater prestige for the institution (always assuming the demand could be adequately met by the college staff). The interface between school and college, and further and higher education was becoming blurred, which meant that those teaching in FE were exposed not only to a much broader range of students than ever before in terms of age, ability, experience, race and sex, but also to new exam techniques, different methods of transmission and changes in curriculum design. New initiatives like TVEI and the proposed restructuring of vocational qualifications resulting from the recommendations of the National Committee on Vocational Qualifications meant that the need for better initial training, in-service and retraining had never been more obvious. External forces, both national and local, were exerting pressure for change in an educational sector with an increasingly aging and demoralized workforce.

Some of the literature on staff development at this time centred around the purpose of the exercise and who should be involved in the process. Was the purpose to serve the needs of the organization, the individual or society? Who should initiate, devise and implement staff development in colleges which managed their organizational structures in diverse ways? Wheeler's (1969) concern with the management of colleges in the light of the tertiary sector growth which started in the early 1960s led him to conclude that a managerial approach was needed in the 1970s. He pointed out that organizational growth often provides a stimulus for staff and students and that this type of challenge can be sufficient to overcome deficiencies in management which can therefore afford to adopt the *laissez-faire* approach exemplified by many college managers in the 1960s. When growth slows down and eventually ceases, organizational problems emerge. It then becomes necessary to adopt a new approach to solve the problems.

Baron (1978) suggests that management by objectives (MBO) is a relevant managerial approach for colleges when they are faced with problems connected with financial stringency. MBO serves to clarify objectives; it can be used to keep costs and resources under control while providing a framework for decision making towards the pursuit of organizational goals; and it can help staff to meet their own needs within an overall framework which benefits the college. Baron, like Wheeler, saw staff development as primarily meeting the needs of the organization.

A similar assumption was made in the ACFHE/APT I (1973) report referred to earlier. Staff development is clearly viewed as the responsibility of management; management identifies the needs of staff and devises programmes to meet these needs. The report put forward four aims for staff development:

(1) to improve current performance and remedy existing weaknesses
(2) to prepare staff for changing duties and responsibilities and to encourage them to use new methods and techniques in their present posts
(3) to prepare teachers for advancement either in their own college or in the education service generally
(4) to enhance job satisfaction.

(ACFHE/APT, 1973, p. 2)

It is also clearly stated that teachers who might be unwilling to accept management's definition of the situation should be encouraged to do so. Thus an element of compulsion on staff to accept management's perspective and to participate was seen as necessary if this type of managerial approach is adopted. In the words of the report (p. 7):

It is possible that some teachers in colleges may object to pressure being put on them to take part in training programmes to meet the needs either diagnosed or thought necessary by their seniors . . . We feel this is a view that management cannot accept under present circumstances (or indeed any set of circumstances) and must seek to change.

The problem with such approaches, however, is that they tend to imply that there can be agreement in the area of objectives. In relation to educational organizations, this is a somewhat optimistic view. In the current situation, whereby colleges of further education are facing numerous demands from a variety of forces, it would appear to be an impossible task. The only common objective seems to be survival. Additionally the idea that staff can be compelled to participate in their own development is rather contradictory, and also goes against what is usually seen as an appropriate managerial response towards professionals. The notion that management can identify the variety of needs staff might have and respond to them, in what could be a rather blanket fashion, is rather difficult to envisage, given the imposition this implies and the time and resources needed for implementation.

Another group of writers stress the part staff play in their own development, defining their own goals and priorities. Sayers and Harding (1974) and Warren, Piper and Glatter (1977), seem to fit into this group aptly displaying what Bradley, Chesson and Silverleaf (1983) call the 'partnership' approach. They attribute the increasing emphasis on the individual's involvement in the process to the growing movement towards the democratization of colleges. The assumption behind this approach is that staff are self-actualizing, and that conflicts of interest between individual and organizational needs and objectives can be solved within the partnership in a harmonious way. Warren, Piper and Glatter (1977) view Staff development as 'a systematic attempt to harmonise individuals' interests and wishes, and their carefully assessed requirements for furthering their careers with the forthcoming requirements of the organisation within which they work' (p. 26). Williams (1981) and Billing (1982) broaden out this partnership model: Williams by including pupils, ancillary staff and governors in the partnership, and Billing by pointing out that not only present but the future needs and objectives of all parties have to be satisfied. He sees staff development as a way of resolving conflicts between the partners, and a way of developing the individual not just within but also outside the organization.

Billing's focus is similar to the one expressed by Alex Main in his book *Educational Staff Development* (1985). He argues for a 'personal growth' model of staff development and makes the point that this is the most appropriate response at a time when resources are diminishing and there is negative growth. He disagrees with the idea that, because of this, the needs of the organization must come first and that 'staff need to change to fit in with the new "mission"' (p. 124). This will create 'passive members of the organisation'. Staff should be treated as self-regulating beings and should be supported by the organization to discover 'self'. That is the 'self as a teacher or manager; the self as a member of the organisation, and the political self – the self in society' (p. 120). Management's role in this situation is to show its commitment to meeting staff needs, not by withdrawing totally but by being around 'to signal that it has provided the funds and that it really cares how the money is used' (p. 120). In this way, staff who face uncertainty and change from without will be 'helped to develop certainties within' (p. 125). Gray (1985) echoes this approach when writing about staff development as part of organizational development in schools. In his view staff development *is* organizational development. As people within the organization discover their true self, so the health of the organization flourishes: self-awareness and fulfilment are prerequisites for organizational growth. This is as true for the students as it is for the staff: 'Schools cannot escape the challenge of student growth to autonomy and liberty and unless teachers are themselves liberated and autonomous they can never begin to fulfil their obligations as key members of the school' (p. 33). This latter group of writers, Main, Gray and to some extent, Billing do not easily fit the classic partnership approach. Theirs is a wider approach, taking a great deal from psychotherapy and social work theory.

Two distinct poles are apparent in the definition of staff development: at one end, there is the rather rigid view that staff needs can be prescribed by management and that staff development is an exercise in making sure that the individual's needs are, or should become, the organization's needs, the individual only being seen in terms of the organization. This lays emphasis on the training aspects. At the other end there is a suggestion of a more developmental approach, extending the aims to include, in the widest inter-pretation, personal growth within and outside the organization, the assump-tion being that such growth is a necessity for personal as well as professional fulfilment.

In some cases, then, the term staff development equates with merely staff training. This rather narrow interpretation limits the exercise to one of moulding staff to fit the needs of the organization. The implication here is that staff are a homogeneous rather than a heterogeneous, group who can be managed in a rather traditional fashion. Objectives might seem clear, when the main need is for the organization's survival at times of restricted growth and cutbacks. This interpretation, however, could be rather unproductive since, when organizational objectives change, people are required to change in direct response. This is a costly exercise, not just in terms of the financial outlay required to train, retrain and update the skills of the workforce, but also in terms of the human cost such erratic changes impose on staff morale, motivation and psychological health.

In the other case, staff development is considered to be a developmental process, aimed at personal and professional growth. This broader perspective seems more appropriate in many respects for professionals working in education organizations, since it appears to take the individual as its starting point, and is concerned with making him or her into an active participant in his or her own growth, acknowledging that change is part of this. Objectives are less clear, motivation individualistic, and management more participatory than imposed. In this way adaptability is engendered and staff are better able to deal with changing situations on both personal and professional levels: thus, an organization's most precious resource – people – assumes greater intrinsic value than money.

But is all this participation, growth, development and what some might call navel contemplation what is required of staff development in the 1990s? Certainly the vocabulary still being used by some staff developers is reminis-cent of the 1960s rather than the 1980s, much less the nineties! The sound of words like efficiency, cost effectiveness, stringency, marketing, monitoring, appraising, and evaluating are harsh to the ears of many an old fashioned educationalist! They are, however, the set texts of the new order. They have often been used in connection with the best known neologism in the staff developers' handbook – GRIST. 'Is it gristable?' became a common response when staff wished to go on a course or to a conference prior to the changes in INSET finding that took place at the end of the 1980s. How and why has this close coupling of GRIST with staff development happened in such a short space of time?

Grant related in-service training was spelt out in DES Circular 6/86, which set out the details of this new government scheme to improve the quality of teaching and further the professional development of teachers. The scheme was intended to 'help local authorities to organise in-service training more systematically so as to meet both national and local training needs and priorities' (DES, 1986). It came into effect on 1 April 1987.

The circular set out the government's proposals for granting financial aid to local authorities for certain kinds of training. Expenditure eligible for this money had to fall into one of two areas; national or local. National priority areas were to be specified each financial year by the DES and local priority areas to be proposed annually by local authorities. National priorities attracted a 70 per cent grant while local priorities only attracted a 50 per cent rate.

The national priority areas for 1986–87 were laid down in the circular. In addition the type of training acceptable under the scheme was outlined and comment was made on the fact that payment would only be made at the higher rate if the training satisfied that description. Local authorities would henceforth have to provide detailed information on the numbers trained, duration and forms of training, evidence of improvements in the planning and management of training, and the results of the authority's or institution's evaluation of the effects of the training. Authorities were also invited to report on

> the extent to which its objectives have been achieved, the effectiveness of the training received and the relevance of that training to needs identified through staff appraisal and through discussions with schools and other institutions.

These requests from the DES meant that many authorities and colleges had to grapple with the new financial arrangements for in-service training, and to monitor more precisely than ever before what they were spending their money on, to obtain the grants on offer. To some extent monitoring was the easier part of the process, given good data collection and computer programmes. But what the DES asked for was a great deal more; they were nudging the authorities into divulging the objectives of in-service training; local priorities were left to the discretion of LEAs, while the DES laid down national priorities. Linked to this was the requirement to evaluate, a more difficult exercise. How could effectiveness of training be measured? How could the training needs of staff be identified through staff appraisal and discussion, when very little of either was going on in FE? Who should or even could judge the relevance of the training? Local authorities were being forced to plan in-service training more carefully than ever before, relating it to their perceived local needs and to a set of national needs outlined by the DES.

Staff development appeared to be a solution to some of the difficulties LEAs were encountering. The coupling was made. Staff development and GRIST became inextricably linked together. Staff development increasingly became 'that which is gristable'. But is it that easy? Can staff development deliver the goods? Can staff development produce efficient, effective, well motivated teachers, with the skills needed to market and deliver the new model further education?

A great deal depends upon how it is done. This in turn depends upon those who are responsible for staff development in the colleges and crucially on the management. Many writers (Glatter, 1972; Greenfield, 1973; Taylor, 1976; Culbertson 1980) see educational organizations as different from those which have to produce profits and goods and question whether the managerial techniques appropriate to business, industry and commerce should be applied to education. Others (Haag, 1982; Walker, 1984) suggest that educational organizations are, or are becoming, more like such organizations, with their formal structures and styles of management. The new Education Reform act would seem to be forcefully tipping the balance towards making schools and colleges more orientated toward becoming businesses and income-generating organizations than has ever been the case before. In this climate it is not only skilful financial management that is required but also the ability to produce a quality product, given the number of schools and colleges currently in the market for customers. This relationship between quality and cost is problematic for educational management.

If staff development is narrowly interpreted as staff training or moulding, the aim being to fit individuals to what is required from the education system at a particular time within a particular type of educational organization, then an autocratic style might be appropriate. However, if the needs and views of staff are deemed to be of crucial importance and the concept is defined as a developmental, on-going process aimed at personal and professional growth, then of necessity management style needs to be more democratic. Importantly also, it could be argued that in terms of implementation the cost and the quality of the final product would differ considerably.

Bush (1986) has classified most of the current theories and approaches to educational management into five models. Each model contains features which might apply more or less to different types of institutions – school, college or university. He takes four main elements – goals, structures, environment and leadership – and illustrates the emphasis each model places on these common elements. The five models he uses are formal, democratic, political, subjective and ambiguity.

He goes on to refer to five factors which influence managerial approach. These are:

1 size of the institution
2 nature of the organizational structure
3 time available to manage and participate

4 availability of resources
5 nature and rate of change in the environment.

Taking the above five factors in order he suggests that, large complex institutions like colleges, where sub-units (like departments) compete for resources and to advance their objectives, become prone to adopting political or possibly ambiguity perspectives. Political and democratic approaches are appropriate where the heads of these units seek to involve their professional colleagues in decision making through the introduction of committees and working parties as part of establishing participation in the organizational structure. The existence of 'free' time is also a prerequisite for establishing greater participation. This is important for both democratic and political approaches, where staff attendance at meetings and such like is necessary if participation in decision making is to be achieved. The managerial approach may also be determined by the extent to which resources are plentiful or scant. When resources are easily available distribution tends to be less contentious than when they are scarce and the possibility of cutbacks and closures looms. Under the latter circumstances groups seek to defend their interests and the formal or democratic perspectives more appropriate to a rich environment become inappropriate. In these situations where conflict is inevitable a political perspective becomes expedient. Stability in the environment creates a situation where planning and prediction can take place; in this type of environment, a formal or democratic approach is possible. Alternatively, instability, creating uncertainty and unpredictability, might necessitate an ambiguous approach.

Another issue which relates to the style of management adopted is that of the skill and ability of the leadership. Human resource management requires certain skills. In a situation where employees are not employed by those who directly manage them and where all are professionals, management requires exceptional skills. Some (Watts 1976; Hughes 1984) have suggested that in such situations skills which encourage staff participation are required, whereby management and staff, because of their mutual professionality, work together towards shared goals each acknowledging the expertise of the other. This approach is, however, not compatible with the rather feudal organizational structure which characterizes many colleges of further education where authority rests firmly with the position in the hierarchy. This type of participation also demands management and staff time, to develop the bonds of trust necessary for it to work and to agree goals and decisions. Time is at present a resource which, like others, is in short supply; decisions often have to be made quickly or not at all. Other resources are also in short supply. March (1974) suggests that specific analytical skills are required of managers who manage professionals in colleges and universities. These can be learnt. What is more problematic, however, is the fact that it takes considerable intellectual ability to apply these skills effectively . . .

The variation in management approach which is influenced by internal and external factors, and the range of abilities and skills managers may or may not possess creates difficulties connected with how staff development is defined and implemented in an organization. Using Bush's models of educational management it might be helpful to speculate how staff development might appear in a college. Five important dimensions can be used to illustrate this. These are objectives, the system, type of participation, records, process, rewards and the purpose.

A formal approach might be identified by a formal, written policy statement indicating aims and objectives based on organizational needs. The system would be college-wide and compulsory. Confidential, written records kept by senior management would be a feature and the process would be top down. Rewards might be consistently linked to performance and merit and the purpose would be to keep staff in their place in the hierarchy.

A democratic approach would also be identified by a policy statement but this would have been agreed between staff and management and would be based on individual and organizational needs. Departments or sections might decide on their system after consultation with and participation of staff, and sharing ideas with other departments. Staff could opt to be involved or not. A contract drawn up and negotiated between the participants with agreed confidentiality would form the basis of the record keeping. The process would be lateral and linked to performance on negotiated and agreed criteria. The purpose in this case might be to involve staff and keep everybody happy.

The statement of policy and aims and objectives associated with a political approach would be negotiated and bargained between power groups, possibly departments. The needs of the most powerful group would be given the highest priority; within the department or section the system would also be determined by those with most power. There would be no sharing of information between the departments. Staff might decide to opt in or out depending on their position in the organization. Secret records would be kept. The process would be two-way and rewards bargained for in terms of the provision of scarce resources. The purpose might be control of powerful groups and individuals in the organization.

The subjective approach has a more individualistic bias. Its objectives are based on individuals' views and experience of staff development, and their perception of their own needs. The system in this case is not consistently applied since those who are able to articulate their views clearly are more likely to have them accepted and their needs taken account of. Within this type of model staff involve themselves when they think they need to and frequent feedback and cross-fertilization of ideas is important. The process is non-directional and the rewards are based on individuals' perceptions of what is valuable. The purpose might be personal growth and development.

The ambiguity model implies that the objectives of staff development are not clear and are related to the external environment. Needs change in relation to pressures. There might be no college-wide system, but one related to the different perceptions of each section of the college. Participation would be by invitation and since differing views on records would prevail there would be different types. Within this multi-directional process rewards would not be linked to overall objectives but would be determined at sub-unit level. The main purpose of the activity would be the survival of the organization and its members.

Such speculation is interesting to the extent that it enables a clearer picture to emerge. Doubtless elements of each model are presently operational in most colleges. The reality for staff suggests that if experience can be used as a measure, the opportunities are there to go on courses, conferences and events; some managers are learning and implementing new found skills; and colleges and authorities have now planned and are monitoring and evaluating their staff development programmes and policies aided and abetted by LEATGS. This is fortuitous since the changes which have already happened and those which are to take place in FE in the ensuing period are gathering force. They will erupt and without doubt cause varying degrees of chaos, disruption, despair, anger and frustration for staff. Amid this rather bleak scenario what is important is that staff are able to come through such a period better trained, more confident and able to provide a better service in qualitative terms for those who need and want to learn.

Staff development can, given adequate funding and resources, help to do this. However, it will fail abysmally if we who are involved in educational enterprise forget that we are essentially dealing with a very precious resource: people. Occasionally, amid the chaos and bustle we need to focus on this. FRAGILE – HANDLE WITH CARE labels are cheap to buy in any post office. The message, however, is priceless – think about it.

References

Association of Colleges of Further and Higher Education/Association of Principals of Technical Institutions (1973). *Staff Development in Further Education: Report of Joint Working Party 1973.*

Baron, B. (1978). *The Managerial Approach to Tertiary Education.* Studies in Education Series, 7, London, University of London Institute of Education.

Billing, D. (1982). *The Role of Staff Development.* Standing Conference on Educational Development Services in Polytechnics, SCEDSIP *Occasional Paper, 6,* Birmingham.

Bradley, J., Chesson, R. and Silverleaf, J. (1983). *Inside Staff Development.* Windsor, Nelson/NFER.

Bush, T. (1986). *Theories of Educational Management.* London, Harper and Row.

Culbertson, J. (1980). 'Educational administration – where we are and where we are going', presented at 4th International Intervisitation Program in Educational Administration, Vancouver.

Department of Education and Science (1986). *Local Education Authority Training Grant Scheme: Financial Year 1987–88, Circular 6/86.* London, HMSO.

Advisory Committee on the Supply and Training of Teachers (1975). *The Training of Teachers for Further Education* (Haycock Report). London, HMSO.

Advisory Committee on the Supply and Training of Teachers (1978). *The Training of Adult Education and Part-time Teachers.* London, HMSO.

Advisory Committee on the Supply and Training of Teachers (1978). *Training Teachers for Educational Management in Further and Adult Education.* London, HMSO.

Glatter, R. (1972). *Management Development for the Education Profession.* London, Harrap University of London Institute of Education.

Gray, H. L. (1985). *Change and Management in Schools.* Deanhouse, Chester.

Greenfield, B. (1973). 'Organisations as social inventions: rethinking assumptions about change', *Journal of Applied Behavioural Science*, 9, 5, 551–74.

Haag, D. (1982). *The Right to Education: What Kind of Management?* Paris, Unesco.

Hughes, M. (1984). 'Reconciling professional and administrative concerns', in T. Bush, R. Glatter, J. Goodey, and C. Riches (eds.), *Approaches to School Management.* London, Harper Educational Series.

Joseph, Sir Keith (1985). Speech by Education Secretary Sir Keith Joseph to the North of England Education Conference, Chester.

Luthans, F. (1981). *Organizational Behaviour.* New York, McGraw-Hill.

Main, A. (1985). *Educational Staff Development.* Croom-Helm, Kent.

March, J. G. (1974). 'Analytical skills and the university training of educational administrators', *The Journal of Educational Administration*, XII, 1, 17–44.

Sayers, S. and Harding, A. (1974). 'Time to look beyond technology to better use of human resources'. *Times Higher Educational Supplement*, 20 December.

Taylor, W. (1976). 'The head as a manager: some criticisms', in R. S. Peters (ed.), *The Role of the Head.* London, RKP.

Tulley, G. (1981). 'Staff development in further education: retrospect and prospect', from Association of Colleges in Further and Higher Education AGM 26/27 February.

Walker, W. G. (1984). 'Administrative narcissism and the tyranny of isolation: its decline and fall 1954–1984', *Educational Administration Quarterly*, 20, 4.

Warren-Piper, D. and Glatter, R. (1977). *The Changing University: A Report on Staff Development in Universities.* Windsor, NFER.

Watts, J. (1976). 'Sharing it out: the role of the head in participating government', in R. S. Peters (ed.), *The Role of the Head.* London, RKP.

Wheeler, G. E. (1969). 'The administration of the larger educational unit', in B. Baron and W. Taylor (eds.), *Educational administration and the social sciences.* London, Athlone Press University of London.

Williams, G. L. (1981). *Staff Development in Education*, Guidelines in Educational Management Series, 3, Sheffield City Polytechnic PAVIC Publications.

Part III

Professional development in the 1990s

Monitoring and evaluating school-centred staff development

Norman Thomas

This chapter sets staff development in the context of children's learning and school practices and raises questions about how teachers and schools are responding to the changing requirements upon them. It argues that the development of individual teachers has to be considered in relation to the changing role of the staff as a team and also allow for the career changes a teacher may seek. Effective development depends on analysing what a school is doing and deciding what changes are necessary to meet internal and external demands. All staff, governors and the LEA have parts to play in forming the plan of action. The evaluation of what is done should take account of teachers' opinions, changes in school practices and in the behaviour and learning of the pupils.

There are a number of traps to be avoided when considering the evaluation of staff development. One is to assume that the process must and should be conducted by a selected individual or team sitting in detached judgement on others. A second is to conceive of the process as one of comparing the functioning of a real, operating teacher with what might be done by the ideal teacher. The first trap leads to a failure to appreciate the vital role of the teacher in the evaluation process. The second discourages a sufficiently specific examination of the job the teacher is trying to do *and also* of the ways the job should change whoever is doing it. A third trap, releated to the second, is to suppose that the evaluation of one teacher's development can be conducted in total isolation from that of others. In practice, one teacher's work may have to be shaped by and shape what others in the staff team do.

The job to be done, and the ways in which it should change irrespective of who is doing it, has to be thought of in terms of the institution concerned and in relation to the education system as a whole. In parallel, the development of an individual teacher should be thought of in relation to the – changing – job the teacher is currently employed to do, and also in terms of the teacher's whole career, of which the present post is only one part.

Applying these thoughts to a teacher in a school; the monitoring and evaluation of a teacher's development should take into account what that teacher is doing and could be doing; what the curriculum, organization and resources of the school are and how they will/should change to respond to shifting internal and external requirements; and what the teacher's longer-term career development might be and how that fits with the needs of the education system beyond the school. In all of this, consideration needs to be given to whether the teacher can manage the desired changes unaided, or whether further training is needed and if so, what.

It is a pity that the issue is not simple; but it is not. It is a pity that there are no precise or universal answers; but there are not. We are dealing with evolution-ary processes: on the one hand with changing educational demands and on the other with the adaptability of the individuals who have to carry out the work to be done. Neither aspect has absolute precedence. Teachers cannot, even in the medium term, ignore the pressures for change for they are, after all, part of the changing scene; but nor can they make impossible leaps.

School determination of in-service training

Given the inherent uncertainties, recent changes in the arrangements for in-service training make it more likely that a reasonable accommodation can be achieved between what children and society require (even they are not always in accord) and what teachers are able to provide. The changed arrangements have – where local education authorities have taken advantage of them – made it possible for teachers to be much more directly involved in deciding what in-service training they require. The details of the arrangements are discussed elsewhere in this book. They were brought mainly into force under the Department of Education and Science's Circular 6/86 which set out the conditions for the payment of specific grants for in-service training in 1987/88. This system has since become the LEA training grant scheme (LEATGS).

Like the more restricted scheme that operated before 1987 the arrange-ments allow and encourage local education authorities to allocate some funds for in-service training to schools and colleges so that they can propose what training should be undertaken and by whom. Teachers are encouraged to think of in-service training as something much wider than traditional courses alone.

The writer had the advantage in 1987/88 of visiting more than 80 schools and colleges which were undertaking self-determined in-service training, of dis-cussing the process with headteachers and other teachers, of observing some of the in-service training in operation, and of reading teachers' accounts of what they had done. This chapter draws on that experience.

School development plans

A school-determined in-service training programme should be part of a broader plan for development. The first questions to be faced when schools formulate development plans are: what is this institution doing at present? How does that match what its pupils' and society now require? And what changes of demand are in prospect? The questions have to be answered, in the first instance at any rate, in terms decided by those undertaking the monitoring.

There is plainly a question to be asked about validating one's ideas and that will be raised later. First it is necessary to examine other implications.

Who should be involved in the monitoring? There are still many schools where the headteacher takes the main and even the sole responsibility. There are others where the headteacher is surprised to find that the teachers wholly agree with whatever he or she had already, privately, concluded. There is nothing to say that these headteachers are necessarily wrong or self-deluding in their conclusions. There seems to be little doubt, though, that the strongest innovative action takes place when the teachers feel that they are full participants in monitoring present action, in deciding what changes are needed and how they can best be brought about. The development plan may well have implications for members of staff other than teachers, particularly nursery nurses and classroom assistants, but also possibly for the school secretary, caretaker and cleaning staff. In so far as they will be affected they should be party to the discussions.

There are a number of complementary issues. Individuals in a school differ in their attitudes and perceptions. These differences are heightened when the teachers carry, as they inevitably do, specific responsibilities for sub-groups of children or aspects of the curriculum or both. Differences of attitude, perception and perspective make it more than likely that different views will be expressed about what the current state of play is and what should be done to enhance development.

There are three main ways of resolving these differences. The first is to allow each viewpoint to stand and to share the resources out so that each contributor can, to some extent, satisfy his or her needs. The second is to establish priorities, taking up some identified needs and not others, perhaps with the promise that those set aside now will be given priority next time round. The third is to create a focus of attention which will accommodate the different viewpoints: for example, to accept that the focus of activity will be to improve children's ability to read and to increase their interest in books; to tackle this consciously through the work done in mathematics, topic work, crafts and so on; and to form closer links with parents in the teaching of reading. A fourth approach is to combine the second and third and even to allow for meeting some exceptional individual need.

A number of factors have to be weighed before a decision can be reached on the best course of action. They concern the urgency of need, the importance of developing a community of spirit in the institution and the resources available. The last relates to the funds and the assistance available, and also to the energy of the teachers. There is little doubt that some teachers, full of enthusiasm for using their new opportunities, took on more than they could reasonably manage in 1987/88. In some cases, trying to follow every proposal led to fragmentation and too little support for anything to be completed satisfactorily. There do seem to be strong grounds for choosing a focus of activity or a set of priorities. It is doubtful whether it is wise to promise to give priority next time to ideas not taken up in the present round: times can change in unforeseen ways.

The development plan covers more than in-service training

The formulation of school development plans of the kind described is a means of dealing with change. The plans are concerned with answering the questions: where are we now? Where should we be going? What must we do to get there? The operation of a plan does not inevitably require funded in-service training, though it often may. It can inform staffing policy, so that the characteristics of a replacement teacher, for example, can be better defined; and it should influence budgeting and purchasing resources. Much of the day-to-day work of the curriculum co-ordinator in a primary school or a head of department in a secondary school ought to be guided by the development plan, as should many staff meetings. The line between this kind of activity and specifically funded in-service training ought to be difficult to draw except by identifying the source of funds. In some schools the opportunity to employ supply teachers has been used to free curricular co-ordinators to prepare materials or papers for use at staff meetings or in the course of teaching.

In the first year of GRIST there was a great increase in the number of visits teachers made to see others at work, either in their own schools or elsewhere. Sometimes the visiting teacher, by prior arrangement, joined in the teaching while observing. The most productive visits were well planned. The visitor and the visited were both clear about the specific purpose of the visit. There was sometimes an exchange of written material beforehand. The people in the place visited knew that time for discussion would be expected and had agreed the part that they would play. Room was left for picking up the unexpected. Almost always the successful visits stimulated the visitor to re-examine his or her own practices rather than, simply, adopt some 'new' technique, though that also happened with profit.

People were brought in from outside to lead workshops or staff in-service days, or as advisory teachers working in classrooms. Sometimes these proved disappointing for the same reasons that traditional courses have proved disappointing. Either the visitor did not deal with the issues that the staff had hoped for, or the issues were dealt with at much the same level as previously.

Quality and effectiveness depend on preparation

The lessons are the same both for visiting and for the arrangement of courses, whether planned for one or for a group of schools. The first requirement is to decide clearly what one wants – something that should be done in the course of settling the school development plan; the second is to choose appropriate people to visit or to invite in; the third is to make it clear to those called upon precisely what is expected of them – and that may call for preparatory visits to or by external contributors. The implications are that more time may need to be spent on preparation than is often allowed; and that the energy and money spent on preparation may actually reduce the number of in-service events that can be set up. Quality is more important than quantity. Fortunately the concentration on quality should have the effect of reducing the weight of in-service training on enthusiastic teachers. The lesson is a difficult one for keen and conscientious people to apply, especially because they are the most aware of how much more is possible in teaching children. Progress can be spectacular but more often has to be steady. Better steady than confused or absent.

The roles of governors and advisory teams

The presumption here is that the staff, under the leadership of the headteacher, make judgements on what the school is providing, on what changes are required to make the work more effective in the light of the children's educational needs, as shaped by the nature of the children and the circumstances in which they live and the school operates. There can be no doubt, under the Education Reform Act and its recent predecessors, that the governors must also be involved in the discussions and in the final decisions about what should be undertaken. Indeed, the involvement of governors is one part of the process of validating the exercise.

Another part of that process ought to be discussion with the local education authority and its advisory team. The discussions may involve inspectors, advisers and advisory teachers. They should rarely have to be about the absolute worth of the proposals. The more likely foci are whether the purposes are clearly enough defined; whether there is a reasonable prospect of the purposes being realized, given the amount of money, time and resources available; whether the chosen methodology is the most suitable in all the circumstances; and where help might be obtained. The discussions among staff members, with governors, and with the advisory team may each lead to some modification of proposals as originally defined. One has to be alert to the possibility that original purposes are being modified. If they are, they should be reshaped by design, not by accident.

Clustering small schools

The opportunities available to teachers in small primary schools – or to a lesser extent to members of small departments or faculties in secondary schools – may be very constrained if funds for in-service training are allocated on a simple per capita basis. It can be advantageous for teachers from a group of schools to operate together in deciding on and arranging the in-service training they require. The prerequisite is that they should have common needs, or at least nearly enough so as to be able to create a common in-service training programme. The setting up of the programme can be more complex when a number of schools is involved. The disadvantage is often substantially out-weighed by the benefits that come from being able to set up a more substantial programme, perhaps invite visiting speakers or workshop leaders, and from the reduction in the sense of isolation that can be felt in small institutions.

Some implications for LEA monitoring

There are surely few local education authorities which do not require some central record of at least the headings of the desired direction of development. LEAs require them to inform their own actions, including the actions of their advisory teams. How far, for example, should schools with similar intentions be brought together so as to minimize the effort and cost of running their programmes?

Any apparent imbalance in the sum of institutional proposals ought to be considered in order to decide whether a counterweight should be applied through central initiatives. For example, in these days of emphasis on mathematics and science, is enough being done about children's aesthetic development? Or, is the LEA aware of a forthcoming circumstance that should be prepared for though it has not yet impinged on individual schools, such as the need for substantial understanding between primary and secondary schools about the meanings of levels 4 to 6 in the core subjects (at least) of the national curriculum? Or, does the LEA know of developmental requirements that are significant authority-wide but that are minority interests within any individual school, and so rarely find a place in a school's development programme? Examples might be the education of 4-year-olds in reception classes, or the educational requirements of children from travellers' families, or the special needs of children with partial hearing. Or is the LEA, with its broader view, aware of needs that are not apparent within a single school, such as multi-cultured education in near mono-cultural schools, whether pre-dominantly white or pre-dominantly black, predominantly working class or predominantly middle class, predominantly urban or predominantly rural?

Additionally, LEAs should be more concerned than individual schools can be about the needs of the system as a whole and of the requirements of teachers as related to their longer term career developments (an issue discussed towards the end of this chapter). Under present conditions it is probably mainly the LEA's responsibility to provide training to increase the effectiveness of curricular leaders and heads of departments within their present schools.

Monitoring and evaluation depend on clear prior definitions

The arrangements for monitoring and evaluating staff development can hardly be satisfactory if the means of deciding what to do and how to do it are nondescript. Nor can the exercises be as time- and cost-efficient as they should be if monitoring and evaluation are wholly *post hoc*. Frank discussion among staff and with governors and members of the advisory service does and should contribute to the monitoring and evaluating process. The results of the discussions should be recorded in writing so that there is a permanent record and, equally important, so that participants can be sure that contributions have not been misunderstood.

Concurrent monitoring and evaluation

Monitoring and evaluation intended to enhance staff development also occur while in-service training is under way. It is almost impossible to imagine any teacher taking part in such training without asking questions about whether what is being done suits his or her own need and the needs of the pupils, and whether there is a reasonable prospect of putting what is being learnt into practice in the classroom. These questions will surely be answered in the negative if the experience is boring, unstimulating or distasteful. The answers are likely to be negative if the circumstances in which the experience takes place are uncomfortable or hostile.

It seems reasonable that the first questions to be asked in evaluating in-service training should be addressed to the teachers who took part and be directed at discovering whether they thought the experience was interesting, well arranged and likely to be influential in their work. Of course, a disturbing and uncomfortable experience can sometimes be a source of considerable learning and that needs to be kept in mind when interpreting what teachers say. But positive learning from a negative experience is likely to be the exception rather than the rule.

The kinds of questions suggested here are often on sheets handed out to members of a course, and they surely are worthwhile if the answers are used to shape future arrangements. The results ought to be conveyed to those responsible for leading the course and to all contributors. In at least one school the results were fed on a week by week basis to a lecturer who was responsible for a number of sessions and who was able to modify his approach to suit the preferences of the teachers concerned.

The teachers' responses may hold lessons about the briefing of speakers and group leaders as well as about their performances; or about the choice of topic and methodology; or choice of rendezvous. They are largely a waste of time if they are used simply to produce popularity charts. They may contribute to the learning generated by the course if the opportunity is taken to stimulate teachers to be more precise in expressing what they want from a training activity.

Teachers also report back to their colleagues. Good schools have always found opportunities for teachers with recent in-service training to inform colleagues about what they have learnt, whether the training was in the form of a course, a visit to another school or a centre or whatever. Often this has been done through oral reporting back at a staff meeting or by arranging one or a series of workshops. Increasingly oral reports are based on written accounts, previously composed, and kept in the school as a permanent record of what has been done. The act of composing a written report, especially where two or more members of staff have shared the experience, enables them to tease out its implications more thoroughly. The questions that need to be faced are not, simply, whether the activity was engaging, what it consisted of and how its messages can be translated into action. They should also be concerned with the extent to which the activity addressed issues relevant to the school development plan and, if it did not, whether a modification to the plan is desirable.

Longer-term reflection

Reporting to the organizers at the end of an activity, or to the rest of the staff on return to school are both short-term responses. By their nature they do not allow time for trying ideas out with children. What seemed a marvellously good idea in that splendid country house where the course was held may prove difficult to put into operation in a cramped classroom with 35 children. That may not mean that the idea was bad, rather that it and the circumstances in which it is to be applied need more adaptation than was at first apparent. What initially looked difficult and inappropriate, on the other hand, may turn out to have aspects that can, after all, be useful.

There has to be instant response to keep the momentum of the initial experience going; but there is also a need for longer-term reflection and that should be built into monitoring and evaluation arrangements. The teacher with responsibility for staff development should mark the calendar a few months ahead to show when the matter will be revived. The arrangements ought not to be burdensome and if there is nothing further to say, time should not be wasted in trying to invent something.

Attitudes and judgements that are unspoken can sometimes be detected in what people do. Perhaps the surest sign that teachers have found in-service activities worthwhile is that they are willing to discuss and join in future arrangements.

The effects of staff development on the school

The purpose of in-service training is not only to satisfy the teachers. Ultimately it will have proved a failure unless it affects the depth and range of children's learning positively. One way in which it might do that is by stimulating change in the arrangements which the school makes.

The kinds of possible changes are many. Perhaps the ways in which the children are grouped for learning will be modified. Maybe the deployment and responsibilities of members of staff will be changed. Techniques for deciding the curriculum can be altered. Schemes of work can be rewritten. Books and equipment can be rearranged to serve their purposes in new ways. School budgets might be differently distributed, and changes made in purchasing policies. New kinds of relationships might be forged with parents, the local community, or industry and commerce.

Whatever is done should to a large extent have been intended in the development plan and should be recorded as having happened. Accounts of these changes – both as anticipated and as realized – might form a significant part of the annual report to governors and to parents, and one would expect them to be of considerable interest to the LEA in its new role under the 1988 Education Act.

Changes in teaching

The changes in teaching can affect the methodologies used, the content of what is taught, the ways in which work is planned and children's progress assessed and recorded. Sometimes the changes are easy to spot. For example, when a teacher of 11-year-olds watched infant-aged children using the computer and disc drive unaided, she decided that her 12-year-olds needed far less help than she had been giving them. They were then encouraged to turn the machines on and off and to feed the disc drives without waiting for close supervision. The educational implications of giving the children more responsibility were significant on a wider front, but this example was easy for the teacher to identify and record. In another case, the purposes of, and techniques used in displaying children's work were changed – a revision that can readily be recorded by the use of the ubiquitous compact camera showing not only the display but also, in the changed circumstances, the children using the display to tell others what they had discovered.

Sometimes the changes are more pervasive and it is hard to remember just what earlier practices were. The technique of clicking a counter to signal when positive reinforcement has been given to a child allows a record of numbers to be kept showing changes. Other changes are best recorded as written accounts or as video-recordings of sample teaching before and (sufficiently) after the in-service training so that comparisons can be made with confidence. When the staffing arrangements allow, it can be helpful to get a 'critical friend' of the teacher's choice to make the accounts. The arrangement may require the employment of a supply teacher to release the recorder from other duties, and this must be a justifiable use of in-service training funds, at least in principle.

What children do and what they learn

The ultimate justification for in-service training rests on the effects that it has on the children. Modifications in what children do and learn at school are intimately but not always simply related to changes of teaching practices, as is clear from examples already used.

Alterations in what children do are generally easier to identify than are changes in how well they learn. The children now given more responsibility in the use of computers may already have been perfectly aware of what to do and capable of carrying out the procedures. The change may simply have been one that allowed them to use existing knowledge. Nevertheless, the development was worth recording because it opened up still more possibilities for independent action in which learning could take place – and not only to do with computers. The teachers counting the number of times they used positive reinforcement need also to be sure that the change in their behaviour is being reflected in changes in the children's behaviour. It would be tedious and far too time consuming to have to make a record of every contrary or depressed act by a child to discover whether the incidence of such events was falling, but it might be worth keeping, over carefully chosen sample periods of time, or of selected children, a record of behaviour that was agreed to be significant, or examining statistics already kept, for example of attendance.

Many schools keep sample collections of children's work and the examination of these can provide considerable evidence of changes not only in individual children but between groups of children over time. The most convenient examples to store are of written work, computer print outs, and painting and drawings; but selected examples can also be kept of three-dimensional work including pottery, models and machines made by children. Some schools are using video-recordings of work in action, and tape-recordings of children. Care has to be taken to compare like with like. There needs to be a thought out system of sampling. It can be misleading if only the work of the most able children is kept. The process of selection can contribute directly to the education of children of all abilities if they are involved in making the choices. For example, if the in-service training has been concerned with increasing the range of language use, then engaging a child in the selection of material to illustrate that variety will help him or her to be aware of the purposes of current teaching and better placed to respond.

Children might also be asked to make judgements of their own work as regards its quality as well as of its range. That can take one closer to identifying the depth of learning. As with all forms of assessment, it is important to be clear against what criteria the assessment is being made. It may be, and it should be that the attainment targets and levels enunciated in the statutory orders for the national curriculum will provide such criteria, and the assessment procedures will make some comparisons over time possible. The chances are that they will be too coarse-grained to be used in relation to much in-service training, which should probably be more specifically targeted.

Whether or not the national curriculum assessment procedures lend themselves to evaluating staff development and in-service training, at least two problems are inherent in monitoring the changes. One is that the principal purposes of staff development, namely to improve the range and depth of children' learning, often take some time to put into effect. A second is that many factors other than the in-service training impinge on the learning that takes place, and it may be difficult and even impossible to be certain that changes in learning are the result solely or mainly of particular in-service training programmes. It would be wrong to abandon the attempt to judge the effects of in-service training and other forms of staff development because making the necessary comparisons is difficult or imperfect. One must be aware that the process should be undertaken as carefully as possible and the results interpreted with common sense.

Career development

This chapter has concentrated almost wholly on staff development in relation to the work of an institution. Another important facet of staff development mentioned earlier is the career development of teachers.

Career development has three aspects. One is improving effectiveness in the job currently being done, and that is close to being synonymous with institutional development. A second is concerned with increasing a teacher's range of abilities, and that may often be of concern in institutional development but may also require a teacher to move on to another school, perhaps run according to different attitudes or beliefs, or in a different kind of catchment area, or with a different age range or size. The third is to do with taking on additional responsibilities in relation to other members of staff. Although the last can certainly happen without moving school, it often does entail movement.

No headteacher worth his or her salt fails to help members of staff to enhance their professional prospects. The 'loss' of good members of staff is usually more than balanced by the lift to morale and the sense of ambition that the promotion of a member carries in its wake, as well as in its bow-wave. There ought to be the opportunity for headteachers, when making school bids for in-service training, to signal the needs for career development among members of staff.

The responsibilities for funding and providing the opportunities surely belong to the local education authority and need to be arranged if not provided by the advisory service. There has been a significant increase in provision for management training of heads and deputies, and perhaps more still should be done for curricular leaders and heads of departments. The training in future should obviously deal with the local management, including financial manage-ment, of schools, and with relations with governing bodies, parents and the LEA. It needs to provide for improvement in the techniques required, for example running meetings and conducting interviews. There is also a need for more general understanding of group behaviour and, perhaps especially, of the management of the curriculum, including the national curriculum.

As LEAs become more concerned with their responsibilities for maintaining the system and giving it direction, rather than with the detailed administration of individual schools, they should also reconsider their role in the initial training of teachers. The development of a policy and action in this regard becomes more, not less urgent in light of the new independence of many institutes of higher education. The contact between LEAs and training establish-ments has not always been as productive and warm as it should be. The placement and support of students in schools for teaching experience has been too passive on the part of LEAs and often of schools also. It will be increasingly in the interests of the LEAs, individually and collectively, to play a more positive role.

Reflection, preparation, action and evaluation

The monitoring and evaluation of staff development require a careful analysis of current practice, an awareness of external changes that will affect future practice, a knowledge of the present capacities of staff, and of training help that can be obtained from outside. On the basis of all that, decisions have to be taken on what should be done, either by determining priorities or by focusing, or a mixture. Unless the ground clearing is thorough and the purposes of action clear the monitoring and evaluation of the effects of the action will be fogged and blurred. How can success be measured if no achievement was defined?

Preparation, monitoring and evaluation take time, money and effort. It has to be faced that they reduce the quantity of staff development that could otherwise take place. But quantity is only useful in so far as what is done is effective in enhancing the learning of the children. Nor is any staff development programme the last word. The results have to be fed back into the discussion about what to do next.

10

Promoting teachers' professional development: a pilot project for primary schools

Chris Day

In May 1988 the University of Nottingham was contracted by Derbyshire County Council Education Department to carry out an independent evaluation of the devolved LEA training grants scheme (LEATGS) funding pilot project. The project began in September 1987 with seven secondary schools participating. From September 1988 these seven schools were joined by eight primary schools and colleges of further education. The evaluation, which was carried out between September 1988 and July 1989, was concerned with the INSET experiences of teachers in the eight primary schools during the 1988/89 school year. The chapter reports these experiences within a political context of devolved funding which is claimed to empower those who are at the chalk face of teaching. By cutting out the middle men (e.g. higher education, LEA officers, etc.) and thus providing the consumers with the power to choose how to spend their money, it is assumed that there will be better value for money. The chapter begins by tracing, briefly, the recent history of in-service developments, particularly those designed at managerial levels outside the schools to effect school improvements. It then reports on the project itself before raising issues concerning the management, conduct and effectiveness of INSET in terms of promoting practitioner research and development. INSET is defined here as,

> those education and training activities engaged in by primary and secondary school teachers and heads, following their initial professional certification, and intended mainly or exclusively to improve their professional knowledge, skills and attitudes in order that they can educate children more effectively.
>
> (Bolam, 1982)

In-service for school improvement

The project which was evaluated was, in effect, one of a series of administratively imposed innovations at national and local levels over the last 15 years designed to improve the quality of teaching and learning in schools. School improvement has been defined as:

> a systematic, sustained effort aimed at change in learning conditions and other related internal conditions in one or more schools, with the ultimate aim of accomplishing educational goals more effectively.
>
> (Van Velzen *et al.*, 1985)

Policy efforts made at political and administrative levels in the UK, both nationally and locally, to improve the quality of schooling, have been well documented (Day 1986; Bolam 1989; Poster and Day 1989). The concern about the contributions of schools to the social and economic growth of the UK which had been expressed by the Labour government of the 1970s (Day, 1986) has been translated into action by the Conservative government of the 1980s and 1990s, first through a series of consultative papers (DES, 1983, 1985) and then via a legislative reform programme embodied in the 1986 and 1988 Education Acts. These established for the first time a framework of national objectives, standards and priorities (through the national curriculum, teacher appraisal, testing), coupled with new government imposed salaries and conditions of service for teachers, and the creation of:

> a market-oriented culture for schools whereby clients (parents) are empowered (via governors, open enrolment, published assessment scores and the possibility of opting out of LEA control) to choose which schools to support and whereby schools are compelled to compete with each other for their clients and thus, in theory, to raise their teaching and learning standards by using their financial, human and physical resources most cost effectively.
>
> (Bolam, 1989)

In order to achieve its objectives the government adopted a strategy which has been described by Peters and Waterman (1982), in the context of 'excellent company' research, as having 'simultaneous loose–tight priorities'. The government has thus been centralized and decentralized in its policies, pushing autonomy down to the shop floor for some functions, but being, 'fanatical centralists about the core values they hold dear' (Peters and Waterman, 1982). The changed management, conditions and attitudes to in-service, which is seen as a part but not a whole of the condition necessary to achieve school improvement, is one example of this strategy in action.

The LEA training grants scheme, which came into operation in April 1987, had four main purposes:

to promote the professional development of teachers and certain other professional groups;

to promote more systematic and purposeful planning of in-service training;

to encourage more effective management of the teacher force and the other professional groups involved; and

to encourage training to meet selected needs which are accorded national priority.

(DES, 1986)

The scheme requires each LEA to submit a plan each year showing how purposes are to be achieved, and the results to date, according to a report by HMI (1989) have been, 'more systematic approaches to the planning, organisation and delivery of INSET by the large majority of LEAs visited'. The managerial perspective in the purposes and monitoring of outcomes is clear. Equally clear, in a report on the first year of the scheme issued by HMI 1989, was the perceived success of the combined centralized–decentralized strategies in terms of teacher empowerment:

> there was substantial evidence that through developed budgets, linked to an agreed institutional staff development plan, there was emerging a strong sense of ownership of the INSET by teachers and a view that the training was far more relevant because it was directly related to issues associated with them and their school or college. This sense of 'owner-ship' and 'relevance' was strong and was resulting in teachers assuming increased responsibility for their own personal and professional de-velopment which in turn was releasing considerable energy and profes-sionalism in many of the schools visited . . .

(HMI, 1989, 3.24)

The introduction of LEATGS in 1987, then, heralded a change from what may be described as a provider–user system of INSET where, 'the emphasis was undoubtedly on raising the individual's professional competence through an enhanced level of scholarship and critical reflection, rather than improving immediate professional practice' (Brown, 1989). In that system teachers determined their own needs and looked predominantly to higher education and teachers' centres to meet them – with consequent problems of match, relevance and transfer and application of learning to their work settings. Essentially, within nationally and locally imposed priorities, schools were given the opportunity to manage their own learning. For many, this was a profound culture shock. New, under- or undeveloped skills were needed, particularly by those who were charged at school level with the management of this new client-led system. It would not be surprising if within the context of the externally imposed multi-innovations with which managers and teachers were having to cope, a destabilization and (at least temporary) deskilling were to occur. The comments of HMI (1989) that the new system was releasing considerable energy and professionalism in teachers needs, therefore, to be examined carefully in terms of the activities undertaken, the learning processes in which teachers engage and their effect on practice.

The next part of the paper provides a brief summary of the evaluation design, a description of the work of the schools and its effectiveness as perceived by heads and teachers who participated in this pilot project.

The project

The design of the project evaluation

The pilot project was evaluated internally, by the schools themselves individually and collectively, by the headteachers, and externally through the contracting by the LEA of the University of Nottingham. The University's role was to collect data from the accumulated documents and perceptions of the value of the scheme from the participants themselves. This was achieved through confidential in-depth tape recorded interviews with the headteachers and staff of all the schools. In effect, the headteachers were interviewed in December 1988 and again, with one exception, in March 1989. Staff in all but one school were interviewed in March 1989. The underlying rationale for using this form of data collection was that it is in the interview that the act of measurement (of worth, effect, effectiveness) comes to life. Despite its potential problems of bias (on the part of the interviewer) and reactivity (on the part of the interviewee):

> The interview, far from being a kind of snapshot or tape-recording – simple report either of fact or of emotional response – in which the interviewer is a neutral agent who simply trips the shutter or triggers the response, is instead inevitably an interactional situation.
>
> (Kuhn, 1962, p. 194)

It is important in evaluations of this kind, which are restricted by time and money, to establish very quickly trust and confidentiality with respondents who have a number of different perspectives, motivations and prejudices; and it is necessary to value and be seen to value what the respondent brings to the interview as much as the agenda carried by the evaluator/interviewer. The purpose in work of this kind is to encourage each interviewee to share freely and openly his/her own perceptions and in doing so, to try to delay until after the interview any attempt to interpret or judge. Essentially, the interviewer is the learner (of the interviewee's opinions, thoughts and feelings), so that if the interactional situation of the interview is conceived in terms of status or power and authority, it is the interviewer who is the underdog during the interview process. While it will be the interviewer who will initiate the questions, it will be the interviewee who determines the nature and quality of the response. To summarize, 'each form of the interview represents a "tentatively" formulated plan of action the investigator may employ . . . Reality "out there" is present only to the extent that it is so defined' (Denzin, 1973).

In this sense:

> The interview is an understanding between the two parties that, in return for allowing the interviewer to direct their communication, the informant is assured that he will not meet with denial, contradiction, competition, or other harassment.
>
> (Benney and Hughes, 1956)

The type of interview often used with each respondent may be described as 'nonschedule standardised' or 'focused' (Merton and Kendall, 1946) in which certain types of information are desired from all respondents but

> the particular phrasing of questions and their order is redefined to fit the characteristics of each respondent. This form of the interview requires that each interviewer be highly trained in the meaning of the desired information and in the skills of phrasing questions for each person interviewed.
>
> (Denzin, 1973)

In a sense, then, the chapter reports professional as distinct from administrative monitoring processes (Eraut *et al.*, 1987). Whereas the latter seeks to determine numbers, resources, budgets, etc., the former seeks to observe and record inputs, processes and outcomes and to 'understand connections between them' (Bridges, 1989). It would include investigations of qualitative aspects of INSET, for example, through observation and/or teachers' perceptions, by investigating how teachers learn and what are the most effective structures and strategies which may be used to enhance this.

The questions asked concerned:

- the effect of the scheme upon teachers' thinking and practice
- the ways in which the scheme had been implemented by schools (organization and processes)
- the response to financial devolution of INSET funds
- the perceived advantages and disadvantages of the scheme generally
- the perceived benefits to the individual and the institution.

The devolution of INSET funds to institutions in Derbyshire

Since 1987 the majority of LEAs in the UK have devolved between 10 per cent and 70 per cent of local priority funding to schools (DES, 1989) although expenditure has to be tied to school development plans and approved by the LEA. In general LEAs have retained control of funds for long, award-bearing programmes, national priority areas, induction of newly qualified teachers and other local priority areas. Devolved funding includes supply cover costs, and usually (though not always) the amounts are determined either through a basic allocation supplemented by a per capita sum or a per capita sum only. The submission by the Director of Education for Derbyshire to the Department of Education and Science (Derbyshire, 1987), indicated that two pilot projects for the devolution of resources to schools had been established. The secondary school cluster was to be given stewardship of approximately 70 per cent of the resources to which it was entitled, the total being calculated on a per capita basis. The primary cluster was to be given stewardship of approximately 35 per cent of the resources, so that the authority was able to monitor, 'how both sets of schools manage the issue of Breadth and Indepth study within the parameters set by their differing circumstances' (Derbyshire, 1987).

The overriding aim of the staff development programme in Derbyshire was 'to enrich the educational experience of the children/students', and, within this, to

increase the effectiveness of staff collectively and individually by:
– helping staff to sustain and enhance their skills and knowledge
– reflecting and promoting curriculum development
– improving job satisfaction and staff morale
– aiding career planning
– providing a balance between the needs of individuals and groups
– focusing on the learning process
– promoting equal opportunities
– relating to the aims and objectives of the institution.

(Derbyshire, 1988)

A number of strategies were suggested to 'increase colleagues' awareness of the range of approaches or techniques' to staff development, although it was emphasized that these were not comprehensive and that further information from the area staff development co-ordinator or appropriate other was available. The strategies listed were action research, classroom observation, counselling/consultancy interviews, courses, cross-curricular initiatives, education/industry links, induction programmes, interagency collaboration, interschool or cross-phase support groups, job rotation, job sharing, modular accreditation of courses, quality circles, questionnaire surveys, school/college-based/focused/initiated INSET, secondments, self-support study, shadowing, shadowing staff, staff libraries or resource banks, staff meetings, task groups, teacher exchange, team-teaching, time logs/diaries, visits to other schools/colleges, working parties (Derbyshire, 1988). The LEA also issued guidelines to assist schools in the formation of staff development. Staff development programmes for 1988/89 were to reach the LEA by 30 June 1988.

The project in action

On 1 February 1988 a letter was sent by Derbyshire's county adviser for primary education to eight schools, calling a meeting to set up the primary school pilot scheme. The meeting involved two primary phase advisers, two area staff development co-ordinators and the heads of the schools which were to become the pilot group. The schools had been selected for a number of reasons:

1 They were geographically close enough to meet
2 They were from two of the four administrative areas in the County
3 they were at different stages of development
4 They included urban and rural, infant, primary and junior, and were clustered around a particular geographical area.

They all received an allocation of £150 per teacher with a minimum protected baseline of £450.

The allocation of money was described by the LEA as 'a sum of money over which the school has more control, and so opportunities for choice and negotiation are increased' (primary schools LEATGS pilot: *The Formulation of a School/College Staff Development Programme 1988–9*, Derbyshire LEA). Other schools in the LEA had a 'notional planning allocation' for 1988/89 as a preparation for 1989/90 when, like the pilot project schools, they would have real money which would require the keeping of accounts. Excluded from expenditure in the devolved budgets were secondments, part-time study awards, other long courses, inductions of newly qualified teachers, headteacher training, training for designated staff development co-ordinators, GCSE/assessment of achievement training, national curriculum training, and the five professional development days allocated annually. At a meeting held on 16 June 1988 it was determined that the project would start immediately, that 'Any activities already agreed but which would take place after 16 June would have to be counted within the allocation', and that the group would meet monthly from the following September. It is clear from the notes of the early meetings that this was new territory for everyone, and that codes of conduct were being created rather than prescribed. Concerns were expressed at a September meeting that the advisers' role should not be to 'check the content' of programmes, but to 'advise and discuss', and it was agreed that, 'the needs of individual teachers must be considered in relation to a whole school staff development programme'.

Headteachers reported back to staff individually, sharing their hopes and fears. At a meeting in one school following the October meeting of head-teachers of the pilot schools, it was reported that,

> It appears that most of the other schools have already allocated all their allowance. I feel that there is a danger in planning too far ahead and therefore not be able to apply for courses that may be arranged at short notice.

We have the equivalent of 10 days supply cover left. Perhaps the best way forward now would be for members of staff to put in a 'bid' for supply cover and expenses so that teachers can have time away from the classroom as part of our staff development project.

In short, the parameters of the scheme, the real authority of the schools to determine the use of the devolved finance, and their new relationship in this with the LEA, were being negotiated *pro tem*.

Many schools (though not all) had already established priorities for individual, group and whole-school developments for the year, prior to the start of the project, usually as a result of full consultation, so that it would be a mistake to suggest that staff and curriculum development planning was new to them.

A summary of the findings

The summary findings were presented in a report to the LEA (Day, 1989). They appeared to have much in common with those of Her Majesty's Inspectors Report on the first year of the scheme (HMI, 1989). Certainly, schools had welcomed the opportunity to have a budget to spend on their own INSET, related to their own identified needs. Teachers had used a wider range of INSET provision than previously and had become more discriminating. Schools had a strong sense of ownership of the INSET and of its relevance. They had assumed increased responsibility and accountability for their own professional and curriculum developments. Problems of administration and management, tensions between individual institutional needs, match between institutional, LEA and DES priorities, and inadequate financial provision remained; and although there were clearly identifiable changes of perception, knowledge of and attitude to INSET by headteachers and teachers, there was as yet no overwhelming evidence that classroom practice was being affected significantly. The impact of the project to date was upon teachers' thinking only. However, 'there can be no simple causal links between training and changes in teaching and learning as there are so many other factors playing a part in the process' (HMI, 1989, para. 2.16).

The in-depth interviews with teachers and headteachers provided both confirmation and elaboration of the responses made by the headteachers to the LEA (Day, 1989). In addition, the data were classified so that they presented major issues of prime concern to those who manage and participate in schemes such as this. The data were discussed under three themes in the original report:

- the school management response to the innovation
- issues of quality in school-centred professional development
- conditions for promoting professional development: relationships between in-service, school and individual culture, and school improvement.

This paper focuses upon the last two.

Issues of quality in school-centred professional development

Types of in-service activity

Between 70 per cent and 95 per cent of the grant in all schools was spent on providing supply cover for teachers to be released from their classrooms to engage in a variety of in-service activities, and it is worth listing some of the different kinds:

- sharing a day's course with other schools
- visiting other schools to look at aspects of good practice: 'When we got there a teacher was released ... not to teach her class to show us, but actually to talk to us and not be teaching at the same time, which was excellent. She had been involved and she knew where things were ... and we were more at ease because we didn't feel we were worrying her'
- time out with a colleague to put together a syllabus/write up policies
- visiting colleagues in other classrooms in their own schools
- exchanges of materials between schools
- in-school days: 'Time to do things together that you normally wouldn't have time to do e.g. working on the Maths curriculum ... We had actually spent time at home on it.'

It was interesting, though not surprising in the first year of the scheme, to note that less emphasis was placed on attendance at courses held outside school. A variety of reasons were given for this. Some, 'didn't really feel that there were many courses which were particularly useful'. There was a perceived shortage of courses which focused upon the needs of infant teachers, and some courses needed to address a narrower target audience. Responses to courses varied. Some were perceived as being too practical: 'When we go on these courses a lot of it is up to us ... We have to do the work.' In others there was too much theory and not enough practice:

> Some of the courses that are run are not as practically relevant to us as we'd like them to be. There's a lot of theory, whereas what we're mainly concerned about is getting in there and doing it at ground level. Some of the courses tend to be overbalanced by the theory of it and not heavily committed enough to the practical application in school, which for the classroom teacher is the priority.

Other teachers credited courses which they had attended as renewing their thinking:

> The course I went on was most worthwhile. It was over five Mondays ... We had two days looking at the National Curriculum, and coming up with ideas that he gave us, instead of trying to pick our brains to see what we

did ... I've tried a lot of the ideas out with the class ... and that course renewed my thinking ...

and being a great aid to self-development:

> For me it's been a great self development to be able to participate in the Science course. It broadened my horizons ... and opened up vistas for me as an Infant teacher that I would never have thought possible ... You're learning different things by meeting other colleagues, by observing what other people are doing ... Whilst you're learning anything, what ever it is, if it's contributing towards school you're developing your skills as a teacher, you're learning different things.

One teacher did, however, speculate as to the value of continuing to emphasize 'lighthouse' school experiences: 'Eventually one will have visited all the schools in your area appropriate to your needs, so where will you progress from there?'

There are two major issues which arise from these experiences. The first must be directed at course providers external to the school who cannot tailor make courses without the guarantee of a minimum audience, but whose responsibility, nevertheless, is to ensure that course purposes, content, processes and target audiences are stated explicitly:

> I do think people are becoming more choosy ... If you go on a course now, and it's fairly expensive, you don't want to go and have three quarters of the course on 'Junior' (as Infant teachers) ... now, if you're spending a lot of money you want it specific and good ... I can't understand why people aren't selling their courses better. We're the customer, and if they gave better run down of the content, and more of an idea of the target, they'd do better ... because when you look through, you get no idea ... 'Science in the Primary School' ... it's very broad ... I want to go on a science course for nursery and infant children ...

The second is directed at those who manage in-service in school, and this concerns balance and the associated danger of parochialism:

> Whilst we have benefited from being together as a staff ... we do not wish to isolate ourselves from the rest of education, so it's important that we find a greater variety of activities.
>
> The work that we're doing in small school teams is far more valuable than sending people off on courses, at the moment, but, perhaps in twelve months time ... we might find that there's a lot of working together going on without having to pay for it. People are getting together ... but they want to know more about it. We'll want a course ...

The abiding problem, however, will remain one of finance. Attendance at longer courses outside school may well prove costly for smaller schools. 'The money for 1989–90 only represents six days'. Thus the pressure is likely to remain on many schools to encourage staff to engage in on-site activities which are self-generated and self-serviced. Those who are, like one teacher interviewed, 'looking for something more long term . . . more intensive' may find it increasingly difficult to have time out of schools with appropriate financial support. In the long term this possible lack of investment in professional development, as distinct from school curriculum development needs, may prove to have a negative effect on the maintenance and enhancement of motivation and knowledge among teachers in schools.

Benefits to the school

'We made it fit our school'. In general, heads and teachers expressed satisfaction with all aspects of the scheme. Minor criticisms only were expressed in relation to its late start and initial administrative difficulties in coming to terms with a new system. Initially:

> it wasn't very clearly explained to staff development co-ordinators what you could do with the money, and in particular the courses that we would have liked to attend just weren't appearing, and therefore we had the opportunity to spend the money as we wished, and as a result we were able to have quite a number of day release events involving one or two staff at a time to deal with curriculum matters . . . As a result, the book keeping was simple, travelling expenses were minimal, and the bulk of the expense has been paid on supply teachers.

The most widely appreciated benefits of the scheme were the opportunities to work outside the classroom on matters related to it during the school day:

> Overall it's been quite successful. It's given us breathing space for examining our responsibility posts. Before everything you have to try and do and cram in at the same time as everything else . . . This has given us the opportunity to stand back, reflect, think things out – some things you cannot do while you're still teaching a class of children and cannot be done out of hours if its something that involves seeing what's happening in each class at a time . . .

and the fact that 'The real bonus was that we got real money', which enabled ownership of decisions: 'I like the idea of buying in cover, buying in the time to work and use the people you've got. They're the only resources you've got'.

Almost all teachers spoke of the value of being able to engage in school-centred work. They related numerous examples of their achievements during the school day working either alone or with a colleague, sometimes off-site and sometimes on-site but outside their classrooms:

> I think that's very good that you can actually work in school without the children . . . for instance, when we organised our own books, because

there's never time. However long you stay after school, an hour isn't long enough. You need a full morning session . . .

This theme of time to stand back, plan and reflect, was a thread which ran through every interview. Teachers appreciated being able – some for the first time in their teaching careers – to work alone or with colleagues on tasks which they had chosen and which they considered to be of direct practical relevance to their school and classroom:

> I've appreciated the fact that we've been able to have time with our colleagues. Usually we're rushing about to do something, or we've got a meeting in ten minutes . . . Everything we've done applies to here, rather than thinking, 'Oh well, we'll go to that meeting. It's about such a thing.' And when you go there you're sometimes disappointed . . . and to be able to come to school and have time here when we hadn't to think about a class . . . to have time when we could go into a room on our own with books etc was really super. We all had a specific target . . . Then we shall pool our work.

Many teachers spoke of the value of being able to work unimpeded by the normal stresses and strains of classroom life:

> I was allowed to go home for the day. Therefore, I could put everything out and there were no interruptions . . . and I really got a lot done . . . If I was having to do it at nights in my own time, then I wouldn't have got it (the syllabus) done. If I'm given time to do a specific job, then I can concentrate on it . . .

> I welcome it with open arms . . . The main problem most teachers face in school is the ability to do things in school itself. You're a classroom teacher, you're so concerned with the practicalities of running your room, monitoring your work, etc., that, really, there's little time left for doing anything else, to do it efficiently, anyway. You can 'surface' touch other things, but to do anything in depth, in intensity you need to be freed from your class, away from it, and in my case (I've just taken over computers), and physically I could not do at home the things that I needed to do . . .

The time bought for teachers not only allowed them to reflect 'on' as well as 'in' action, but also to work together in depth. Headteachers were able to release people from their isolation in school time, to complement the time spent working at home:

> If I buy in a supply teacher, and I take another class, and I can get two people working together then, and it's much more productive than getting people to work in isolation or to have to do all the work at home . . . People do spend quite a lot of time at home, but I've backed that up

with support in school, and I think now the staff are beginning to feel happier about this ... directed time hours can't be used for staff development ...

This issue of isolation related particularly to small schools where:

If you take out one teacher from the classroom you take out 50% of the staff ... they're doing everything. They've got the same paperwork that everyone has, and they've got to research it and evaluate it and it's the same two people doing it all ...

Nevertheless, the opportunities afforded by the scheme provided 'a comfortable cushion' from previously experienced isolation, for teachers who were 'just grateful to get away from the constant book work and doing it in classtime':

It's provided a comfortable cushion that we've never had before. We've always felt we were isolated and were we doing it right ... Now I worry less, because I've heard [others] who I always think are impregnable, admitting that they didn't know how to fill in this form or that form ... We've had more free time to talk to each other more and exchange each other's ideas. We've gone away and found other things.

Headteachers commented particularly upon the positive response of most staff:

It's given me a lot of pleasure in seeing my staff work as hard as they have done, but being able to do it without the encumbrance of a class, pressures of progress, next day work etc.
We as a school got to grips with what we could do and we really felt that we were able to meet our own needs.

They commented upon the high motivation of many:

They've seen for the first time that I can take them out of the classroom, that the classroom's not disrupted, that there's continuity, and at the same time they can look at a piece of work that they've volunteered to do, and the motivation is high, and they've had chance to sit down and thrash it out – and that's never happened before ...

and their purposeful involvement as a whole staff:

For me, it's been the main 'plus' this year. It's been getting the staff together, getting them to talk about school curricula, where they see weaknesses. .. Where we ought to be looking at as a team, not 'You've been told to do this'. We've got a long way to go, but at least people do feel involved now.

Most of all, they, like their teachers, appreciated that the scheme had enabled them to review their curriculum and to act upon the review in a more concentrated period of time than would previously have been possible:

> The opportunity to sit down and discuss subjects in depth, which has really brought us together as a complete thinking unit, where previously we've not really had this opportunity. Staff meetings at school don't give the length of time that we've had on the full or half days, and we never really felt as if we'd gone far enough before we had to call a stop to it . . . It's made us think again about what we're doing and our aims and objectives. Sometimes we can lose sight of those. The use of our own funding has given us the opportunity to spend time on certain elements of the curriculum in a shorter period of time than otherwise we'd be able to. Therefore, we feel we're at the beginning of making improvements to the curriculum which really have been sadly in need of attention for some years. But despite all the staff meetings and all the time spent together there are always other important points to discuss as well – the ordinary, everyday running of the school, planning various events. All these take time. At least we've been able to put aside time to do that, and hopefully, over the next two or three years we would be able to improve the curriculum provision and spend time on those subjects that need the extra time.

Problems associated with the scheme

The problems identified varied between schools and between staff in individual schools. They concerned:

- Finance: 'The money allocated doesn't anywhere near cover what we are expected to achieve according to the new expectations'.
- Directions: 'You're not allowed to choose now, you're told that you've got to go on certain courses.'
- Planning: 'If there is a weakness, it is that everything has to be decided in advance . . . I don't know how I'm going to spend the money next year . . . I can't project much further than Christmas . . .'
- The plight of part-time teachers: 'I have to give extra time, without much choice, in order to keep up to date with what's going on. I couldn't not attend staff meetings, because I'd miss out.'
- Continuity of teaching: 'The main thing is we always seem to have supply teachers in the school. We never seem to have a settled week where all the staff are there . . . Not too many days out because it's taking me away from what the job is about.'

> 'I'd like to go on more courses, but a) it's difficult, it breaks the pattern of your week at school. When you're with a class all the time you miss the day with them . . . If you're in the middle of a project it can be quite disruptive.'

'What stops me applying for more courses is the hassle of getting supply teachers.'

Those in small schools, however, perceived an advantage for children in experiencing different teachers from time to time:

> In a small village school I don't mind the continuity being broken two or three times a term, because these children have me for three years, and x for four years. So to bring someone new in is a breath of fresh air . . . as long as they know what they're doing . . . I like the children to have another person's voice – that's why I use television and radio drama. It's a break from the 'boredom' of us . . .

Discussion

In 1978 Rubin claimed that, 'Any attempt to improve children's learning depends on some form of teacher growth' and that, 'the best teachers must have periodic occasions for reflection, for readjusting their tactics to shifting social situations, and for utilizing new processes and procedures.' The broader issue of teacher learning does, however, concern its quality. A number of factors will affect this. For example, the design of the in-service event or programme, the psychological, social and intellectual stage of the learner and his/her state of readiness to learn. For the purposes of this paper, I would like to focus upon the state of readiness and the demands made upon the teacher who is also a designer of professional and curriculum development in a model of in-service which has become predominantly school-initiated and school-based.

It was clear that most of the teachers interviewed perceived that they had gained significantly from involvement in a project in which INSET was:

> integrated with and part and parcel of concrete programme changes and problems experienced at the classroom and school level . . . intensive and ongoing . . . linked . . . to organizational development efforts . . . directed at specific skill and conceptual development over time . . . [planned] at the school level.
>
> (Fullan, in Hopkins, 1986).

Additionally, though, many teachers had been their own developers. Some, as noted elsewhere, had, 'found their new role demanding both in terms of time as well as physical and emotional energy' (Kennedy and Patterson 1986; Day, 1990). Within the context of school-based curriculum development doubts concerning the intellectual rigour of self-created learning opportunities have been expressed by Rudduck:

> I remain somewhat sceptical about the intellectual rigour and coherence of courses of study created by busy teachers in their own schools: creation must be disciplined by conscious articulation of the

problematics of the relationship between materials and form . . . Major
works of curriculum creation could be more safely left to others provided
that we could rely on confident critique and adaptation from teachers.

(Rudduck, 1987).

These views should at least serve as warnings to those who manage an
in-service programme which is predominantly school-based: 'Too much can
be asked of teachers, and simplistic policies that are not aware of the broader
issues can have disastrous results' (Kennedy, 1989).

Nevertheless, in terms of the activities undertaken by teachers in the project,
most went beyond what was described as 'swapping recipes'. Indeed, they had
been almost obliged to do so by the nature of an innovation which demanded
that professional learning opportunities be policy related; but because the
locus and focus for policy making and implementation (albeit within an
externally imposed framework) was the school, teachers were prepared, at
least for the present, to commit themselves. However, although perceptions of
the purposes and processes of INSET were beginning to change as teachers
made the link between curriculum, personal, interpersonal and institutional
development, there was little evidence that this was yet affecting their classroom practice.

Conditions for teacher empowerment: relationships between in-service, school and individual culture and school improvement

Collaborative school cultures

Headteachers used a variety of strategies to determine the kinds of learning
which were to be promoted and the establishment of priorities within
individual schemes. In general, staff were widely consulted about their own
needs and those of the school, with the Head taking final decisions:

> We all put bids in . . . stating what we thought our needs were, personal as
> well as school. Our bids were put into [headteacher] who then assessed
> the needs of the school against our needs and the money he'd got
> available to pay for it and it was sorted out from there on. He prioritised it.
> As a school we generally discuss things before we get to that stage, and so
> the others have agreed. So even though staff were not actively respons-
> ible for making the decision they put their oar in before the decision was
> actually taken . . . The existing staff know each other very well, and so it's
> easier to make decisions . . .

In schools represented by this statement there was already a climate of
collaboration and consultation. In some, this had been established partly as a
result of their use of GRIDS (guidelines for review and internal development

of schools), which involved a systematic individual and institutional needs analysis.

> No decisions are ever made without a team of three or four being involved in the decisions . . . and even then, it is most rare for a decision to be taken without a follow-up going to the staff meeting . . .

> We've always got on well together, talked about things. This last year it's all been put on a slightly more formal basis. We've got things down in writing perhaps that we didn't have before. We always have been pretty good at communicating. We've had a good background of working together in curriculum and spreading the responsibility from one or two people working together to seven or eight . . .

It is clear from these statements that the scheme had benefited those schools with a more 'democratic' ethos in which decisions concerning school development were based upon active staff participation, and where staff were treated, in the words of one teacher, 'as adults'. This feeling of 'having a say', of opinions being valued, and of the locus for need identification and decision making having been moved closer to the source of action (the school itself) was perhaps the most significant benefit reported across the pilot schools:

> If people feel that their opinion is valued, then they contribute more . . . and then they started coming up with ideas . . . and then when we had a staff meeting . . . we split up into teams [to work on review of maths] and we bought supply in so that people could have time during the day, which they thought was marvellous, that they were valued to the point that you would provide cover to let them work on things . . .

> We've been able to have the things that we felt we needed . . . It's been nice to feel that we could choose for ourselves . . .

There were, however, examples where the locus of decision making was within the school, but not yet within the staffroom:

> I wouldn't say that the staff development programme has been a direct result of staff themselves saying what they wanted to do. That's what it ought to be really, but the first few meetings we had . . . what they suggested was to spend a lot of money looking at . . . in other words, they didn't require a great deal of input or thought . . . The focus they were giving for courses were all in directed time . . .

Where there had been no climate of collaboration there had been occasions when, 'one or two of us feel we are being pushed out because our views aren't quite the same as the younger people. We're not being asked, we're being told'. This kind of statement served to reinforce the view expressed by a teacher in another school that:

> I wonder, if we hadn't been in agreement, then it might not have been as easy... We have regular meetings and we decide on the issues... It could have been difficult. If you had a very dominant person who disregarded everyone else...

Where the unspoken values underlying the successful operation of the scheme clash with the prevailing culture of the school, then problems will arise. For example, if there has been no active school development policy, if staff have been used to identifying their own needs, or if they have not involved themselves in in-service – despite encouragement – then this kind of in-service opportunity may not be fully appreciated by some or welcomed by others. There were examples of resentment among some staff: 'It's been limited to a few... It seems that the hierarchy or the things that are "in", they're the one's who are going to get the time... There was nothing in the bids for personal development.' Others indicated feelings of worthlessness:

> A lot of time is given to young teachers to go on courses... but you get to the middle or towards the end of your teaching career and you think, 'Well, did I ought to go? Would it be better for other people?' You tend to go on courses now – which I feel we're going to be dictated – that deal with your area of the curriculum... because of the money... which is not always what you want.

This point was also recognized by a headteacher: 'Some heads talked of, "members of staff who prefer to work in their own way..." and of the fine line between upsetting people, making them feel that their contribution is worthless, and allowing them to continue'. Others commented adversely on the apparent refocusing of in-service priorities from meeting individual to meeting institutional needs:

> It's giving you a very narrow view, whereas before this you were able to choose whichever course took your fancy... I feel we're being pushed into one channel... so I feel that it's going to be detrimental to your own development and what you're able to put over to the children...

Whose needs?

Part of our staff development policy is that money will be set aside for people to pursue things that they are interested in solely for themselves... everybody agreed on that... I think people feel quite strongly about that, and I agree with it. I always try to bear in mind the individual needs and what people want to do, because if we're doing our own staff development, with an emphasis on staff, that's what it should be about, but obviously we're having all these things coming at us and we've got to address those needs. So I'm feeling reluctantly that it's got to be those things first ... and then the personal if we can fit them in. I don't necessarily agree that's how it should be, but we're under these pressures.

The evidence from the teachers in this project suggests that they were generally sympathetic to these problems, and that they understood at this time that institutional needs must take precedence over personal needs. They also recognized, however, that, 'People's needs change from one year to the next', so that sensitive leadership is required in processes of prioritization. 'Where money is tight', one teacher commented, 'there's a danger that individual needs will be squeezed out'. Although external contexts may change, teachers will always feel the need to be valued during their professional lifetimes and this must always be remembered when considering the balance between identifying and meeting individual and institutional needs.

Policy-oriented in-service

These comments from teachers and a headteacher in three of the schools highlighted the dilemmas facing schools who try to manage staff and curriculum development within limited budgets. The second statement above indicates the effect of external innovation upon decisions made regarding the content of in-service, and this was referred to by many of the teachers: The comment below is representative: 'Most of the money will be focused upon the changes required under the National Curriculum. It's up to me as head to find out what we can do best to fit our children into the scheme of things that are required.' Some teachers were more sceptical about the effect of this upon teacher and school autonomy: 'I feel sceptical about how much autonomy we'll have – with the National Curriculum and testing and assessment, and "money" being the watchword at the moment, I can't see us having much freedom to choose ... I'm quite cynical.' Others regarded it as helping to motivate and focus:

> The National Curriculum helped us ... Through this imposition ... we can say, 'Are we sure we're addressing it. We're doing these things wonderfully well, but we're not doing much of that, are we?' Because nobody felt personally threatened ...

Individual and school improvement

The scheme had clearly provided opportunities for different kinds of change at different levels. For one teacher, developments had been accelerated:

> I am open anyway to new ideas and to change ... by nature I am curious ... because I'm the kind of person I am that would have still happened anyway. I would have made it happen. It's just made it physically more possible for me to do it.

Others' horizons had been broadened:

> It's given me chance to free [named teacher] out of class to get some really
> super ideas because she's been really hidebound in there . . . She's been
> able to go to teachers' centres and other schools . . .

Others felt less isolated. They had learned that 'you're not stuck in school on
your own now . . . and that . . . you've got to keep on learning and keep on going
on courses . . . It's given a different angle . . .'

There was evidence that both headteachers and teachers were much 'more
sophisticated about the way we're going to use the money'. Teachers had had
their consciousness raised about the financial costs of in-service, and had
become more discriminating, more concerned with value for money:

> Now when we go on a course we find out more about it . . . Whether it's
> worth the money or not . . . we're more discriminating . . . It's a way of
> making sure the money is well spent . . .

> It's much more important now, and we want some feedback afterwards,
> because it's costing us money . . . The fact that we used to go [to in-service]
> at half past four it didn't seem as valuable somehow as going in school
> time . . . so I think we've really got to seeing some end result of these
> courses with plenty of evaluation afterwards . . .

> You've got to look at it in £ s d now. The staff meeting last night was £100
> because there were ten people there for an hour, and it was £10 per
> hour. And if you look at an in-service day, it is costing something in the
> region of £800. I've got to find value for money in this . . . say someone
> has two days' supply, that's cost £120 to replace, but there's also the
> teacher's salary in that. So, really, those two days are costing me upwards
> of £250–£300. And if it's for a deputy head it's even more . . . I've got to
> get something on paper for that, and that's coming back into good
> practice, or to change our practice within the school. Otherwise I'm not
> spending the money well.

Headteachers were unanimous in acclaiming benefits in terms of change of
attitude to professional development among their staff, and perhaps this was
the most significant success of the year-old scheme:

> I feel that the staff work cohesively together now in identifying the needs
> . . . the fact that we have changed from thinking that in-service is all about
> courses so that it has been more school-focused – that is a major
> change . . .

> It's made us discuss things more. It's made us more aware . . . We've had
> more time to look at the documents and do things . . . The obvious
> answer would be from the results of the work with the children, but . . .
> you also have to keep your staff happy. If your staff are happy and are

interested in what they're doing, then that reflects upon the children . . .
So, look for a happy staffroom!

It's part and parcel of how we see the school as a whole. I am trying to
move people to a different approach in the classroom . . . But it would
have happened much more slowly . . . But I've still got members of staff
who prefer to work in their own way . . .

It is making a difference in school, because people are getting down to
really talking about what is important, the way we must be going, really
sorting ourselves out . . . To some extent, because of the National
Curriculum, it would have had to have happened, but it would have
happened much more slowly . . . I found it very difficult before directed
time came in to get people together on a regular basis. So directed time
has helped. Then staff development money has been an extra bonus, a
marvellous bonus really, because you can do that during the day, when
people are fresh . . . rather than at the end of the day when people are
tired . . .

High on everyone's agenda was the effect on practice, highlighted by a
comment from a deputy head:

It's very difficult to keep an overview of it and not get too obsessed with
having the trappings of what's good but really it's not happening in the
classroom. Having the wonderful documents . . . but if there's nothing
happening at the end of it all, then it's a complete waste of time. Really, it's
'How does this apply to us? What are we going to do in the classroom? . . .
If we go out of school, if we don't bring it into school and if it doesn't do
anything – whether it sparks off a discussion or whatever – then it's a total
waste of money . . . Now it's got to be part of your staff development plan.
That side of it I find sad, that you can't just go away and do something for
your own benefit . . . For me, whether something had worked or we'd got
'value for money' would be if I saw something change in the classroom
for the children . . . That's really what I'm after. If I could honestly say that I
could walk in a classroom and see some practice that had been the
product of the staff development . . . The other thing is getting the staff to
work together . . . to talk . . . all these are a process to try and get
something better for the children, so ultimately that's how I would judge
it.
Q: Can you say that now?
A: No . . . I don't see it as years. It's an expanse of time . . . Hopefully,
people will move a little bit. You have to keep in your mind the overall
picture . . .

Nevertheless, there was evidence of some change in some teachers' classroom
thinking and practice.

Most of those teachers who associated the scheme with change in classroom

practice, spoke in terms of 'reinforcement' of current practice or trying out of
new ideas gained from visiting other schools or attending courses rather than
significant changes:

> Not really, because most of the work we were doing before. It has,
> perhaps made us a little bit more conscious as far as science is concerned.
> We do a little bit more than we did before.

> I haven't changed anything that I'm already doing, in the classroom . . .
> We're only just getting it into practice. We have put quite a lot of thought
> into it . . . There must be concrete experience in what we do . . . It's
> reinforced what I'm already doing. . . .

> It's not changed dramatically. But certainly I've seen lots of ideas which
> I've incorporated into my way of working.

In three instances teachers did claim that there had been radical change in
their practice and thinking about practice. Interestingly, the first teacher
worked in a small school, where opportunities for experiencing a variety of
practices of teaching are by definition likely to be limited:

> It's stimulated me to do something different in my classroom. It's a jolly
> good idea. We stagnate if we stay in school too much. In that way it's good
> that I'm getting out and about, seeing other people's classrooms, how
> they work, and then coming back and doing something a little bit
> different myself . . .

The second, who was 'trying to change' as a result of challenges to her
thinking about practice was concerned that her own point of view might be
ignored – a potential hazard for managers and a reminder of the need for moral
as well as practical support over time for those in the processs of changing:

> I've found it has challenged the way I have thought . . . and I am in the
> process of trying to change . . . Yes . . . particularly on the Maths and
> Languages . . . but I hope that people will listen to what I have to say . . .
> but I'm a bit apprehensive – But I just have a feeling some things are being
> swept aside, that things we have done, and have done well in the past, are
> being questioned. I'm quite prepared to be questioned, but I hope that
> our points of view are going to be well listened to . . .

A third teacher had been motivated to, 'try things that I didn't do before . . . It's
made me do more practical things with children'.

Towards a culture of collaboration

The project provided an illustration in practice of what Purkey and Smith
(1985) described as an 'inverted pyramid' approach to changing schools, for it

recognized that while the LEA had legal responsibility for in-service work, for this to be effective, schools must be given 'strategic independence' (Finn, 1984) so that the inevitable tensions between system-wide uniformity and school-level autonomy might be reconciled, or at least become productive. Bruce Joyce (1989) reported that the contributing authors of the 1990 *Yearbook of the Association for Supervision and Curriculum Development* (of which he is editor) 'appear to have concluded that creating conditions where education personnel are growing productively and school improvement is an embedded feature of collegial life requires a major restructuring of the workplace':

> The challenge is to create an ethos that is almost an inversion of the one Lortie so accurately described in *Schoolteacher* (1975). That is, vertical and horizontal isolation and separation of roles will be replaced by integration and collaboration.
>
> (Joyce, 1989)

Almost all the in-service which occurred in the schools was related to their school development plans. Writing in an industrial context in the early 1980s, Ackoff makes a similar point about the interdependency implicit in any act of corporate planning, proposing three operating principles of interactive planning–participation, continuity and co-ordination and integration:

> It is better to plan for oneself, no matter how badly, than to be planned for by others, no matter how well ... no parts of an organisation can be planned for independently of any other unit at the same level ... planning done independently at any level of a system cannot be as effective as planning carried out interdependently at all levels
>
> (Ackoff, 1981)

The gains which may be achieved through interdependency have been well documented. Rosenholtz (1989) in America identified learning-impoverished and learning-enriched schools. The characteristics of learning-enriched schools were:

- collaborative goals at the building level
- minimum uncertainty
- positive attitudes of teachers
- principals supported teachers and removed barriers for them
- principals fostered collaboration as opposed to competition.

The characteristics of learning impoverished schools were:

- no clear goals or shared values
- teachers rarely talked to one another
- teachers perceived the school to be routine
- norms of self-reliance flourished, as did isolation.

(from Rosenholtz, 1989)

In England, paradoxically, the in-service strategies and curriculum reforms pursued by national and local government, have given added impetus to the breaking down of traditional school and teacher autonomy cultures so that professional development activities are now more likely to be based upon planning and learning as a reciprocal and mutual process (Holly and South-worth, 1989) within a growing culture of collaboration (Nias, 1987). For this emerging culture to flourish, however, some headteachers and their staff need to change from being, 'over developed individuals in under developed schools' (Reid, Hopkins and Holly, 1987). They will need to acquire, 'a range of knowledge, skills and attitudes not demanded in schools which have worked within a framework of centrally determined policies, plans and budgets and with few requirements as far as accountability is concerned' (Caldwell and Spinks, 1988). Conversely, education managers themselves will have to take account of these needs and provide appropriate support for the implementation of the system innovation. Even then they can only be certain that they are working to reduce the negative and increase the positive forces (Figure 10.1) which pertain to the link between in-service and teaching, rather than the link

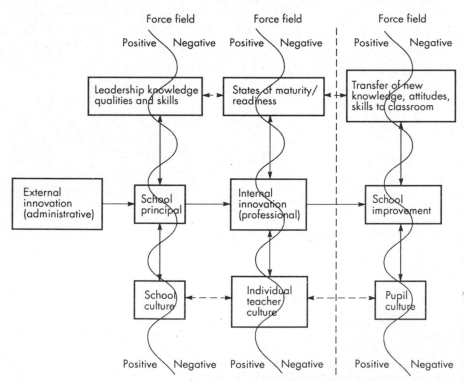

Figure 10.1 Variables in the success of externally initiated, self-managed staff development and school improvement

between teaching and learning, which is more properly the province of school self-evaluation:

> From an LEA standpoint INSET evaluation should focus on the link between INSET and teacher attitudes and behaviour, while school-based evaluation should focus on the link between school policy and practice and pupils attitudes and achievements.
>
> (Eraut et al., 1987)

Professional development: end piece

We should not, therefore, expect too much of INSET. In reporting on an OECD International School Improvement Project (ISIP), David Hopkins wrote (1987):

> From what has already been said it should be becoming apparent that school improvement is to do with curriculum development, strengthening the school organization, changes in the teaching-learning process, and teaching styles. Its focus is the classroom and the school; it is content and process oriented. Within this concept of school improvement, the teacher is receiving more priority in the change process, but not at the expense of the school leader, the subject department or the faculty; therefore the collaboration among all school personnel becomes central. This approach also focuses attention on the process of strengthening the school's capacity to deal with change.
>
> Those involved in ISIP do not expect profound structural changes in the school. The accent is on making the best of the school's staff and resources, increasing flexibility and the adaptation of the school to ensure students a good transition to an active life. Differential treatment of schools, and more school-focused improvement efforts, will be the main characteristics of the improvement strategy.
>
> Improving the competencies of a school to manage itself, to analyse its problems and its needs and to develop and carry out a strategy of change, is a key approach for school improvement in the eighties and beyond.

References

Ackoff, R. L. (1981). *Creating the Corporate Future: Plan or be Planned For*. New York, Wiley.

Bolam, R. (1982). *In Service Education and Training of Teachers: A Condition for Educational Change*. Paris, OECD.

Bolam, R. (1989). 'School-based INSET: research and experience in England and Wales', paper presented to an International Conference on School-based Innovations:

Looking Forward to the 1990s, Hong Kong Educational Research Association, December.

Benney, M. and Hughes, E. C. (1956). 'Of sociology and the interview', Editorial preface, *American Journal of Sociology*, 61.

Bridges, D. (1989). 'Identifying INSET needs: a school improvement perspective', in R. McBride (ed.), *The In-Service Training of Teachers: Some Issues and Perspectives*. Lewes, Falmer.

Brown, G. (1989). 'The changing face of INSET: a view from a university department of education', in R. McBride (ed.), *The In-Service Training of Teachers: Some Issues and Perspectives*. Lewes, Falmer.

Caldwell, B. J. and Spinks, J. M. (1988). *The Self-Managing School*. Lewes, Falmer.

Day, C. (1986). 'Staff development: some problems in promoting school professional learning and change', in C. W. Day and R. F. Moore (eds), *Staff Development in the Secondary School: Management Perspectives*. London, Croom Helm.

Day, C. (1989). *LEATGS: Evaluation of a Pilot Project for the Devolution of INSET Resources to Primary Schools, 1988–9*, Mimeo, School of Education, University of Nottingham.

Denzin, N. K. (1973). *The Research Act*, Chicago, Aldine Publishing.

Derbyshire County Council (1987). 'LEATGS 1988–89', letter dated 7 October.

Derbyshire County Council (1988). *Staff Development and Professional Review*, 25 February.

Department of Education and Science (1983). *Teaching Quality*. London, HMSO.

Department of Education and Science (1985). *Better Schools*. London, HMSO.

Department of Education and Science (1986). *Local Education Authority Training Grant Scheme: Financial Year 1987–88*, Circular 6/86. London, HMSO.

Eraut, M., Pennycuik, D. and Radnor, H. (1987). *Local Evaluation of INSET: A Meta Evaluation of TRIST Evaluation*. Bristol, National Development Centre for School Management.

Finn, C. E. (1984). 'Toward strategic independence: nine commandments for enhancing school effectiveness', *Phi Delta Kappan*, February.

HMI (1989). *The Implementation of the Local Education Authority Training Grants Scheme (LEATGS): Report on First Year of the Scheme 1987–88*, London, DES.

Holly, P. and Southworth, G. (1989). *The Developing School*. Lewes, Falmer.

Hopkins, D. (1986). *In-Service Training and Educational Development*. London, Croom Helm.

Hopkins, D. (1987). *Improving the Quality of Schooling*, Lewes, Falmer.

Joyce, B. (1989). 'Staff development as cultural change', paper presented at International Conference of Hong Kong Educational Research Association, November.

Kennedy, K. (1989). 'Policy and practice in school-based curriculum development', Paper presented to the International Conference of Hong Kong Educational Research Association, 13–16 December.

Kennedy, K. and Patterson, C. (1986). 'Enterprise kids – case study of a year 10 transition education course', in B. Fraser (ed.), *School Development Through Transition Education*. Perth, Western Australian Education Department.

Kuhn, M. H. (1962). 'The interview and the professional relationship', in Rose, A. M. (ed.), *Human Behavior and Social Processes*. Boston, Houghton Mifflin.

Merton, R. K. and Kendall, P. L. (1946). 'The focused interview', *American Journal of Sociology*, 51.

Nias, J. (1987). 'Learning from difference: a collegial approach to change', in W. J. Smyth (ed.), *Educating Teachers: Changing the Nature of Pedagogical Knowledge*. Lewes, Falmer.

Peters, T. J. and Waterman, R. J. Jnr. (1982). *In Search of Excellence: Lessons from America's Best Run Companies*. New York, Harper & Row.

Poster, C. and Day, C. (eds) (1989). *Partnership in Education Management*, London, Routledge.

Purkey, S. C. and Smith, M. S. (1985). 'School reform: the district policy implications of the effective schools' literature'. *The Elementary School Journal* (USA), 85.

Reid, K., Hopkins, D. and Holly, P. J. (1987). *Towards the Effective School*. Oxford, Basil Blackwell.

Rosenholtz, S. J. (1989). *Schools, Social Organisation and the Building of a Technical Culture*, New York, Longman.

Rubin, L. (1978). *The In-Service Education of Teachers: Trends, Processes and Prescriptions*, Boston, Allyn and Bacon.

Rudduck, J. (1987). 'Can school-based curriculum development be other than conservative?' in N. Sabar, J. Rudduck and W. Reid (eds), *Partnership and Autonomy in School-Based Curriculum Development*. University of Sheffield, Division of Education.

van Velzen, W., *et al.* (1985). *Making School Improvement Work*. Leuven, Belgium, ACCO.

11

The role of appraisal in staff development

Helen McMullen

There is no doubt that staff development is a high priority for teachers and headteachers, particularly at the time of the introduction of the national curriculum, with all that that implies; but staff development must be more than the identification of in-service needs. It must be part of a systematic process of review and development for which the government has legislated under the local education authority training grant scheme and this legislation ensures that every school will have an appraisal system. If appraisal systems are to be a means of enhancing the professional development of teachers, as they are claimed to be and indeed have been found to be in surveys of practice (Turner and Clift, 1988), we need to be able to demonstrate that they are worth the considerable investment which they require.

In this chapter four main issues will be examined:

1 What is actually meant by staff development?
2 What are the possible alternatives to a formal staff development policy?
3 The school culture which needs to exist for staff development to be seen as a positive.
4 Management activity and the implications which arise out of a formal system.

The relationship between staff development and appraisal

In practice a range of meanings can be and often are, attached to staff development; but this chapter is written on the premise that a staff development programme is a planned process of development which enhances the quality of pupil learning by identifying, clarifying and meeting the individual needs of the teaching staff within the context of the school as a whole.

Staff development should relate to the individual, the interested groups and the whole school. Its primary aim should be to increase the quality of pupil learning by the development of the staff potential and it should seek to recognize the specialized needs of the individual teachers. Hewton (1988) reminds us, however: 'that the effectiveness of organisations depends upon the quality of life provided for those who work within them' (p. 37). Fernstermacher and Berliner (1985) maintain that 'staff development has become an activity that encompasses much more than a single teacher acting as individual, it is understood that this person's activities are a part of the larger environment of the school.'

Drummond (1986) also argues that professional development should embrace personal development (individualized learning) and staff development (the collegiality of group learning/co-learning). Turner and Clift (1988), in their study of a project funded by the Leverhulme Trust, found that one of the main differences between the views of appraisers and appraisees on staff development was whether appraisal should serve institutional or individual needs. For the most part they found that if appraisers were senior members of staff, the desired outcomes were concerned with the maintenance and improvement of the institution as a whole and that appraisal and staff development was viewed mainly as a management tool.

Eraut (1986) believes that the product determines the purpose of appraisal; therefore if the product is an action plan for development the appraisal interview will become a staff development interview, but if the product is an agreed appraisal of a teacher's performance for insertion into his or her file, the appraisal foreground will put staff development purposes very much into the background.

The ACAS agreement (1986) emphasized the developmental rather than the accountability aspect of appraisal and made staff development one of its main aims. Turner and Clift (1988) also found that most schools focus on staff development as the main aim of appraisal.

For many teachers appraisal linked to professional development is the least threatening and *Quality in Schools* (DES 1985) states that those managing the teacher have a clear responsibility to establish a policy for staff development based on a systematic assessment of every teacher's performance.

A staff development policy which is part of an appraisal system can act as a focusing device for both management and teachers. To understand the needs of the individual and the establishment a vision is necessary of how things might improve in the future. This requires a strategic, corporate and longer-term view which may override the shorter-term wants of individuals. Effective needs analysis requires more than the systematic collection of information. It involves careful negotiation, commitment from all parties and consensus where the views of individuals and groups of teachers may not coincide.

Circular 6/86 (DES, 1986) sent to all LEAs required that proposals for the annual in-service training grant should be based on systematically identified needs and regular consultation with individual teachers.

> The Secretary of State will wish to assure himself that these proposals are related to systematically assessed needs and priorities are set within balanced and coherent overall policies and plans and build appropriately on the strength of current arrangements.
>
> (p. 7)

This circular expected that schools and local education authorities would take account of the expressed needs and views of teachers when setting up training. A draft circular sent to all education authorities in 1987 (*LEA Training Grants Scheme Financial Year 1988–89*) re-emphasized that proposals for in-service should be based upon needs identified by regular consultation with individual teachers.

A staff development policy, however, requires clear aims and a rationale for those aims, a co-ordinating mechanism to help to avoid overlaps and to encourage individuals and groups to work together on developments and a definite commitment to a course of action. How can these aims be met if they are not based on a thorough assessment of the needs of the teachers?

The alternatives

It is quite possible for a school to have an implicit staff development policy which has evolved over a period of time and has never been formally thought out, discussed or written down. Critics of a formal policy, according to Hewton (1988), may argue that a staff development policy (particularly if linked to appraisal) may inhibit flexibility and prevent a rapid response to a new situation, particularly if resources are already committed and in-service needs identified. A policy requires that a considerable amount of time be devoted to its development, particularly if all staff are to be involved in the exercise, and its implementation may be costly.

There is much going on in schools which could lead to staff development needs being identified, albeit in an haphazard way. Teachers usually have some idea how well or how badly things are going; there may be discipline problems, either within a particular classroom or around the school; a vague sense of dissatisfaction may exist among some or all members of staff and teachers' morale may be low. The general school climate may lack something, displays may look shabby and parents may be expressing some dissatisfaction. These could all be indicators of staff development needs.

Hewton (1988) discusses needs blindness, which he believes may stem from complacency, tradition and possibly out-of-date and incorrect assumptions about what is happening in and around a school; but this may not tell the whole story. Even if needs are identified, how might they be justified and interpreted and from whose perspective? How may possible differences between the wants and needs of individual teachers with no clear evidence or justification to substantiate them be resolved? This will, to a large extent, depend upon how sensitive the headteacher and members of the senior management team are to these indicators and how they translate their perceptions into actions. It may result in no action at all, or action which is haphazard, unfair and unequal. This situation could remain until deliberate steps are taken to change the norm.

It is necessary for a headteacher to have a conscious awareness of the effect of his or her endeavours upon those with whom he or she works, to be sensitive to the differences, personalities and characters which exist within the group, and to try and ensure that the work they do is rewarding and satisfying. Failure to take account of personal interactions may result in low morale among the staff and poor professional performance. It does not follow, either, that a happy staff is an effective staff. A headteacher one's overriding concern should be to provide the pupils with the best possible education.

The school culture

The development process has two purposes. First, it indicates the sequence of events to be pursued cither by individual teachers alone within small groups, or the staff as a whole, and secondly, it reinforces the point that professional development is not a series of unrelated events but a long-term process. But before any of the formal elements of staff development can be introduced, it is necessary to build the sort of working atmosphere in which professional growth can be encouraged.

Bradley (1983) suggests that schools which make a positive contribution to an individual's development are characterized by certain organizational features such as problem-seeking rather than problem-solving initiatives in which responsibilities are delegated with power to take action and delegation is accompanied by participation.

Within such schools teachers are encouraged to discuss issues openly and share the ownership of both the problems and the solutions. The teachers in these schools see themselves as part of a team and there is an atmosphere of consistency and trust. Evaluation within the school is seen as an essential element of the development process. It is non-threatening and stems from an expectation that things can always be improved. The achievement of such an atmosphere in a school demands continuing good management with a vision. Each headteacher must identify priority areas and targets in order to establish a positive atmosphere within the school, where development will be seen in a positive light. Bradley (1983) identifies several issues which the headteacher should address in order to facilitate the development of individuals:

- fostering a collaborative and participative team approach
- making maximum use of the talents of each member of staff by creating an

efficient structure of responsibilities within the school and then delegating effectively
● considering what actions will encourage staff to take responsibility for their own development.

Certainly if a team approach is to be developed, individuals require clearly defined areas of responsibility with the authority to take decisions. The purpose and the limits should be made clear and also how success will be judged.

To encourage staff to be actively involved in their own development a headteacher needs to be able to identify what motivates the staff to continue learning, to find ways to positively influence these motivating factors, and to know how the school organization can maximize them.

Many elements which positively contribute to establishing a participative team approach will be present in the day-to-day opportunities provided by the activities which the headteacher undertakes with individual teachers through regular informal discussions within the classrooms, around the school and through regular, planned and purposeful staff meetings where discussion and debate are encouraged.

But the quality of staff development will be greatly enhanced in a school where teachers are:

● encouraged to plan and evaluate their work jointly with colleagues
● involved in visits to other classrooms and other schools
● encouraged to attend courses
● encouraged to keep up to date on specific curricular areas (and educational developments in general)
● able to lead seminars, both school-based and externally
● encouraged to study and question their own practice
● involved in management decisions.

Managing aspects of staff development

The strategies which are now outlined evolved in part, as a result of the experience gained by working closely with teaching staff. It is essential to remember that the formal aspects of appraisal should, if possible, be established only when the informal system has succeeded in creating the positive climate previously discussed.

The formal system needs a careful structure, and a clear framework. The framework can be broken down into distinct phases: preparation, observation, the interview and evaluation. As working relationships develop between the headteacher and staff, further knowledge and understanding will be gained. Pure objectivity, according to Bell (1988), is unattainable and self-awareness will always be clouded by self-perception. However, to achieve some degree of objectivity the system must be closely related to the aims and overall educational objectives of the school.

Preparation

All members of staff need to be well briefed about the purpose of the activity and about the processes to be used. It is important to involve those who will be appraised in the development of the scheme rather than just imposing it upon them.

The process will require both the appraiser and the appraisee to be involved in some preparatory activities such as gathering up-to-date information and setting the agenda. The teacher should be in possession of documentary evidence such as current job description, and have knowledge of how this relates to the overall staff structure, policies which relate to the aims and objectives of the school, schemes of work and organizational information. The headteacher, as an appraiser, must have current knowledge of the teacher's classroom skills with regard to approaches to learning, the classroom environment and the organization of the teaching and learning programme. Such preparation must include observation of lessons – but that raises the question of by whom.

Consultation between both parties prior to the interview is essential to ensure that both are aware of what is to be discussed. However, the agenda must not be too prescriptive. It must cope with a range of circumstances as deciding on a specific agenda may well exclude important matters from discussion.

Classroom observation

There seem to be two purposes of classroom observation. One is to enable the headteacher to reach a judgement about the person being appraised while the other is the sharing of ideas in order to improve practice.

Teachers must have confidence in the fairness of the process at all times and as most teaching and learning takes place in classrooms, classroom observation offers a practical procedure for collecting some data about teacher performance. However, there is no doubt that the lesson observed may not be typical and information should be gathered over a period of time. The way in which observation data is collected and shared with teachers is an important factor in the success of the interview. Observation data must be seen in a constructive way as contributing to improved classroom performance. However, collecting data is a time-consuming activity and requires the observer to have certain skills.

The interview

Much has been written about the interview process, and therefore I will not examine this issue in detail, other than to state that a climate should exist in which genuine dialogue can take place. Attention should be focused upon past successes and the data available should be used to indicate areas for improvement and ways in which this might be achieved. The focus should be on the performance of the defined job.

The interview should emphasize development rather than deficiencies in performance. The emphasis should be on helping teachers to consider their own position, defining their own problems and discovering, through discussion, their own practical solutions. Whatever the news about the outcomes of appraisal, teachers, according to Turner and Clift (1988) invariably express satisfaction with the time of exclusive and uninterrupted discussion with their headteacher afforded by the appraisal interview.

For some teachers this may be their first opportunity for sustained discussion with the headteacher. Most teachers value the opportunity afforded by the formal appraisal interview for feedback and communication about their work from someone whose professional credibility they respect and who has the power to bring about changes. Turner and Clift (1988) believe that irrespective of the empirical validity of headteachers' criteria of judgement, they are the ones who will determine the outcomes of appraisal.

At the end of the interview, an agreed statement should be prepared setting out the action to be taken by both parties by an agreed date. Targets should be specific and realistic. Once individual needs have been identified, the means of satisfying them have to be found. In order to ensure that the process does not degenerate into a paper exercise, the effectiveness of the system should be monitored and evaluated on a regular basis.

Staff development programme – one school's experience

Within the school of which I was headteacher a planned staff development programme appeared to be a natural progression following staff discussions prompted by the staff themselves and the local education authority self-evaluation scheme. As a staff we had examined the school's aims and questioned how we met these aims. We had examined what we considered good practice within the classroom, areas of concern and the relevance of job descriptions.

It was essential at this early stage to look at the motivating forces which were at work within the school. Teachers vary considerably in what motivates them and this had to be taken into account. However, I considered that most teachers were motivated by the excitement of children developing and learning, by an enthusiasm for a particular subject, by recognition, interest, praise and encouragement, by being given an opportunity to contribute to the staff and excel, by a challenge to their professional skill by the inspiration of others or by career prospects.

Prior to the school planning to introduce a formal scheme it was crucial to examine the existing procedures for evaluating the professional performance of individual teachers. There was a danger that a staff development programme which was originally initiated to develop the professional awareness of teachers could have become a paper exercise or just another administrative chore if provision had not been made to monitor staff reaction, attitude and involvement in the mechanics of the process, even in the very early stages of the programme.

As headteacher, it was important for me to recognize staff reservations and I therefore spent some time stressing the positive side of the scheme: that it was intended to discover areas of strength and give full scope for development, that it was a necessity and could not be avoided if individuals were to make progress in the real world, that it was part of professional life and that it was much better to participate in a scheme which was efficient and open rather than be involved in something which was subjective and carried out in a devious manner.

The objectivity of a planned scheme needed to be stressed along with the fact that an individual would be appraised on his or her practical merits over the full range of school work, with support being given. The equality of treatment and the fact that it was to happen at every level with a two-way exchange of ideas, was an important factor to the success of the scheme, as was the consistency of looking ahead and building on achievements to develop a relevant curriculum and organization. Throughout staff discussions, therefore a co-operative, involved attitude was critical and all parties needed to acknowledge that the scheme was objective, open, focused on the job, operationally simple, systematic and developmental. Appraisal has been part of good industrial management practice for many years; I therefore believed that educational institutions could benefit from the experience and knowledge of industry's well established appraisal processes.

In industry appraisal was the principal means by which staff discovered answers to questions such as 'What is expected of me?' 'How am I getting on?' 'How can I do better?' 'How can I further my career?' The industrial scheme needed to be adapted to meet the needs of schools, but the key features had many similarities, such as regular meetings between manager (headteacher) and employee (teacher), an agreed and negotiated job description, an agreed standard of performance, agreed targets for the forthcoming period which were realistic, relevant, attainable and objective, regular reviews, evaluation of performance and relevant and regular in-service training opportunities.

If as headteacher I was to help each teacher examine his or her own performance and evaluate its effectiveness, I needed to be in possession of information about each member of staff. In order to meet the needs of the educational establishment, the teacher, too, needs to be in possession of certain information which will inform his or her practice within the school.

This knowledge needs to include information about the terms and conditions of employment, the workings of the teaching profession, to whom and for whom the teacher is responsible. The teachers required professional information about the school philosophies, policies, organizational routines and the support available.

The teachers had acquired the practicalities of different teaching techniques over a period of time, and as headteacher, I needed to be aware of the level of each teacher's expertise in using appropriate teaching techniques within the classroom. I also needed knowledge of the teacher's ability to manage children, both individually and within groups, and the experience the teacher had had to date in managing pupils.

Not only did I need to have knowledge of these factors in relation to each teacher, but I needed to possess the relevant professional information, qualities and skills. This was perhaps where my role as headteacher as a manager differed from managers within industry, as it is not a requirement that industrial managers possess shop floor skills.

Teacher performance within the classroom and the standards of performance that children were expected to achieve featured as important discussion points in the staff development programme. Targets and objectives needed to be stated in specific terms, but this required professional skills, judgement and a knowledge and understanding of the school's guidelines and schemes and what was expected nationally.

As headteacher I needed to be aware of the teacher's classroom skills with regard to approaches to learning and the effects of classroom environment and organization on the learning programme. I had to question whether the teachers could interpret their own observations within the classroom to discover starting points and motivating factors for the pupils and whether they could provide for the needs of all the pupils within the group with good provision for the majority and extra provision for those at the extremes of ability. I was required to have knowledge of whether teachers could assess response and reaction and whether they knew when to intervene in the learning process.

The skills of organization and planning are fundamental to teaching; therefore I had to know whether the teacher could plan for group and individual learning, create a learning environment and use that environment as a teaching tool. The majority of teaching took place within the classroom. Observation within the classroom was therefore the best practical procedure for collecting data about a teacher's skills and performance. Without regular classroom observation – both formal and informal – the staff development programme would have little relevance or value, although it must be acknowledged that teaching cannot be broken down into specific perceived components.

It was crucial that both teachers and I saw the observation within the classroom as a co-operative, constructive venture. Observation needed to be supportive and evaluative and to concentrate on the significant matters of

teaching. It was not seen as a process for highlighting incompetenc[
failure. Classroom observation gave the staff development progr[
credibility and relevance.

With this knowledge I was able to have meaningful discussions with
individual teachers which helped them to develop an overall philisophy and a
sense of direction: 'A teacher will know if he is succeeding only if he has a clear
idea of what he regards as success' (Surry Inspectorate).

> A respected appraisal scheme and a well conducted interview can serve
> to reinforce the informal messages that people get which tell them that
> they are doing well and this in itself is a form of reward and a source of
> further motivation.
>
> (Everard, 1986)

The interview should be constructive, developmental and forward looking, not
threatening or punishing. In fact, teachers regard the formal interview as the
most valuable aspect of the staff development process.

The interviews needed to be conducted at regular intervals and were
structured by guidelines agreed by staff. The actual agenda needed to be given
careful consideration and it was emphasized to the teachers that it was a
two-way process. Other issues which needed to be considered were whether
anything should be written down and who would have access to this information. Teachers were naturally concerned with the confidentiality aspect. I
found it useful to agree with the individual teachers which points discussed
would remain totally confidential and which aspects I was free to discuss
whenever appropriate.

Within the interview, I needed to adopt a style appropriate to the teacher's
situation and each teacher had a right to receive a constructive, responsible,
balanced feedback about the work he or she was doing within the school.
Some time within the interview was devoted to setting future targets, and
discussion time was allowed. Listening was often the key to a successful interview. It was agreed that the outcome of the interview should be of benefit to
the teacher and to the school; essentially my role as headteacher within staff
development interviews was to assist teachers to work towards solving their
own problems.

Teachers needed to be helped to understand and believe in the results that
they were expected to achieve. They had to be given the resources to do so,
helped in measuring progress and achievements, and these achievements
needed to be recognized.

Day, Johnston and Whitaker (1988) suggest that it is the responsibility of the
head teacher to ensure that every child and teacher in the school receives the
best possible education. In order to achieve this, I had to keep up to date with
developments and in the understanding of effective teaching and learning and
to have the skill to enable the teacher to do the same. The outcome of a
successful professional development programme, therefore, seemed to

depend on the attitudes of all those involved, the resources available, and the access to professional support and guidance.

From this experience, it became clear that a school should expect from a successful structured staff development programme a questioning approach to classroom practice, a greater analysis of strengths and weaknesses (and a desire to remediate the latter), receptivity to new ideas and a willingness to explore different approaches to learning. The staff will, and did, question curricular plans and programmes with a greater awareness of knowledge, skills, attitudes and concepts which were to be learned. The staff did discuss their careers, their performances and their relationships. They were prepared to be critical of themselves and share their knowledge, skills and experience with other members of staff. They offered professional support to each other but, perhaps most important of all, they achieved a high level of professionalism.

Emerging issues

Hewton (1988) argues that an effective staff development policy is both the right and the duty of all teaching staff, but the benefits of staff development which are built around the appraisal interview will depend upon how it is perceived by the staff and how prepared they are for it. Staff development and appraisal, even in its most costly form, will not necessarily lead to improving the educatiom provided by schools. The Suffolk (1985) project stated that appraisal schemes will not solve all the problems found in schools. They can, however, provide a systematic framework for ensuring that difficulties are registered and appropriate action implemented to try to overcome weaknesses, support strengths and encourage potential.

However, there are costs and resource implications. The costs of appraisal are of two kinds – direct money costs and opportunity costs. The collection of reliable and valid evidence about professional performance of individual teachers is labour intensive, particularly if headteachers are involved in this activity. Skill training will be required in appraisal interviewing skills as interviewing involves many activities, listening, negotiating and target setting and personal attributes of sensitivity and perceptiveness. Although some of these may be possessed by interviewers already, others may not. Therefore some training will be necessary to raise awareness of the problems likely to be encountered. As a result of the appraisal, training needs must be satisfied and support, to ensure the attainment of goals, must be available. A scheme will lose credibility if ideas and expectations are raised during an interview and not followed up. There is little doubt that staff development within a structured situation, within which staff can develop as professionals, is the key to the quality of the education which is offered to pupils in primary schools.

In my view, the school needs to ensure that staff development does not take place by chance, but with an ethos/climate in which professionals collaborate to solve the problems of improving the learning that the school enables the pupils to undertake. This will depend, however, on a careful sequencing of stages structured in a way that clarifies how teacher needs are identified and met and how the results are evaluated and fed back into the education/training cycle which is necessary to meet the current changes in education.

Although Turner and Clift (1988) in their project found that appraisal rarely produces tangible changes, it is still seen as being of considerable benefit to individuals, particularly as part of a whole staff development project. If appraisal is to serve a developmental function, it must start from an understanding that the teacher's roles are multiple and complex. Teaching is not a context-independent activity. Additionally, as Jennifer Nias (1988) points out, the self is a crucial element in the way teachers themselves construe the nature of their job. This suggests that the linchpin for success is prepared to be self-evaluating – an issue in itself.

References

Advisory Conciliation and Arbitration Service (1986). *Teachers' Disputes*, London, ACAS Independent Panel Report of the Appraisal and Training Group.

Bell, L. (1988). *Appraising Teachers in Schools*. London, Routledge.

Clarkson, M. (1988). *The Emerging Issues in Primary Education*. Lewes, Falmer.

Department of Education and Science (1985). *Quality in Schools, Evaluation and Appraisal*. London, HMSO.

Day, C., Johnston D. and Whitaker P., (1988). *Appraisal and Professional Development in Primary Schools*. Milton Keynes, Open University Press.

Eraut, M. (1986). *Teacher Appraisal and/or Teacher Development*. Times Educational Supplement.

Everard, K. B. (1986). *Developing Management in Schools*. Lewes, Falmer.

Fenstermacher, G. and Berliner, D. C. (1985). *Determining the value of staff development'*, *The Elementary School Journal*, 85, 3.

Hewton, E. (1988). *School Focused Staff Development*. Lewes, Falmer.

Holly, M. L. and McLoughlin C. (1988). *Perspectives on Teacher Professional Development*. Lewes, Falmer.

Jasman, A. (1987). 'The Assessment of Progress and Achievement', in *Curriculum Studies in Education*, Suffolk, Driffield.

Nias, J. (1988). 'What it means to feel like a teacher – the subjective reality of primary school teaching' in J. Ozga, *School Work: Approaches to the Labour Process of Teaching*. Milton Keynes, Open University Press.

Suffolk Education Department (1985). *Those Having Torches: Teacher Appraisal – A Study*. Ipswich, Suffolk LEA.

Surrey Inspectorate (1984). *Professional Development*. Ewell, Surrey Media Centre.

Trethowan D. (1987). *Appraisal Target Setting*. London, Harper Education Press.

Turner, G. and Clift, P. (1988). *Studies in Teacher Appraisal*. Lewes, Falmer.

Whitaker, P. (1983). *The Primary Head*. London, Heinemann.

12

Staff development, local management of schools and governors

Derek Esp

The local management of schools introduced by the Education Reform Act will affect everyone working in schools. The focus will not be on budgets alone but on the effective delivery of the national curriculum and the survival of the school in a competitive education market place. For staff, the reforms herald a new era where the national curriculum, nationally determined attainment targets for pupils and teacher appraisal, will break into the traditional autonomy of the individual teacher in the classroom. Local management of schools (LMS) will give powers to schools that enable them to have greater control over the use of resources, both material and human. The local education authority will be there to monitor adherence to the national curriculum and the efficient and effective use of resources but the real powers, responsibilities and accountabilities are to be at the level of the institution. The school will be accountable to parents and will be subject to the ebb and flow of consumer demand within the social market. School governors will have responsibilities which cannot be shrugged off at the annual meeting with parents where they will be called to account. The Education Reform Act provides the framework within which schools can develop as relatively autonomous institutions.

The delegated budget

There is nothing new in the idea of the delegation of financial responsibility to schools. The White Paper following the 1944 Education Act (CMND 6523 of 1944) on the principles of the government of schools stated that within broad headings of the approved estimate, the governors should have the latitude to exercise reasonable, responsible discretion. Behind this statement lay the assumption that LEA schools and their governors should be capable of exercising responsibilities in the manner of independent schools. The 1986 Education Act gave governors increased powers which foreshadowed the Education Reform Act in 1988. That Act has increased the powers of governors substantially beyond those envisaged in 1944. They share responsibility with the LEA and the headteacher for ensuring that the school curriculum is broad and balanced, and meets the requirements of the national curriculum. They must ensure that courses for pupils of compulsory school age leading to public examinations are for approved qualifications and follow approved syllabuses. They also have to see that the law on collective worship and religious education is complied with and that information about the curriculum and pupils' achievements is available to parents and others. They will help the headteacher to decide what other subjects should be taught in the school. All this goes far beyond the delegation of a budget and enters the heartland of professional expertise. Governors will have increased powers over pupil admissions, and will be given full information about the costs of running their school and all other schools within the LEA. At the secondary schools and primary schools with more than 200 pupils governors will be responsible for managing the school budget.

LMS has far reaching effects for the management of schools. It affects all aspects of management and changes personnel and other management functions considerably. DES Circular 7/88 described the fundamental nature of the changes as follows:

Local management of schools represents a major challenge and a major opportunity for the education service. The introduction of needs-based formula funding and the delegation of financial and other managerial responsibilities to governing bodies are key elements in the Government's overall policy to improve the quality of teaching and learning in schools. Local management is concerned with far more than budgeting and accounting procedures. Effective schemes of local management will enable governing bodies and head teachers to plan their use of resources, including the most valuable resource, their staff to maximum effect. They will be establishing their own budget needs and priorities and will need to be more responsive to their clients: parents, pupils, the local community and employers.

(DES, 1988 p. 3, para. 9)

This declaration of intent makes clear the purpose of LMS as a major piece of social engineering. Within the national and local framework provided the governing body will control the running of a school within its delegated budget. The head and the governors will have freedom to deploy resources according to their own educational needs and priorities. Governing bodies will be able to delegate management of schools' budgets to the headteacher and there is provision for the establishment of committees by governing bodies, including non-governors as well as governors, and the delegation of functions such as finance or staffing. This would be within a framework set out by the full governing body. The aim is for LEAs to hold on to not more than 10 per cent of the school's budget initially. This is then to be reduced to 7 per cent once schemes are established. This gives school governors control over most of their school's budget.

Schools will be exercising their new responsibilities in the context of an open market where parents will be able to shop around. This will encourage schools to develop marketing policies and to become more readily responsive to consumer pressures. Schools below the mandatory size for delegated budgets will demand to be put on the same footing as LMS schools. All teachers and support staff will be working in this new context. Indeed, some of them will be working for other new categories of relatively autonomous schools i.e. grant-maintained schools and city technology colleges. All these changes require a fundamental review of management structures and styles, consultation, information and other procedures in schools. How will staff and governors respond?

Teachers and governors have understandable reservations about the pace of change and the volume of work involved. The greater accountability that comes with relative autonomy is not universally welcomed. Teachers are fearful of the local determination of personnel policies and practices; some heads are apprehensive about what they see as additional responsibilities and administrative burdens and governors are also apprehensively seeking survival training. A flood of training materials is now on the market in response to the anxiety abroad. It is not enough to help the head, the governor, the teacher governor, the head of department or the parent governor to understand their own role. There is a need for mutual understanding and skilled collaborative working if the relatively autonomous school is to release and use the energies, expertise and dynamism necessary to meet the challenge. In order to do this it is essential to understand something more of the changes taking place and the likely opportunities and difficulties. Studies of innovation in schools have confirmed that those schools that look at opportunities rather than at problems are most likely to succeed in the introduction and implementation of new initiatives. It is an essential task to create and nurture a positive climate and the high expectations that are the characteristics of effective schools.

It is people in schools who will implement the necessary legislative changes. Hence the need to encourage a positive response to change. Change facilitators at national or local levels sometimes assume that legislation is sufficient to deliver the change. This is not the case. School improvement studies show that change requires a great deal of groundwork within the institution and that people often require a great deal of time to modify their approaches or attitudes. Work done by 15 countries engaged in the OECD International School Improvement Project revealed something of the complexity facing national and local authorities when they attempt large scale reforms. For example, advice is given to national authorities on the staff development programmes for headteachers. Policies for the development of school leaders focused on improvement should take account of the key requirements for effective development programmes. In brief they are:

- an adequate period of time for learning
- scope for reflective learning
- a focus on concrete situations
- application of learning in collaboration with colleagues.

These requirements suggest that development programmes must be closely related to the actual work and functioning of the school; that they need to extend over a considerable period of time; that preparation and follow up are crucially important; that they should foster a team development approach by involving as many other members of the school's personnel as is feasible; that they should make considerable use of experience-based methods (such as peer consultation, investigative school-based projects, job exchanges and so on) rather than simply relying on formal courses (Stego *et al.*, 1987).

Development planning and staff development

It is evident that effective development programmes for staff and governors can best take place when authorities, i.e. LEAs, churches, DES, City Technology College Trust or Maintained Schools Trust, plan and are enabled to fund the training needs determined by national priorities and programmes. This requires an understanding of the effort required at school level to deliver the desired improvements. A systematic and positive system of external monitoring has to be in place. The school will have to establish a school development plan which incorporates the development of curriculum content; teaching and learning strategies; the training and development needs of staff and governors and marketing plans, including positive dialogue with local community interests and parents. The existence of a school policy framework can serve to stimulate a regular review of development and training needs and can be a powerful vehicle for transmitting information to the bodies providing support at local and national level. A realistic assessment of needs in the school development plan and an effective external monitoring of the effectiveness of training provision by HMI, local advisers and others contracted to provide a monitoring service may help to reinforce a more realistic view of the training required to improve and maintain standards.

Positive attitudes do not develop without systematic planning and evaluation of the school's work. The new responsibilities require that the development of the school is reviewed systematically. Staff development must be seen in the context of the school development plan which addresses educational priorities for development, action plans and a systematic review. The whole process involves an active partnership between school staff and governors. The Department of Education and Science school development plans project has provided useful guidelines for governors, headteachers and teachers. Development planning encourages governors and teachers to answer four basic questions. Where is the school now? What changes do we need to make? How shall we manage these changes over time? How shall we know whether our management change has been successful? As the DES booklet says, 'The distinctive feature of a development plan (DP) is that it brings together, in an overall plan, national and LEA policies and initiatives. The school's aims and values, its existing achievements and its needs for development (Hargreaves *et al.*, 1989, p. 4). The processes in development described in the DES guidelines include an annual audit of the school curriculum and resources. INSET and staff development planning are seen as an essential component of the school development plan, not least because it is essential to match the needs of the school with the professional development of teachers.

Staff development, set in the context of the school development plan, is an essential requirement for success, especially where a number of key national initiatives are being attempted simultaneously. Every member of staff and every governor will be required to make fundamental changes in their role and expectations. School management will have to review management styles, especially in schools which have been weak in the field of consultation and co-operative working. The hoped for new model army of the school governors will come fresh but unprepared for the complexities of encouraging school improvement. People will need time to develop confidence in exercising their new roles if the effect of all these changes is to lead to improved teaching and learning at the chalk face.

Staff and governors will need more than an information briefing or training in specific skills through survival packs. The extent of the problem can be seen in the difficulties facing change facilitators even where more limited changes are attempted. Advisory teachers can help to develop new approaches in the classroom but even here the improvement may disappear with the advisory teacher at the end of the project. This will happen where teachers have not fully accepted or felt ownership of the innovation. This also happened in LEA schools which were given locally managed budgets before the implementation of the Education Reform Act. Even in the relatively successful pilot schemes there was, sometimes, little real involvement of staff and governors. In Lincolnshire one of the Project Seven schools which pioneered the delegation of budgets from 1983 did so largely through the enthusiasm and commitment of the head. There was evidence that senior teaching staff and the governors were not greatly involved. The subsequent delegation scheme for all secondary schools has attempted to put much greater emphasis on the training required through all phases of the innovation. In the description of a revised scheme of delegation

The principal aim for the local management of the schools is to create the climate and mechanisms which allow the school to plan and implement the most effective use of the available resources for the maximum benefit of pupils.

The first objective is to create the circumstances where elected members, chief officers, teachers and governors will have the ability to create a climate of ownership and hence participation in the management of schools. The changes required permeate all aspects of the work of the LEA as well as all paid and voluntary participants at school level.

The effective management styles and conditions observed in the 'good school' are no different after the Education Reform Act than they were before its arrival. However, a period of rapid and extensive innovations puts strains on any institution and reveals the existing strengths and weaknesses very rapidly. Management at school level is now in the front line of the national campaign to improve standards and make the education system more responsive to consumer demand. On the face of it schools are being asked to cope with massive changes at a time when the interventionary powers of the LEA are being reduced. LEAs will experience withdrawal symptoms, particularly where they have taken a large number of decisions on behalf of schools and have kept them closely protected and supported. The schools which have done some growing up through pilot local management schemes may be better prepared than those which have been kept more dependent on the LEA. Whatever their state of readiness there is no doubt that all schools will seek, and will require, considerable support and advice, even when they achieve successful planning, staff development and a real partnership between teachers and governors.

The role of governors

The Education Reform Act still gives the LEA an important role in co-ordinating, supporting and stimulating effective staff development through the LEA training grant scheme. Similarly, programmes such as TVEI extension schemes will also provide resources and support for staff development. Central government funding will also be channelled through LEAs for governor training, in addition to the many national initiatives to develop support materials. Many LEA staff development strategies and the TVEI extension structures will continue to provide mutual support and co-operation networks. The continuing need of schools to belong to a network for mutual help and support in the field of staff development is seen also in the new category of grant maintained school. The grant-maintained schools are already aware of the need to secure training and other support. The growing network of city technology colleges is also seeking to create a new structure of mutual support where each college will develop training provision, an aspect of curriculum innovation or other pioneering work on behalf of all the CTCs. All of this indicates the need for relatively autonomous schools to be supported and stimulated by some kind of support system. The International School Improvement Project observed that a supportive external system was vital for school leaders. When introducing large-scale educational reforms aimed at improvement, school systems should ensure that adequate training, support and resources are given to school leaders to enable them to lead the implementation of the changes within their schools. School systems should consider how well equipped external support agencies are for providing help (Stego *et al.*, 1987).

Training is an important aspect of staff and governor development. The pattern of training provided in the school for staff and governors will need to bring everyone along together as innovations are introduced and implemented. For example, an attempt to introduce supported self-study approaches in school may be hampered if governors are not fully aware of what is happening. Thus problems can arise over issues such as the reason for two pupils getting different homework! It will not be enough to depend upon old patterns of training provision even where they existed. New governors are coming into schools at a time when pressures are greatest. Governing bodies have new powers, if they want to take them up, which were not there before, and this brings burdens of work which were not there before. New governors are therefore having to learn a job which is new to them, and which is changing even while they try to learn it (Eiles, 1989). This implies the need for an integrated training and development programme which brings staff and governors together for briefing, discussion and a core of common training. In addition some staff and governors will require specific skills. In a recent survey of teacher governors items identified for training in rank order included local financial management, the responsibilities of teacher governors, the legal position of teacher governors, interview techniques, meetings procedure, consultation and reporting back, report writing and public speaking (Richardson, 1989). It is clear that everyone cannot do everything however. Some governors and staff will 'major' in staff recruitment techniques, for example. The decisions about who does what will be better made if the school has a clear framework of management and policy planning where all staff and all governors understand the whole management structure and where there are systematic arrangements for staff and governors to meet in order to review together the school's progress in the light of the school development plan.

There will be considerable training requirements for the senior managers in the school. Again, this should not run ahead of the training of the core of the school governing body engaged in policy decisions and major resource decisions. Behind the Education Reform Act and its recommendations is the model of the independent school where management might be concentrated in a small high-powered governing body with the major role going to the head and the chairman of governors, backed up by a competent bursar who will, in some schools, report directly to the chairman. In the independent sector the composition of the governing body can be planned without the constraints of legislation. Even so the principles of governor recruitment are a good guideline for the maintained school sector. Ideally the members of a governing body should between them be able to speak with knowledge and experience on the whole range of matters which are likely to come before them for decision. The care taken in governor selection will influence the scope and content of training required. The same comment applies to the experience of senior members of the school staff. Expertise, commitment and continuity are required and the experience required of governors may include education, law, finance, business, central and local government and buildings.

The LEA school moving into LMS does not have to raise fees but it does have major management responsibilities. In terms of complying with the national curriculum, the inability to expel pupils and the need to relate to the varied demands of parents and a community on its doorstep the LEA school has a management task as great as that of the independent school. However, it does not have such complete control over the appointment of its governors. It could be a sensible strategy, therefore, to enable the senior staff of the school and a core of governors to undertake some management training together in joint staff and governor working parties on curriculum, resources, buildings and other aspects of the school development plan. Such joint training can help staff and governors to achieve mutual understanding and support. The school will also gain from a pooling of experience as part of the training and development process. In this framework the large supply of training materials can be used sensibly and effectively beyond the survival kit phase of staff and governor training.

The school will need to develop a unified approach to the LEA when negotiating its budget requirements, bidding for special funds or representing its needs for training and other support services. Within the community, the school will be most effective where staff and governors together can engage in positive discussion of the school's progress and performance with parents and others.

There has always been benefit to the school where the head and the chair of governors have met regularly and have developed a positive relationship. As a result of the introduction of LMS it is even more vital than ever that, as in the independent school, the head and the chair develop a special rapport. Leadership on the part of the chairman is especially important, as is the sympathetic rapport with the head. The training of governors must form an integral part of the overall planning for staff development in the school. The ability of the school to create effective staff development policies and training will affect the quality and relevance of governor training. There are aspects of governor training that are common to all schools. The ongoing development of the knowledge and skills of governors must also be related to the school's own stage of development and priorities.

The management of professional development

The review of TVEI-related training by Hall and Oldroyd (1988) provides guidance on the management of professional development and in-service training. The same principles apply to governor training and joint staff/governor training initiatives. The objectives of a school staff development programme are outlined and many of these objectives apply to governor training, e.g. to increase knowledge of, and participation in, the school community; to enable participation with fellow professionals; to assist people to participate in the planning of the school curriculum; to provide a caring environment in which praise and encouragement flourish; to specify and evaluate roles and responsibilities; to give each governor the right to an annual governor development discussion; and to keep governors up to date with educational developments. Within the context of a school staff development plan it will be easy to identify common elements of training and those aspects of training that need to be provided separately for all governors; some governors or individual governors with key roles (e.g. chairs of working parties and special initiatives). All this implies that the school has already developed a systematic assessment of individual and institutional needs aimed at a balanced programme of personal/career and staff development across the whole organization. Such a school will have designated someone to be the deputy head (staff development), the staff development officer, the INSET co-ordinator, the staff development co-ordinator or the professional tutor. In the very small school the role will be exercised by the master of all trades – the headteacher! Many larger schools will have established a staff development INSET panel. Once a year it would be useful for this panel to meet with governors to discuss governor training needs and useful areas where some or all governors could participate in the staff INSET programme. This will bring the training of governors into the cyclical model of curriculum and staff development inherent in the school development plan.

An effective programme of training for governors will have regard to awareness raising, identification of training needs, and other aspects which form part of an effective staff development programme. External advice will be needed and this can be provided by national organizations concerned with governor briefing and training, the staff of the LEA and other external advisers e.g. providers in of school based INSET in higher education. Governors, like teachers, need more than an initial impressive burst of training activity. They need continuing support and advice, access to regular information and opportunities to develop their competence. There are various ways in which this might be achieved. For some years schools have provided staff presentations to governors on areas of work, new developments and key problem areas. Service on a standing sub-committee or on an *ad hoc* joint working party with teaching staff is a good means of providing development opportunities to governors. Governors should receive a regular newsletter, perhaps one of those provided nationally for governors. Individual governors may come with special expertise that can be tapped for the benefit of governors and staff. A study group of governors and staff can work together to produce a short report on the latest LEA circular or national initiative requiring a school response. A governor can attend an external course and prepare a report for the full governing body. Special attention needs to be paid to the training of key governors who may need opportunities to meet people, discuss working practices (e.g. interviewing of staff) with another school or with technical experts, and to develop special skills such as chairing meetings or dealing with the press. Obviously governors will have limited time to spare and training programmes must be selective and realistic in terms of time required of governors. This is another good reason for making part of every governors' meeting a training event.

The school, and the governing body will benefit from a regularly available 'critical friend'. A number of LEAs have provided a liaison officer who attends governing bodies to give help and advice. In addition the school management team and the governors might gain great benefit from some outside help in terms of an external change agent to help them to develop or review their training programme. Such help might come from the LEA or from another external source of help. Neighbouring schools, or schools within a consortium, 'family grouping' or other LEA networks might develop joint training opportunities. Two neighbouring schools and governing bodies may pair to help each other. Even within the market economy of the education service the tendency of schools to get together co-operatively will still be encouraged by LEAs, by various nationally funded projects and by the basic common sense of sharing and spreading best practice to the benefit of the community. The best endowed establishments should be encouraged to share their facilities for training with other schools. This kind of development may well occur across the great divide between LEA-maintained, DES-maintained and independent schools.

It is necessary to remember that governors bring great experience of life with them. Some training will be essential: some will be desirable for the added value it can give to the individual governor and the school. Any training activity for governors, like the school development plan, the staff development plan, the curriculum development plan, the annual meeting with parents, the review of results and performance indicators must all have one end in view: the improvement and enhancement of the quality of teaching and learning in the classroom. Training programmes and planning processes that divert energies unduly from the prime purpose of the school must be avoided. All these activities must be objectively appraised in terms of what they are delivering in terms of better policies, better management decisions, better staff and governor relationships and better educational outcomes.

The local management of schools provides a new context in which the management style and the structures of the school can be reshaped to allow for real participation in discussion of priorities by staff and governors. Team building will include the positive creation of joint staff and governor working groups. These will provide opportunities for development and mutual support. Staff and governor training must be considered together within the overall mission statement, aims and objectives and priorities articulated in the school development plan. In this context best use can be made of the externally provided funds and materials for staff development and governor training. Quite properly the emergency training packs have started where people are and in many cases have been aimed specifically at heads or governors. Other initiatives have encouraged schools to use materials in ways which will build up the confidence and competence of staff and governors together. Schools will survive and succeed in the context of the social market where staff (teaching and non-teaching) and governors are enabled to develop effective teamwork which mobilizes the total 'firepower' of the school.

References

Department of Education and Science (1988). *Education Reform Act: Local Management of Schools*, Circular 7/88. London, HMSO.

Eiles, C. (1989). 'The new governing class', *Education* Journal, 20 January 1989, 155. London, Longman.

Governing Bodies Association and Girls' Schools Association (1988). *Guidelines for Governors*, Document 208. London.

Hall, V. and Oldroyd, D. (1988). *Managing Professional Development and INSET: a handbook for schools and colleges*. National Development Centre for School Management Training. Bristol.

Hargreaves, D., Hopkins, D., Leask, M., Connolly, J. and Robinson, P. (1989). *Planning for School Development*. London, Department of Education and Science.

Independent Schools Joint Committee (undated). 'The governing and financing of independent schools', A joint Committee working paper. London.

Lincolnshire County Council/BIS Systems (1988). *LMS Handbook*. Lincoln, LCC.

Ministry of Education (1944). Government White Paper, 'The principles of government for schools', Cmnd 6523. London, Ministry of Education.

Richardson, R. (1989). 'The lone rangers', *Education* Journal, 20 January 1989, 50. London, Longman.

Stego, N. E., Gielen, K., Glatter, R. and Hord, S. M. (1987). *The Role of the School Leader in School Improvement*. An International School Improvement Project publication from OECD. ACCO Leuven/Amersfoort.

Index

ACAS, 165
accountability, 47, 50, 56, 144, 160, 165, 176, 178
Ackoff, R. L., 159
action research, 89, 95–6
  see also school-based model (Branston approach)
advisers
  increased pressure on, 32
  LEA (role/functions), 50–52
  recruitment of, 52–3
  role, 55–6
  role in staff development, 58–60
  training, 53–5
Advisory, Conciliation and Arbitration Service, 165
Advisory Committee on the Supply and Training of Teachers, 68, 77, 111
advisory and inspection service (of Nottinghamshire), 39–47 *passim*
advisory service (development), 50
advisory service (role), 38
  developmental aspect of formal inspections, 39–41
  evaluation of inspectors, 46–7
  mode of operation (changing), 41–5
  prospect for the future, 47–8
advisory teacher (staff development role), 49, 84, 180
  development of advisory service, 50
  innovation and staff development (strategies), 56–8

LEA adviser (role/functions), 50–52
  management implications, 60–61
  recruitment of advisers, 52–3
  role, 55–6
  role in staff development, 56–9
  summary and conclusion, 61–2
  training, 53–5
advisory teams (role), 129, 131
aims statement, 18, 19
ambiguity approach (management), 117, 119–20
Anderson, S., 30
Andrews, S. E., 57
anticipatory socialization, 6
appraisal (staff development role)
  alternatives, 166–7
  emerging issues, 174–5
  managing aspects of staff development, 168–74
  relationship between appraisal and staff development, 164–6
  school culture, 167–8
apprenticeship model, 5–6, 9, 21
assessment procedures, 134–5
Association of Colleges of Further and Higher Education, 110, 113
Association of Principals of Technical Institutions, 110, 113
Association for Science Education, 85
attainment targets, 135, 176
Audit Commission, 51, 57, 61
autonomy, 155, 159, 160, 178
award-linkage, 97, 100

Baron, B., 113
Bell, L., 168
Benney, M., 141
Berliner, D. C., 165
Better Schools (DES), 14, 68, 138
Billings, D. E., 4, 114
Birch, P. A., 60
Birnbaum, I., 50
Blackie, J., 50
Bolam, R., 50–57 *passim*, 77, 137, 138
Bradley, J., 114, 167
Branston approach
  background and rationale, 88–92
  1st year, 92–6
  2nd year, 100–103
  3rd year, 103–4
  teachers as experts, 104–8
Bridges, D., 141
Brown, G., 139
Burgess, Robert, 36
Burnham scale, 55
Bush, T., 57, 117, 119

Caldwell, B. J., 160
Callaghan, James, 24
career development, 135–6
Centre for Adviser and Inspector
    Development, 54
Centre for Performing Arts, 50, 59
Certificate of Pre-Vocational Education,
    96
Chesson, R., 114
city technology colleges, 178,.179, 181–2
Classroom Action Research Network
    conference, 95–6
classroom behaviour analysis, 89, 95
classroom observation, 45, 169, 172–3
Clift, P., 164, 165, 170, 175
clustering, 84, 87, 130
co-learning, collegiality of, 165
co-operative inspection, 43–5
co-operative teaching, 84
co-ordinator
  county, 67, 72, 73, 74, 75
  in-service, 67, 70, 72
collaborative school cultures, 152–5,
    158–61, 174–5
collegiality of group learning and
    co-learning, 165
Collins, G., 54
community service (planning), 32–3
confidentiality, 173
Conservative government, 138

consultant (knowledge linkage role), 56,
    59
consumer choice, 176, 178, 181
continuity of teaching, 150
costs of appraisal, 174
county co-ordinator, 67, 72, 73, 74, 75
county evaluator, 67, 71–2, 73–5, 77
course-based model, 7–10, 21
courses, short, 68
Cowan, B., 16–17
criteria for evaluation, 18, 20
cross-phase clustering, 87
Culbertson, J., 117
cultures, school, 152–61, 167–8, 174–5
curriculum
  Branston approach, 89, 94–6, 103–8
  descriptions group, 89, 94–6, 103
  development, 83–4, 98–9
  of learning group, 104, 107
  mapping, 107
  see also national curriculum

Day, Chris, 93–4, 99–100, 138, 144, 151,
    173
Dean, J., 52–8 *passim*, 60
defender (knowledge linkage role), 56
delegated budget, 176–9, 180–81
democratic approach, 117, 119, 153
Denzin, N. K., 141
Derbyshire project, 137–61
DES, 5, 50, 55, 141, 177, 180
  Better Schools, 14, 68, 138
  *Education (School Teachers' Pay and
    Conditions of Employment) Order*,
    15
  Education in Schools, 13, 68
  further education staff development,
    111, 116
  GRIST initiative, 67–73, 75–8
  In-Service Training Grant Scheme,
    13–14
  James Report, 11, 12, 68, 77, 78
  LEATGS, 14–16, 67–71, 116, 126, 139,
    165–6
  Quality in Schools, 165
  Teaching Quality, 138
  Warwickshire LEA and, 26, 27, 31–2,
    36
deskilling, 139
development planning, 179–81
direction problem (primary project),
    150
Drummond, 165

Education (School Teachers' Pay and
    Conditions of Employment) Order,
    15
Education Act (1944), 50, 176–7
Education Act (1986), 138
Education Reform Act (1988), 86, 94,
    117, 138
    advisory service (role), 38, 42
    advisory teacher (role), 50, 54
    governors (role), 129, 133
    local management of schools, 18, 35,
        50, 176–7, 180, 181, 182
Education in Schools (DES), 13, 68
education support grants, 24, 27, 61–2
Educational Staff Development (Main),
    114
electro-acoustic music, 49, 57, 58–60
enhancement courses, 7, 8
Eraut, M., 141, 161, 165
evaluation
    of Branston approach, 93–4
    criteria for, 18, 20
    initiatives, 35–7
    of INSET, 85–7
    of inspectors, 46–7
    of primary school project, 140–41
    in school culture, 167
evaluation and monitoring, 34–5
    GRIST initiative, 74–5
    school-centred staff development,
        125–36
Everard, K. B., 173
examinations, 112, 177
    GCSE, 32, 77, 96, 102, 104
'excellent company' research, 138
experience-based methods, 179
'experience capital', 55
experts, teachers as, *see* school-based
    model (Branston approach)

Fernstermacher, G., 165
finance, 150
    delegated budget, 176–9
    monitoring and, 31–2
    see also funding; grants
Finn, C. E., 159
Fiske, P. A., 52
formal approach (management), 117,
    119
formula funding, 47, 177
Fullan, M., 151
funding, 156
    in Branston approach, 97–8

formula funding, 47, 177
primary school INSET, 81–2
primary school project, 141–2, 143
school-centred staff development, 128
see also grants
further education, 110–20

GCSE, 32, 77, 96, 102, 104
Gentle, K., 53
Georgiades, N. J., 8
Glatter, R., 114, 117
governors, 47
    role, 129, 131, 176–8, 180–83
    training, 183, 184–6
grant-maintained schools, 178, 179, 181
grant-related in-service training, 26–9,
    31, 34–6, 110, 115–17, 128
grant-related in-service training
    (management of), 67–9
    findings, 71–6
    implications, 76–8
    methodology, 70–71
*Grant Related In-Service Training in
    Warwickshire*, 26–9, 33, 35
grants
    education support, 24, 27, 61–2
    LEATGS, *see* local education authority
        training grant scheme
Gray, H. L., 114
Greenfield, B., 117
GRIST, *see* grant related in-service
    training; grant related in service
    training (management of)
group approaches (professional
    development), 3
    school-based model, 10–11, 13
    school-focused model, 11–12, 13
group learning, 165
guidelines for review and internal
    development of schools (GRIDS),
    152–3

Haag, D., 117
Hall, V., 69, 184
Harding, A., 114
Hargreaves, D., 180
Havelock, R. G., 56, 58
Haycock Report (1975), 111
headteacher, 127, 135
    appraisal and (role), 167–8, 170, 173
    in inspection, 44–8 *passim*
    primary school project, 143
Henderson, E. S., 7, 11, 68, 76

Henning, A., 30
hero-innovators, 8
Hewton, E., 10, 165, 166, 174
HMI, 139, 144
Holly, P. J., 160
Holmes, B., 57
Hopkins, David, 151, 160, 161
Howarth, G., 51
Hoyle, E., 11, 59
Hughes, E. C., 141
Hughes, M., 118
human resource management, 118

in-service co-ordinator, 67, 70, 72
in-service training
    activity (types), 145–7
    advisory teachers (role), 49, 51–2,
        54–62
    days, 16–17, 33, 104–5
    for enhancement, 7, 8
    grant related, *see* grant related
        in-service training
    policy-oriented, 155
    professional development through,
        7–10
    promoting systematic planning, 72–3
    remedial, 7, 8
    school-based model, *see* school-based
        model (Branston approach)
    school-focused model, 11–13, 21,
        80–87
    school determination of, 126–30
    school development approach, 12–18
    for school improvement, 138–40
    top-up courses, 7, 8
    Warwickshire scheme, 23–37 *passim*
    see also INSET needs and
        programmes; INSET in primary
        schools
In-Service Training Grant Scheme, The
    (DES) 13–14
individual approaches (professional
    development), 3
    apprenticeship model, 5–6, 9, 21
    course-based model, 7–10, 21
individual development, 96–100
individual improvement, 155–8
individualized learning, 165
industrial action, 59–60, 88, 89
Industrial Training Boards, 111
information, 33–4, 102–3, 171–2
information technology, 55, 58
initial training, 7, 111

innovation, 178
    school-focused model, 11–12
    strategies, 54, 56–8
innovator (knowledge linkage role),
    56–7, 58
innovators, hero, 8
INSET needs and programmes
    funding, 81–2
    identifying needs, 82–3
    modes of delivery, 83–4
INSET in primary schools, 80
    evaluation of INSET, 85–7
    needs and programmes 81–4
    pilot project, 137–61
    providers of INSET, 84–5
inspection
    advisory and inspection service, 39–47
        passim
    cooperative, 43–5
    evaluation of, 46–7
    formal (developmental aspect), 39–41
    partnership in, 43–5
inspectors, 32, 40–41
interaction, 95
International School Improvement
    Project, 161, 178, 182
interviews
    appraisal, 169, 170, 173, 174
    cooperative inspection, 45
    GRIST management, 67–8, 70–71
    primary school project, 140–41, 144
'inverted pyramid' approach, 158–9
Isaacs, S., 37
isolation, 149

James Report (1972), 11–12, 68, 77, 78
Johnston, D., 173
Joseph, Sir Keith, 24, 110
Joyce, Bruce, 159

Kendall, P. L., 141
Kennedy, K., 151, 152
Kirkman, 54
knowledge linkage roles, 56–9
Kuhn, M. H., 140

Labour government, 138
Lambert, K., 60
launch pack (Branston approach), 89–92
Laycock, Paul, 95
leader (knowledge linkage role), 56–7,
    58
learn, readiness to, 151, 181

learning for learning group, 94–5, 103
Letch, R., 52
Leverhulme Trust, 165
Lewis, J. A., 53, 56
Lincolnshire, 180
link inspector, 40
local education authorities, 5
    advisers (role/functions), 50–52
    monitoring by, 130–32
    see also Derbyshire project;
        Nottinghamshire (advisory service);
        Warwickshire (management of
        professional development)
local education authority training grant
    scheme, 52, 80, 98, 120, 164, 181
    Derbyshire, 137–9, 143
    DES circular, 14–16, 67–71, 116, 126,
        139, 165–6
    Warwickshire, 28, 30–31, 36
local management of schools, 18, 35, 47,
    183
    advisory teacher (role), 50, 61
    delegated budget, 176–9
    development planning and staff
        development, 179–81
    teacher as expert, 97–9, 105

Main, Alex, 114
main professional grade teachers, 45
management, 139
    approach (further education), 113,
        117–20
    implications (staff development),
        60–61
    by objectives, 113
    of professional development, 184–6
    skills, 118–19, 139
    styles, 180, 181
    teachers (effective), 73
    see also local management of schools
Manpower Services Commission, 24, 25,
    26, 111
manufacturing industries, 111
March, J. G., 118
Matthews, P., 52
Merson, Martin, 35
Merton, R. K., 141
modular curriculum, 96
monitoring, 38, 39, 179
    finance and, 31–2
    LEA implications, 130–32
monitoring and evaluation, 34–5
    GRIST initiative, 74–5

school-centred development 125–36
morale, needs and, 166–7
Moreland, Dr Neil, 35–6
motivation, 149, 168, 170, 173
music, electro-acoustic, 49, 57–60 *passim*
mutual support, 181, 183, 186

National Association of Inspectors and
    Educational Advisers, 54
National Committee on Vocational
    Qualifications, 112
national curriculum, 19, 35, 86–7, 135
    advisory service and, 38, 47, 48
    advisory teachers and, 52, 61–2
    local management of schools and, 176,
        177, 183
    teacher empowerment, 155, 157
    teachers as experts, 105, 107
national priority areas, 73–4, 116
needs, morale and, 166–7
Nias, Jennifer, 160, 175
'notional planning allocation', 143
Nottingham University, 137, 140
Nottinghamshire (advisory service),
    39–48

OECD, 161, 178
Oldroyd, D., 69, 184
Olsen, M., 30
Open University, 55
opportunity costs (of appraisal), 174
oral evaluation, 86
organizational development, 114, 115
organizational skills, 172
Owen, R. G., 77

part-time staff, 33, 150
partnerships
    approach, 114, 180
    in inspections, 43–5
pastoral care, 54, 96, 105–6
Patterson, C., 151
Peters, T. J., 138
phase inspector, 40, 41
Phillimore, L., 8
Piper, D., 114
planning
    coherent (development), 30–34
    development, 179–81
    framework (overall), 83
    for the future, 29
    of INSET, 72–3
    skills, 172

policy-based model, 12–18, 21
policy-oriented in-service, 155
political approach (management), 117, 119
pop music, 49, 57–60 *passim*
Poster, C., 138
pre-vocational education, 89, 96
preparation (for appraisal), 169
primary schools, INSET in, 80–87
primary schools (promoting
    professional development), 137
  collaboration, culture of, 158–61
  in-service for school improvement,
      138–40
  professional development, 161
  project, 140–44
  quality (issues), 145–52
  teacher empowerment, 152–8
Primary Science Review, 85
probationary year, 38
problem-seeking, 167
process-oriented activity, 102
product-oriented activity, 102
professional development
  control of, 105–6
  management of, 184–6
  promoting (primary schools), 137–61
  purpose of, 23–4
  school policy and, 96–100
professional development (LEA
    management of)
  coherent planning, 30–34
  evaluation initiative, 35–7
  GRIST and Thomas Report, 26–9
  initiatives, 24
  LEA (Warwickshire), 25
  planning for the future, 29
  purpose of professional development,
      23–4
  quality, evaluation and monitoring,
      34–5
  secondments, 29–30
  TRIST in Warwickshire, 25–6
professional development (in 1990s)
  appraisal (role), 164–75
  monitoring and evaluating
    school-centred staff development,
      125–36
  pilot project, 137–61
  local management of schools, 176–86
professional development in schools
  GRIST initiative, 67–78
  INSET in primary schools, 80–87
  school-based, 88–108

staff development in further
    education, 110–20
professional development of teachers
  conclusions, 20–21
  group approach, 3, 10–12
  individual approach, 3, 5–10
  professional development, 4–5
  school development approach, 3,
      12–18
  some implications for schools,
      18–20
professional development of teachers
    (supporting)
  advisory service (role), 38–48
  advisory teacher (role), 49–62
  approaches, 3–21
  management in a LEA, 23–37
professionalism, 14, 139, 174
  teachers as experts, 88–108
providers of INSET, 84–5
public relations policy, 45
pupils, 134–5
  -teacher interaction, 95
  -teacher ratio, 101
Purkey, S. C., 158

qualifications, 177
  see also examinations
quality
  evaluation and monitoring, 34–5, 48
  school-centred development,
      145–52
Quality in Schools (DES), 165

readiness (to learn), 151, 181
Reading Association, 85
recommendations (recording), 40
recruitment of advisers, 52–3
Reid, K., 160
remedial courses, 7, 8
reporting process (inspection), 41
researcher, teacher as, 88–108
resources, 15, 16
  allocation (development plan), 18–20
  Branston approach, 94, 98–9
  devolution of (Derbyshire), 141–2
response sheet (Branston launch pack),
    90–92, 103
Rickaby, Dave, 96
Ridger, M. L., 23
role models, 6
Rosenholtz, S. J., 159
Routledge, M. D., 77

Rubin, L., 151
Ruddock, J., 151–2

sabbatical leave, 68
Sanday, A. P., 60
Santinelli, P., 77
Saunders, M., 68
Sayers, S., 114
school(s)
    -centred development, 145–52
    clustering, 84, 87, 130
    culture, 152–61, 167–8, 174–5
    determination (of INSET), 126–30
    development approach, 3, 12–18, 21
    development plans, 18–20, 127–8
    effects of staff development, 133–5
    grant-maintained, 178, 179, 181
    implications of professional
        development, 18–20
    improvement, 138–40, 155–8
    leader (role), 179, 182
    leavers, 102
    local management, see local
        management of schools
    see also primary schools
school-based model (Branston
        approach), 10–11, 13, 21, 87
    background and rationale, 88–92
    1st year, 92–6
    2nd year, 100–103
    3rd year, 103–4
    professional development and school
        policy, 96–100
    teacher as expert, 104–8
school-centred staff development
        (monitoring and evaluating), 125
    career development, 135–6
    effects on school, 133–5
    LEA monitoring, 130–32
    in-service training, 126–30
    reflection, preparation and action,
        136
school-focused model, 11–13, 21
    in primary school, 80–87
school policy, professional development
        and, 96–100
secondments, 8, 78
    changing nature, 25, 27, 29–30
self-appraisal, 45
self-audit, 18, 19
self-development, 146
self-evaluation, 86, 160–61, 170, 175
self-regulation, 114

service industries, 111
Shuttleworth, Kay, 50
Silverleaf, J., 114
skills, 111, 112, 172
    managerial, 118–19, 139
Smith, M. S., 158
social engineering, 177
socialization, anticipatory, 6
Soulbury Committee, 62
Soulbury scale, 55
Southworth, G., 160
Spinks, J. M., 160
staff development, 4
    development planning and, 179–81
    effects (on school), 133–5
    in further education, 110–20
    management systems (SDMS), 30
    managing aspects of, 168–74
    role of advisory teacher, 58–60
    role of appraisal, 164–75
    school-centred, 125–36
    strategies, 56–8
staff development (governors and LMS)
    delegated budget, 176–9
    development planning, 179–81
    governors (role), 181–3
    governors (training), 184–6
Stego, N. E., 179, 182
Stillman, A., 49
subjective approach (management), 117,
    119
Suffolk project (1985), 174
supply cover, 33, 84, 143–4, 145
Surrey Inspectorate, 173

target outcomes, 18, 19–20
task-led approach, 13
Task Group on Assessment and Testing
    report, 98
Taylor, W., 4, 117
Teacher Education and Training
    (James Report), 11, 12, 68, 77,
    78
teachers
    advisory, see advisory teacher (staff
        development role)
    career development, 135–6
    empowerment (conditions for),
        152–8
    exchange, 84
    as experts, 88–108
    as governors, 182
    professional development, 137–61

teachers – *cont.*
  -pupil interaction, 95
  -pupil ratio, 101
  see also headteacher
teaching
  changes in, 133–4
  continuity of, 150
  team approach, 5, 167–8, 179
Teaching Quality (DES), 138
team-teaching, 5, 167–8, 179
team leaders (Branston approach), 92–3,
  94
technical and vocational initiative (TVEI),
  112
  extension schemes, 181
  TRIST, 24–7, 31, 34–5, 68
tertiary sector (growth), 112
Thomas, Norman, 27, 35, 36
Thomas Report (1988), 26–9, 33, 35
time (directed), 148–9, 157
Tolley, Dr G., 110
Tomlinson, John, 35
top-up courses, 7, 8
trainer (knowledge linkage role), 56–7,
  59
trainers (need for), 33
training
  of advisers, 53–6
  days, 16–17, 33, 104–5
  of governors, 183, 184–6
  governors' role, 181–3
  in-service, *see* in-service training
  initial, 7, 111
  national priority areas, 73–4
  support grant, 68–9
*Training Teachers for Educational
  Management in Further and Adult
  Education* (ACSTT), 111
TRIST, 24, 25–6, 27, 31, 34–5, 68
Turner, G., 164, 165, 170, 175
tutor (role), 89, 96, 105–6
TVEI, *see* technical and vocational
  initiative

unemployment, 111, 112
universities, 76–7
University of Nottingham, 137, 140

validators, inspectors as, 43
Van Velzen, W., 138
vocational education, 111

Walker, R., 50
Walker, W. G., 117
Warren, X. X., 114
Warwickshire (management of
  professional development), 73
  coherent planning, 30–37
  GRIST and Thomas Report, 26–9
  initiatives, 24
  LEAs, 25
  planning for the future, 29
  purpose of development, 23–4
  secondments, 29–30
  TRIST in, 25–6
Waterman, R. J., 138
Watkins, R., 68
Watson, Len, 4, 100
Watts, J., 118
Wheeler, G. E., 112
Whitaker, P., 173
Whittle, J., 55
whole-school approach, 31, 32, 96
  GRIST initiative, 72, 74, 76
  INSET in primary schools, 80, 82, 86
  school development, 3, 4–5, 12–18
Wilcox, B., 50
Williams, Fred, 96, 114
workshop sessions, 60, 83
Wright, N., 16–17

*Yearbook of the Association for
  Supervision and Curriculum
  Development* (1990), 159
Young, Lord, 24
youth service (planning), 32–3
youth unemployment, 111